For Kate and Sadie

ALAN RYAN

BERTRAND RUSSELL

A Political Life

ALLEN LANE
THE PENGUIN PRESS

ALLEN LANE THE PENGUIN PRESS
Published by the Penguin Group
27 Wrights Lane, London W8 5TZ, England
Viking Penguin Inc., 40 West 23rd Street, New York, New York 10010, USA
Penguin Books Australia Ltd, Ringwood, Victoria, Australia
Penguin Books Canada Ltd, 2801 John Street, Markham, Ontario, Canada L3R 1B4
Penguin Books (NZ) Ltd, 182–190 Wairau Road, Auckland 10, New Zealand

Penguin Books Ltd, Registered Offices: Harmondsworth, Middlesex, England

First published 1988

Filmset in Monophoto Garamond

Printed in Great Britain by
Butler & Tanner Ltd, Frome and London

British Library Cataloguing in Publication Data

Ryan, Alan, *1940–*
Bertrand Russell: a political life.
1. Russell, Bertrand   2. Philosophers –
England – Biography
I. Title
192   B1649.R94

ISBN 0-7139-9005-8

CONTENTS

PREFACE

I FIRST read Russell when I was sixteen. I read *A History of Western Philosophy* and John Stuart Mill's essay on *Liberty* within weeks of each other and came as close as I expect to come to the experience of religious conversion. One of my school-teachers had told me that Russell was 'an old fool' – this was the autumn of 1956 and Russell had just denounced the British invasion of the Suez Canal zone; I concluded, rebelliously, that he must be a very good thing. The *History of Western Philosophy* showed how right I was. It was dazzlingly clever and astonishingly funny: reactionaries, time-servers and obscurantists were mocked to death; clear-eyed, sceptical but generous liberals were praised in eloquent tones. The news that political and intellectual seriousness could also be fun was a revelation. It was less fun for my teachers. When the poor wretch who taught us 'religious knowledge' tried to teach us St Thomas Aquinas's Five Ways to the knowledge of God, it was a pleasure to meet him with Russell's demolition of each of them. When he irritably retorted that a man with four wives couldn't be an authority on such matters, it confirmed my belief that the pious and respectable were illogical, too.

Through the years of the Campaign for Nuclear Disarmament, the Committee of 100, and the Cuban missile crisis of November 1962, I admired the bold clarity with which Russell wrote about nuclear war and the need for Britain to abandon nuclear weapons and pursue a neutralist foreign policy. During the long-drawn-out horror of the war in Vietnam the feeling that he was often shrill and hysterical, and had become the mouthpiece of his moral and intellectual inferiors, never outweighed admiration of his refusal to grow old, calm down, and become respectable. When it emerged after his death that he had generally been right about the atrocities perpetrated in the course of the war, and about the deceptions the American government had practised on Congress and the American people, this admiration grew stronger.

Today I am more sympathetic to middle-aged teachers faced with cocksure sixteen-year-olds. Few of Russell's essays on social and political issues have stood the test of time quite unscathed, and the *History of Western Philosophy* too often seems casual, unfair and prejudiced, and too ready to shade the truth for the sake of the *bon mot*. Still, the verve and lucidity of this and almost everything else he wrote remains astonishing. When he was awarded the Nobel Prize for Literature in 1950, his first response was, 'They don't like my philosophy.' The truth is that one can reject his ideas – he rejected most of them over the course of his ninety-seven years – but from first to last he wrote so well that he will always be the envy and despair of other philosophers.

This book is concerned with one side of Russell's life: his life as a polemicist, agitator, educator and popularizer. It is not about Russell's philosophy, as he understood philosophy; he thought of philosophy in the strict sense as an ally, perhaps even a branch, of science, inquiring into the most general truths about the world and the mind. Morals and politics were realms of opinion and emotion, not science; only in a loose sense could there be a moral or political philosophy, as distinct from the analysis of the *logic* of moral or political discourse. And it is with Russell's ideas about ethics, religion, politics, education, the pros and cons of socialism, the historical fate of liberalism and, above all, with his ideas about war and peace that this book is concerned. I shall not press my readers to share my view that Russell was one of the last great radicals, but I shall be sorry if none of them are moved to read him or remain untouched by what they read, especially readers thirty years younger than myself. For Russell always touched a particular chord with the young – just as he always irritated the middle-aged.

He always believed that it was to the young that we must look for salvation. In the First World War, the young conscientious objectors of the No-Conscription Fellowship found in him both a leader and a father confessor, a man whose mind and emotions retained the quickness and flexibility of youth – though he was forty-five to their twenty. Fifty years later, the young radicals who clustered round him in the Committee of 100 and the Bertrand Russell Peace Foundation had the same experience. He in turn found comfort in the thought that if middle-aged and elderly politicians were too stuck in their ways to see the need for dramatic change, the young were not. They had no vested interest in the corrupt old order, and no accumulated pride, guilt and resentment to stop them embracing new ideas. Russell once explained the attraction of G. E. Moore's moral philosophy to 'Bloomsbury' by pointing out that Moore's conception of 'the absolute good' made it look as if the members of the

Bloomsbury Group were 'absolutely good'[1]. It is not too cynical to observe that one attraction of Russell's politics to the young is that it is on them that he pins his hopes – after all, so did Plato, and both of them may have been right.

It is Russell's ideas about society and politics which concern us, and this book is not primarily a biography. There are several reasons why not. The first is that Russell's own *Autobiography* is in general much too good to invite competition; only where it is particularly misleading do I try to supplement it.[2] Ronald Clark's enormous biography, *The Life of Bertrand Russell*, has subsequently put into the public domain almost everything Russell's executors, collaborators, former wives and close friends are willing to see published.[3] It provides a more detailed and more accurate account of Russell's daily life than even the *Autobiography*. It would be absurd to duplicate it, even though I do not wholly like either the tone or the emphasis of the book: in his concentration on Russell's emotional odyssey, and his relations with Ottoline Morrell and Constance Malleson, Clark makes him gloomier, more sentimental, more religiose and more monotonously concerned with his sexual relationships than I find him, and in the process the content of Russell's writings is too often ignored – Clark praises *The Principles of Social Reconstruction*, for instance, as Russell's best and most considered piece of political writing, but says little about what is in it, though much that is useful about the frame of mind in which Russell wrote it.[4] Clark gives the impression that Russell engaged in intellectual and political work only to take refuge from his private ecstasies and miseries, but this is wholly belied by Russell's exuberance, vitality and stamina. The *Autobiography* itself is sometimes sentimental; but Russell knew that this was only one facet of his character and one he did not wholly like.[5] But Clark's account of the final twenty-five years of Russell's life is excellent. Russell's career as nuclear disarmer, 'world ombudsman', campaigner against American involvement in Vietnam and the rest raises few complicated intellectual issues but a host of biographical ones, which are handled with great tact and good sense, and my own account is very much in Clark's debt, even where I disagree with him. Katharine Tait's *My Father Bertrand Russell* provides a third reason for not writing another biography of her father.[6] Although hers is professedly an unintellectual, self-centred essay in reminiscence, it is, as even her father's *Autobiography* sometimes is not, an account of a man who was very likely to write what Russell wrote.

As an account of Russell's ideas, this book's aim is to explain what Russell thought, to show where it makes sense and where it does not. As history, it is the story of an aristocratic liberal who tried to influence a mass audience in an age when birth alone would no longer get him a hearing, when he would have had to work through a mass political party to gain any kind of power himself, and when the means of communication had changed from the nineteenth-century quarterly reviews to mass-circulation newspapers geared more to gossip and entertainment than to political enlightenment and persuasion. In so far as Russell was a tragic figure – and to some degree he was – his tragedy was not personal but the tragedy of an intellectual class and an intellectual style.

The organization of what follows will be familiar to anyone who has used a Michelin 'Green Guide'. Each chapter opens with 'a little history' to set the discussion in the context of Russell's own life and the politics of the day, and then tackles his main ideas on the subject in hand. No stars are awarded to the ideas, but readers will guess which I think are worth the whole journey and which only 'merit a detour'. I begin at Russell's cradle where his own radical commitments began, and spend my first chapter on his parents, his upbringing, and the liberal tradition into which he was born – all too literally, for even his birth was made the occasion of a demonstration in favour of the liberal principle of sexual equality. Until 1914 his concerns were predominantly mathematical and logical, so that if he had been run down by the proverbial bus in 1914 he would have been remembered for his work on the foundations of mathematics and for his elegantly despairing essays on the meaning of life, such as 'A Free Man's Worship'. But before 1914 he wrote a good deal more about religion, and about the nature of moral truth; he also stood in a by-election, failed to become a candidate in a general election, and turned down several chances to stand elsewhere. So Chapter Two gathers together Russell's ambivalent answers to the question whether there *can* be such a thing as 'moral philosophy' at all, along with his views about religion, and the politics of Edwardian England, and in so doing ranges on beyond 1914. (The only portion of what follows that non-philosophers *may* find difficult is the discussion of Russell's moral philosophy; it may safely be skipped, for part of my argument is that Russell's strictly philosophical views on ethics made no difference to his moral and political commitments.) Thereafter chronology and subject keep step. Chapter Three covers the high point of Russell's political existence, his opposition to the First World War and his account of how to prevent its recurrence. Chapter Four explores further his recipe for peace, with an inquiry into his views on socialism, especially as practised in Bolshevik Russia, and his doubts about the 'scientific' reconstruction of society. All this raises two large questions – can drastic change be brought about peacefully, and will a scientifically planned society not be liberticide? The answer to both questions lies in a theory of education, and Chapter Five considers Russell's views on sex, marriage, child-rearing and schooling. Chapter Six turns again to Russell's fears concerning war and peace, and his thoughts about the fate of liberalism; the 1930s were generally miserable years for him, but *Freedom and Organization* (1934) and *Power* (1938) were among the best things he ever wrote – and *Which Way to Peace?* (1936) is an important expression of extreme defeatism, even if Russell soon repudiated it. Before turning to Russell's last years as nuclear disarmer, amateur world statesman, demagogue and radical hero, in Chapter Seven I step back to consider Russell's extraordinary role as a mischievous sage – a role which culminated in his Order of Merit in 1949 and his Nobel Prize in 1950. Russell's uncertainty whether to be sage or entertainer, politician or gadfly, was partly temperamental, but partly a response to dilemmas which face any politically engaged intellectual in the twentieth century, and I try to give a non-portentous account of these, too. Finally, Chapter Eight turns to Russell's views on war and peace in the nuclear age, his defence of world government, his advocacy of British disarmament and neutrality, his growing conviction that the United States was a greater threat to peace than the Soviet Union, and his last battle against American participation in the war in Vietnam. I am, I hope, more anxious to get the story straight than to decide with the benefit of hindsight who was right and who was wrong. But it would be idle to pretend that I find Dean Rusk, General Westmoreland, the editors of *The New York Times* – or Lloyd George and the War Office of 1916 – as sympathetic as Russell.

It remains to express thanks and acknowledge debts. My first and deepest debt must be to Michael Cherniavsky, whose readiness to take seriously the intellectual enthusiasms of schoolboys enabled me to get a liberal education in all senses of the term. The Bertrand Russell Archives at McMaster University have, in the persons of Ken Blackwell, Carl Spadoni and Sheila Turcon, provided endless help with sources. They, together with Dick Rempel, Louis Greenspan, Nick Griffin and Katharine Tait, have talked me through every topic discussed below, and I am very grateful to them. Martin Ceadel, Dick Rempel and Adam Roberts have read several chapters of the typescript and saved me from a good many errors, while Kate Ryan has very helpfully read it for intelligibility to the lay reader. The generous help of the British Academy and the Social Studies Faculty of the University of Oxford took me to McMaster University to plunder its resources. I have very much enjoyed myself. I hope the reader will enjoy the result.

ONE

A LIBERAL UPBRINGING

RUSSELL'S career defies summary analysis; his life was much too long and his activities too various. His philosophical allegiances were no more stable than his emotional allegiances, and his political allegiances no more stable than either. He sometimes thought of himself as the last representative of eighteenth-century Whiggism, but at other times was a Guild Socialist and the voice of the New Left.[1] Russell took an active part in politics only sporadically; he contributed to the Free Trade controversy of 1904, stood for parliament in 1907, 1922 and 1923, was one of the most influential opponents of the First World War, a central figure in the campaign against British nuclear weapons and a controversial figure in the fight against the American presence in Vietnam. He was, however, always an audible and visible presence in the ranks of social and political radicalism. He was always welcome in magazines such as the *New States-man*, and published an astonishing number of essays and books defending a radical view of politics, economics, sexual morality, educational practice and, above all, approaches to war and peace.

What gave him the authority to speak for intelligent radicalism was two very distinct qualities. The first was his astonishing intelligence; his work in formal logic and the foundations of mathematics gained him a Fellowship of the Royal Society at the age of thirty-six – but the analytical approach to philosophy which he constructed on these foundations has dominated philosophy for the past eighty years, and shows no signs of loosening its hold.[2] The analytical brilliance was allied to a clarity of mind and facility of expression which he could display as easily in discussing transfinite numbers as in pronouncing on the absurdity of American sexual morals. Morals and politics were, he said, no part of philosophy and his views on them were not 'philosophical'. None the less, it was the authority he had gained by his work in philosophy strictly defined that made him so fearless a combatant in the political arena, and it was that fearlessness which made him so effective. Although we are concerned with what

1

Russell thought of as his unphilosophical career, I try to convey something of the flavour of that philosophy in Chapter Two.

The other source of his self-confidence was social. He was, after all, as thoroughly a part of the aristocracy as it was possible to be. True, his grandfather's earldom was a new creation, but Lord John Russell had been born a younger son of the Duke of Bedford and had thus been born into a world which took its place in parliament and government for granted. Though Bertrand Russell himself often dismissed his earldom as so much humbug, and made little use of the chance it offered to take his views to the House of Lords, he took for granted the access it gave him to the leaders of government.[3] Having a grandfather who had been both Prime Minister and Foreign Secretary allowed him to take it for granted that he should write to President Wilson to implore him to keep America out of the First World War and, forty years later, to write to his successors demanding an end to nuclear brinkmanship.[4] His tastes and standards of conduct were essentially aristocratic; that was why he praised China for preserving the civilities of the eighteenth century and was slow to remark on the horrors of everyday life for the bulk of its population. But it was also why he was never frightened to speak his mind, and why he was at his best when preaching against fear. He had an aristocratic contempt for cowardice, whether it was an intellectual timidity that shut people off from the excitements of science, or the political servility that led the British government to support America in Vietnam.

Russell really belonged to two aristocracies, though membership of them overlapped. Besides being a member of the aristocracy of birth, he was a member of the aristocracy of exceptional talent. How these could overlap is illustrated by Russell's relationship with Gilbert Murray; Murray was Australian by birth, a wonderful Greek scholar, and the husband of one of Russell's Stanley cousins. He and Russell shared tastes in classical poetry, quarrelled drastically, but not irremediably, over the First World War, and corresponded intensely and uninhibitedly on poetry and the prevention of war for half a century. (Murray was a leading light in the League of Nations Union when Russell was a .complete defeatist who thought the League quite useless.) They might have known each other just as well had there been no family links; but family links helped to bring them together at country houses and urban dinner tables, and so strengthen such intellectual ties. The intellectual network which spread out from Cambridge and the Apostles exemplifies the way in which an unofficial aristocracy operated. The Trevelyan family produced senior civil servants and great historians; Keynes combined a passion for King's

College, ballet and macroeconomics with a readiness to kill himself in the public service. The enthusiasm of Bloomsbury for sexual unorthodoxy, and the association of the 1930s' Apostles with homosexuality and treason have obscured the extent to which most of their members devoted themselves to academic excellence and public service. These were Russell's friends; it was taken for granted that they would govern the country, if not in active politics then behind the scenes in administration, and if not there then through an osmotic process of infiltrating their ideas and ideals into those who did control parliament or staff the civil service – 'permeation' as Sidney Webb liked to call it. What Russell's friends had in common was a consciousness of their right to set the standards to which society ought to conform; for the most part, too, they shared the liberal belief that economic and social reform should free the poor and control the capitalist without intruding on the private and personal freedoms they so much prized.

To say that when Bertrand Arthur William Russell was born on 18 May 1872 he was born into the upper reaches of English liberalism is therefore literally true, and quite inadequate. The Russells had been defenders of liberal causes since the end of the seventeenth century; in 1683 Lord William Russell had been executed for his part in the Rye House Plot, a martyr in the battle against royal despotism and Catholic intolerance; Bertrand Russell's grandfather, Lord John Russell, had rectified injustices done *to* rather than by Roman Catholics by promoting Catholic emancipation in 1829; he had next helped to push through the great Reform Bill of 1832; Russell's godfather, John Stuart Mill, was the intellectual conscience of English liberalism in the mid-nineteenth century. Every cause Russell espoused had roots in the politics of his parents, grandparents and godparents; his birth itself was the occasion for a demonstration in favour of equality of opportunity for women – Russell's midwife was Elizabeth Garret Anderson, the pioneering woman doctor. Her medical studies had been paid for by Russell's mother, but she was still debarred by her sex from practising as a doctor and so had to attend in the lowlier capacity of midwife.[5] Russell's behaviour towards the many women in his life may not have been all it should have been; but from the cradle, he shared his parents' conviction that anything less than perfect equality of opportunity was simply wicked.

Russell's parents were on the radical edge of Liberal politics. His father, Viscount Amberley, was briefly Member of Parliament for Nottingham; he lost his seat in the election of 1868, and even if he had not died prematurely in 1876, his unorthodox views would have kept him out of office. His chief offence was to be a passionate advocate of birth control, just as Russell and his second wife Dora were in the 1920s. In the 1920s it took some boldness to advocate birth control in public; in the 1860s and '70s it was a recipe for social ostracism. After Mill's death, Gladstone learned that John Stuart Mill had spent a night in prison at the age of sixteen for distributing birth control leaflets in a working-class district, and hastily resigned from the committee which was raising money to commemorate 'the saint of rationalism'.

Behind the arguments over birth control lay an economic theory which has since been wholly discredited but which in its day was almost universally believed. It held that since wages depended on how many workers came forward for employment, the level of wages reflected working-class habits of procreation; those habits in turn reflected the level of wages. If wages rose above the level needed to keep body and soul together, too many children would be born, and the wages paid would in due course be too low to support them all. Poverty and misery would cut back their numbers, so that wages would oscillate around subsistence levels. The checks on population were said to be 'war, misery and vice'. Birth control was a branch of vice – or, rather, 'vice' was a pious label for all those forms of sexual activity which were intended not to result in children, sex between married couples employing birth control among them. The radicals were undeterred by the label, and insisted that if the working class could be taught to limit the number of offspring they produced, their lot would be improved without drastic social upheaval. Russell's parents felt that an even more powerful argument for birth control was the welfare of women. The toll which unrestrained breeding took on women of all classes needs no stressing. Whether it was worse in Victorian England than earlier and elsewhere is doubtful, but Victorian England was committed to progress and improvement. Kate and John Amberley insisted that women could no longer be treated as machines for producing babies; it was no longer tolerable just to urge resignation on bereaved or worn-out mothers.

John Amberley's political mentor was John Stuart Mill, and a close friendship existed between Lady Amberley and Mill's stepdaughter, Helen Taylor. Amberley was less of an out-and-out libertarian than Mill, and as pragmatic about state intervention as his son was to be. Mill and he disagreed over the Contagious Diseases Act, for instance; this was an Act which gave police in garrison towns and towns with naval dockyards the power to detain suspected prostitutes and have them examined for venereal disease. More soldiers and sailors were lost to venereal disease than perished in battle.[6] The War Office was also sensitive to the charge that

4

troops and sailors often infected their innocent wives and children when they got home. Mill, however, saw the Act as an insult to women. He did not quarrel with the desire to have a healthy army and navy, only with the assumption that it was the prostitutes rather than their customers who should be liable to detention and inspection. An infected prostitute would infect many customers, but she must have caught the disease from a man in the first place, and since the trade existed only because there were customers for it, let them be inspected and treated. In this instance, Amberley was more utilitarian than utilitarianism's most distinguished adherent; it seemed to him simpler to search out a few prostitutes than to control their numerous clients. Subsequent experience suggests that such Acts fail because they are punitive, but it was Florence Nightingale rather than Mill who predicted that.[7]

One reform for which Mill, the Amberleys and Russell all fought, both in print and on the hustings, was female suffrage. Like Mill, John Amberley took it for granted that women should have the vote, on whatever terms men had it. This, too, was an unpopular opinion in the upper reaches of society, though it was shared by more people than were willing to declare it. In 1870, when Mill and Amberley were both out of parliament, a Women's Suffrage Act astonished both its supporters and its opponents by passing on first reading, and even when defeated on second reading it still got 184 votes.[8] Once it was seen that more than a handful of cranks supported the measure, timidly liberal souls came out of hiding.

On matters of war and peace, the subject which dominated Russell's political career, his father held strikingly unorthodox views for his day. Amberley came as near as anyone in the nineteenth century to advocating what the twentieth century would recognize as pacifism. It is true that liberalism was generally and intrinsically anti-militarist; free traders such as Cobden and Bright wanted to see nations exchanging goods rather than cannon-fire and thought that a country which reduced its armaments and its treaty obligations, and took an intelligently restrained view of its vital interests, need never embroil itself in war. Amberley went beyond the usual liberal position, and thought that a league of nations might outlaw warfare altogether. In this he anticipated ideas about world government which his son was preaching some seventy years later. He also encountered some of the tensions his son encountered between on the one hand the desire to abolish war and on the other the idea that a league of nations might have to impose good order by force.[9]

The difficulty was recurrent and was constantly felt by Russell himself. He never believed that war is the worst of all evils; secular liberalism does not believe in the sanctity of life, and absolute pacifism is hard to reconcile with the utilitarian and consequentialist approach to politics which Russell adopted. Moreover, radical liberalism is a moralistic doctrine, and although liberals saw that Britain would be ill-advised to set herself up as the policeman of Europe – even if it were feasible, it would involve the creation of a large and costly standing army of just the sort they hated – they felt an acute urge to interfere on behalf of liberalism in Europe. Mill admired the moral virtues which war brought out more than Amberley or Russell did, and half accepted the idea that conscription could be a prop to public spirit in a democratic society. Yet Russell, too, saw that other people felt that war brought out morally valuable qualities in those who took part, and he sympathized sufficiently with a taste for excitement and adventure to understand that the onus lay on him and other pacifists to find room for energy, courage and high spirits without mass slaughter.[10]

Perhaps the most radical person in Russell's background was his mother. Kate Amberley was the daughter of Lord Stanley of Alderley; her family were of the same political persuasion as the Russells – Whigs with radical inclinations – but they had opposed her marrying anyone with such far-fetched ideas as Amberley. The truth was that her ideas were a good deal bolder than his.[11] Her enthusiasm for female emancipation infuriated the most powerful woman in the country, if the story is true: 'I wish I could *whip* that Kate Amberley,' Queen Victoria is supposed to have said. Kate Amberley took her stand on Mill's *Subjection of Women*; since there were no respectable grounds for treating women as the subjects of men, they had better be admitted to full equality and recognized as capable of controlling their own property, making their own living, and lending their voices to the nation's politics.[12] The implications for such Victorian shibboleths as the sanctity of marriage were bleak; at a time when most people affected to regard divorce with horror, Kate Amberley declared that marriage was a contract like any other and should be dissolved if both parties agreed, due provision being made for the interests of any children. Everyone knew that this was the implication of treating men and women as strictly equal in law, though Mill himself had neatly ducked the issue by saying that the reorganization of marriage ought to wait until women could make their views felt in the political arena. Kate Amberley was a firm believer in 'the voluntary principle' in marriage, which meant that she and her husband were entitled to regulate their lives as they chose, whatever their respective families might think. On the political front, she joined the Women's Suffrage Society in 1869, and was a popular platform speaker until her death in 1874. It was the closeness of her friendship with

6

Mill's stepdaughter and amanuensis, Helen Taylor, which emboldened her to ask whether Mill might agree to be godfather to her newly arrived son. It was a delicate question, since Mill was a firmly avowed agnostic and might flinch at a relationship which seemed to imply beliefs he did not have. In fact Helen Taylor was able to reply that 'Mr Mill says if you wish it he does not think it would conflict with his opinions to enter into that relation.'[13]

Mill died less than a year after Russell was born; he therefore exerted no personal influence on his godson, though his *Autobiography* played an important part in Russell's education, and Russell later recalled with some surprise that he had learned a great deal from Mill before he had learned that Mill was his godfather 'in a non-religious sense'. Since Kate Amberley also died when her son was barely two and John Amberley scarcely eighteen months later, neither of them had time to exert much direct influence on him either. Russell's *Autobiography* shows how powerful a place his dead parents had in his imagination, however. He soon picked up from his grandmother the impression that his parents had been either slightly mad or rather wicked. The family had busily destroyed such of his parents' papers as might have led to scandal, and Russell in due course discovered the reason for that at least. His parents had employed a tutor for his elder brother, Frank; this tutor, Douglas Spalding, had consumption and Russell's parents had felt he ought not to marry. But they felt 'it was unfair to expect him to be celibate. My mother therefore allowed him to live with her, though I know of no evidence that she derived any pleasure from doing so. This arrangement subsisted for a very short time, as it began after my birth and I was only two years old when my mother died.'[14] Though he learned of this only some years later, it is hard to believe that his family's alarm and disapproval were hidden from him during his childhood.

It is all the harder to believe, given the character of the person who had the greatest part in moulding his character during childhood and adolescence. This was his grandmother, Countess Russell. The Amberleys had appointed Douglas Spalding and an agnostic friend of his, John Cobden-Sanderson, as guardians for their sons – Cobden-Sanderson was Russell's other godfather – but the family overruled their choice, and confided them to their grandmother's care. Writing in 1931, Russell offered a detached but entirely plausible account of her effect on him. She was affectionate enough during his childhood but intellectually constricting then and morally insufferable once he reached adolescence. It is hard to believe that he found the Pembroke Lodge household anything but bleak, dull and repressive. Visitors certainly thought the large empty house in Richmond Park no place for a lively small boy. Russell's grandmother was a devout Liberal in her politics, but a great believer in sin; Russell maintained that she succeeded all too well in transmitting that sense of sin to him: 'when asked what was my favourite hymn, I replied "Weary of earth and laden with sin"'.[15] Russell's *Autobiography* is ambivalent about the effect of all this, sometimes suggesting that he was happy enough most of the time, and sometimes maintaining that all that kept him from suicide was the desire to learn more mathematics. Those who suspect that a strong sense of sin is an aid to strength of character will find support in Russell's summing up of his grandmother's impact: 'her fearlessness, her public spirit, her contempt for convention and her indifference to the opinion of the majority have always seemed good to me and have impressed themselves upon me as worthy of imitation. She gave me a Bible with her favourite texts written on the flyleaf. Among these was "Thou shalt not follow a multitude to do evil."'[16]

Her antipathy to sexual passion impressed him less. Nor did he acquire her religious leanings. Russell's views on religion are not easy to summarize, as we shall see. He was always hostile to organized religion and to the social role of the churches, and thought the moral code of orthodox Christianity repressive and mean-spirited. For all that, his hostility was directed at the institutions of organized religion rather than at the spiritual needs they failed to serve. He had a good deal of sympathy with what one might call a 'religious view of the world', so much so that his daughter has described his mind as 'essentially religious'. That is something of an exaggeration. Like most people, he sometimes tried to drum up in himself convictions he did not really possess for the sake of pleasing other people. The most obvious published example of this is 'Mysticism and Logic' which shares the oddly florid and mystical tone of his correspondence with Lady Ottoline Morrell and the essays he wrote for her in the early 1900s; but the same tone occurs often enough in the *Autobiography*.[17] During childhood and early adolescence he took on trust the Christianity to which his grandmother subscribed (she was a Unitarian, and only debatably a Christian at all, but her grandson plainly felt he lived in a Christian household). That his faith lay lightly on him seems plain from the ease with which he lost it. He was reading Mill's *Autobiography* and came across the passage where Mill remarks that the 'First Cause' argument for the existence of God won't do, because it provokes the question, 'What brought the first cause into existence?' The point was conclusive, and his belief was gone.[18] It would be hard to believe so quick and rationalistic an account of the matter, were it not backed up by an entry in Russell's own journal on the day the loss occurred. Russell was by then eighteen years old, and had given up most of whatever belief he had once held. He records that he had disbelieved in personal immortality for some two years; and one of his tutors had been an agnostic who was quite ready to discuss his unbelief with him.

What survived of Countess Russell's puritanism and gives some colour to the idea that he had a religious temperament was a sense of the incompleteness and unsatisfactoriness of the world. It is hard to leap directly from the thought that the world is a vale of tears in need of divine redemption to the thought that the loss of God does not matter because the world is not a vale of tears after all. Indeed, his dislike of the world he found around him, and his sense that it had to be justified by a better future or had to be spurned for spiritual disciplines such as mathematics, was almost Manichean. Its effects on his moral and political views are many and various. There were times when it drove him away from any interest in practical matters, and he thought the only thing worth caring for was the truth of mathematical and logical theories which possessed the timeless and indestructible perfection that mystics had ascribed to God himself. At other times it drove him to work his heart out for the innumerable social and political causes he subscribed to, as if he might save his soul by making the world a little less imperfect. Always it coloured the style and tone of his writing, sometimes in the direction of a world-weary cynicism and disgust, sometimes in the direction of encouraging utopian hopes for an earthly paradise of guilt-free, energetic, creative and fulfilled humanists. In all this we may detect the impact of his Russell grandmother.

His grandfather, the first Earl Russell, but much better known as Lord John Russell, was twenty-three years older than his wife and died at the age of eighty-two in 1878, when his grandson was six and two years after the boy came to live at Pembroke Lodge. He had retired from political life in 1868, but his achievements were part of the air his grandson breathed as he grew up. He had been twice Prime Minister as well as leader of the House of Commons and Foreign Secretary. His life was a standing record of adherence to liberal decency, even if his judgement had sometimes been wayward and his competence as a party politician infinitely inferior to that of Palmerston and Gladstone. The eighteenth-century rationalism which was to surface in his grandson also stirred in him. He much admired Napoleon, who was no liberal but who had done much to destroy the absurdities of feudalism all over Europe and had brought modernity to

9

slumbering backwaters by a combination of brute force and personal authority.

Pembroke Lodge was much visited by politicians of a liberal hue, Gladsone among them. Russell tells an alarming tale of being left alone after dinner to entertain Gladstone while the ladies retired; the Grand Old Man spoke only once; 'This is very good port they have given me,' said Gladstone, 'but why have they given it to me in a claret glass?'[19] Russell's journal records many more solid encounters than this, with innumerable dinners spent arguing about Home Rule and the possibility of a federal constitution for Britain with the men whose votes and decisions would help to bring them about or defeat them. Russell grew up as the Liberal Party to which he was the heir – the party of his grandfather and Gladstone – began to break up over Home Rule. Family arguments reflected conflicts outside, for his Stanley grandmother was deeply opposed to Gladstone's plans for Irish Home Rule, though Russell recalls the fact merely to observe that 'formidable though my grandmother was, she had her limits'; she had sworn to tell Gladstone where he had gone astray, but faltered when the time came to do it; 'His hawk's eye could quell even her'. Elsewhere, he says that Gladstone reduced her to the demureness of a pussy cat.[20]

The details of Russell's childhood and adolescence do not bear very closely on the content of his later political allegiances, though they have much to do with the way he adopted and defended them; the lack of maternal affection, the puritanical sexual outlook of his grandmother, and a fear of the streak of madness which ran through the family, all coloured Russell's character more than his intellect.[21] They explain his early priggishness and the violence of his revolt against it, his early sexual diffidence and his anxiety later to make up for missed opportunities. These are not in themselves doctrinal matters, though they make a difference to what doctrines a person finds attractive. For instance, a constant theme of Russell's social and political thinking was the ultimate loneliness of each individual. A solitariness which only intense personal relationships or overwhelming intellectual passions could overcome seemed to him to be the central fact about the human condition. Although he was properly sceptical about how much social reform could do for a metaphysical condition, it is plain that essays such as *The Principles of Social Reconstruction* are motivated by a hunger for fellowship with the rest of suffering humanity. Indeed, when Russell came to explain why he did not consider his social and political writings as contributions to philosophy in the strictest sense, he wrote, 'I wrote on these matters as someone who saw the sufferings of mankind and suffered with them.' He did not add a great deal to the nineteenth-century liberal view of politics narrowly considered, and nothing to nineteenth-century liberal economics narrowly considered; what he did add was a different and in some ways deeper view of human nature than his predecessors had possessed, and a view of social, economic and political life which rested on this. His upbringing had predisposed him to look for such insights, even though it did so precisely by being so inadequate an emotional basis for life.

Russell's account of his early years in the *Autobiography* is not, as his godfather's *Autobiography* so largely was, a sort of extended reading list with commentaries on the books that most affected him. By the time Russell wrote the first volume of the *Autobiography* in 1931 he had become much more interested in his own emotions than Mill ever allowed himself to be, and, having earned his living as a lecturer and popular journalist for the best part of a decade by then, he had a lively sense of what made for 'human interest'. Nevertheless, his education bears a little scrutiny. He was taught at home by a succession of governesses and tutors. It was not an unusual education for someone of his class, although it seems to have been dictated by his grandmother's fears of what school might do to his morals more than by hope of what his tutors might do for his brains; his older brother Frank had behaved more or less disgracefully throughout his time at Winchester. So, he was taught by a succession of tutors and governesses, under the not particularly interfering eye of his grandmother. It is a familiar story that the great passion of his youth – indeed of his entire life before 1914 – was mathematics. He often said, though with what truth one cannot tell, that the desire to learn more mathematics was all that kept him from suicide in the worst moments of his adolescence.[22] The first experience which suggested to him that he might be more intelligent than average was when he found it easy to master Euclid, and the one occasion when he took anything on trust was when his brother Frank insisted that if he did not accept Euclid's axioms, without explanation, they could not prove any of the theorems. He got his own back in due course by showing how to reduce mathematics to logic. His education was not narrowly mathematical; he read Latin, Greek, French and German, read quantities of history – and early and late drew the same rationalist and liberal morals from the history he read. Before he went up to Trinity College, Cambridge, at the age of eighteen he had mastered the economics of Mill and Marshall (a factor of some importance in persuading him that Marx's economics had nothing to offer). He had also read Mill's *System of Logic*, some Comte (which he thought little of) and some Carlyle.

Russell's *Journal* shows how much his interest in philosophy owed to his doubts about religion but, whatever the incentive, the result was that by the time he went to Cambridge he had a more sophisticated sense of the philosophical climate of his day than one would expect from an undergraduate freshman.[23]

Before turning to Russell's career before 1914 and his views about religion, morals and politics in those years, it is worth pausing to contemplate the intellectual and practical dilemmas of the liberal faith which Russell inherited. This is not to say that Russell devoted much attention to them before 1900; his picture of his own absorption in his emotional life, his worries about his absence of faith, and his desire to learn more mathematics ring true enough. He was, however, interested in politics both at home and in Cambridge, and more so when he went to Paris and Berlin in 1894–5 and wrote his first published book on *German Social Democracy*. The Boer War provoked him to deeper and more anxious thought about politics and imperialism as the century ended. Until 1914, he relied unhesitatingly on the outlook of what came to be called 'advanced liberalism' – reformist rather than *laissez-faire* liberalism. It was many years later that he declared allegiance to the plain prose style and libertarian political theory of John Stuart Mill. None the less, the tensions in Mill's ideas were tensions in nineteenth-century liberalism generally, and they illuminate, and are often identical with, the tensions in the advanced liberalism which Russell espoused as well.

Mill tried to provide nineteenth-century liberalism with its creed. If rank-and-file liberals thought him intimidating, he was one of liberalism's claims to rationality. What influence he exerted on Liberal Party practice it is impossible to say, though one distinguished historian of the liberals suggests that if he had so wished, his influence would have been very great indeed; his impact on Gladstone was certainly profound. Anyone who reads even the driest parts of Mill can see at once that he was engaged in a political campaign. The weapons were philosophical, but the results were to be practical. The defeat of superstition, rigid old habits, intolerance of novelty would leave the field clear for liberal politics, and a liberal society, a programme which Russell heartily endorsed. There were problems at all points, however. Mill argued, as did Russell almost throughout his life, that the only rational basis for social morality is the pursuit of happiness, the doctrine generally known as utilitarianism. (It is true that Russell qualified this by saying that 'happiness' was not a very satisfactory name for the goal of morals and politics, but then Mill had already done something very similar by claiming that only some sorts of happiness were really worth pursuing. Russell and Mill largely agreed on *what* was to be pursued, if not on how best to describe it.) If happiness was the ultimate good, it followed that more was better than less, and the test of social and political policy must be its tendency to create as much happiness as possible. The 'greatest happiness principle' was the touchstone of utilitarian politics. Yet it was an uncertain guide to policy, and one which contained some nasty dilemmas – Mill earned a reputation for abandoning his utilitarianism whenever it threatened his liberalism, and has often been praised for so doing. Russell was never as systematic a utilitarian as Mill and therefore never faced quite the same problems; but he, too, frequently abandoned his utilitarianism when it ran counter to deeply felt intuitions about freedom or other deeply held values.

It is, as critics have said, not obvious that *maximizing* happiness really is what governments ought to do. Some kinds of happiness are very much better than others, and some kinds of happiness do not seem worth promoting at all. The sadist's happiness has never been thought worth promoting, to take one very obvious example. Even within the realm of orthodox politics, there are many issues which are not very amenable to a utilitarian account. Liberals who wished the state to go beyond repressing force and fraud and to see to the education of its subjects were uneasily conscious that there was no guarantee that a state which promoted education, say, or a high regard for philosophy and the arts, would create more happiness. One might reply that few educated people wish that they had remained uneducated, so that in educating people we give them something which they are, after the event, glad to have had. Yet it is not at all clear that they are glad because they are happier. In any case, to justify compulsory education by saying that the educated will be glad in the end looks suspiciously like a paternalistic view of the state's relations with the citizenry, and liberals are hostile to paternalism. Tory paternalism could justify dragging the uncultivated into a cultured condition; liberalism could not.

The trouble goes philosophically deeper than that. Liberalism is 'about' the pursuit of liberty. What constitutes liberty is contentious; but, whatever it is, liberty and the pursuit of happiness may conflict. If what we value most highly is human happiness, freedom can only be a means to that happiness, and who can say that free choice will invariably be the best route to happiness? Quite apart from exceptional cases – if I seize the man who is about to plunge unknowing over the edge of the cliff, I interfere with his freedom, but only as an exceptional measure[24] – the case for freedom as a means to happiness may be pretty unreliable. Certainly, freedom is *often* a means to happiness and best defended as such. The freedom to dissolve an unhappy marriage and enter a happier one is clearly justified on utilitarian grounds; freedom of choice in employment and in matters of individual consumption are similarly justified. The right to vote is a political freedom whose warrant is that governments which have to secure re-election mind more about the happiness of their subjects than governments immune from this constraint.

Yet the argument can be turned around. Suppose that we discover how to control beliefs and attitudes by indoctrination. The citizens' happiness can now be secured by ensuring that they choose what they will enjoy and enjoy whatever they have chosen. A well-organized and benevolent administration would ensure that when its subjects lost their free will they also lost the ability to cause themselves misery. So long as the administration could always match tastes and results, happiness would be achieved. The lack of freedom cuts no ice: what use is the freedom to make ourselves unhappy? Ordinarily, we wish to retain our freedom because we do not trust others to make the right choices for us, because they either do not know our tastes or do not have our interests at heart. The utilitarian backed by modern science can deal with the first point, since he looks forward to the day when the administrators know what we want because they have conditioned us to want it. The second point demands no larger a leap of the imagination; we see already innumerable public officials who are benevolent, hard-working, intelligent and entirely devoted to the happiness of the public. If there was less economic and social conflict, there would be more such people, and people such as they, equipped with the right techniques, could ensure that their own successors were even more reliably and rationally benevolent then they. It is frequently suggested that Bentham would have welcomed this as utopia; the Webbs, who were close, if disapproving, friends of Russell, had leanings in this direction; more surprisingly, so did Russell.[25]

In its fully developed form, it is the not-quite-fantasy world of Aldous Huxley's *Brave New World*, where the Director makes sure that alphas, betas and gammas get what they want and want what they get. Life lasts only as long as it is pleasant, but while it lasts it is a life of constant sensual enjoyment. Huxley was only one of many nineteenth- and twentieth-century writers who have explored our ambivalence about the consequences of taking the pursuit of happiness as the only goal of life; Dostoevsky's Grand Inquisitor is more substantial than Huxley's Director, but his offer to take away our unhappiness by taking away our liberty is just the same.[26] It was Huxley's model which Russell knew best. He had known Huxley when both frequented Garsington, and Huxley had drawn on him for *Crome Yellow*; it seems clear, too, that Huxley plundered Russell's work for the ideas behind *Brave New World*.[27] Most of the machinery of *Brave New World* first turned up in *The Scientific Outlook*; and when Russell suggested the need for a new drug with the euphoric qualities of alcohol but no tendency to create hangovers, Huxley obliged with the invention of 'soma' and the slogan, 'a gramme is better than a damn'. The question Russell tried to answer was not whether *Brave New World* is achievable – Russell thought it was within the bounds of possibility – but what we are to make of it as an image of a happy society. For Russell did not dismiss out of hand the suggestion that we ought to try to build a brave new world for ourselves. Mill did, when he declared that Socrates dissatisfied was better than the fool satisfied; but Russell moved between extremes. He could advocate virtual anarchy at one moment and a completely controlled society at the next, and his writings of the 1920s and '30s do just this. This was not a matter of temperament merely; if freedom is primarily valuable as a means to happiness, it is genuinely hard to know what to say if it looks as if the systematic abolition of freedom would be an even better route to human well-being.

Russell was pulled in two directions, then, by the moral and philosophical commitments of liberalism, by his belief in freedom and his belief in happiness. Mill was never tempted by Bentham's picture of happiness, and his essay on *Liberty* was a hymn to our right to make ourselves as dissatisfied as we wished; the romantic defence of liberty was a good deal more persuasive to most readers than his attempt to show that the dissatisfied pursuer of liberty and self-development was really happy after all. Nor was Mill ever tempted by the simple visions of political and economic liberty which made other liberals intermittently popular. Palmerston, for instance, was a jingoistic liberal and hugely popular; Mill merely insisted that liberty was more than national independence. Cobden and Bright were pacifists who identified freedom with free trade; again Mill refused to limit freedom to commercial liberty, though he agreed on its importance. When Russell argued for freedom, it was in the spirit of *On Liberty* rather than in a Palmerstonian or Cobdenite spirit that he argued; all the same, he was more tempted than Mill by Bentham's recipe for orderly happiness. Russell had seen just how dangerous mankind could be. Mill loathed Napoleon III, but the emperor was small beer compared with Hitler and Stalin; the minor intolerances of Victorian England paled beside the madness which led to the horrors of Nazi Germany. That is not the whole story; Bentham remarked that he would cheerfully give up the freedom to make himself unhappy. Mill held that this was the renunciation of all that made us human. Russell sided with both of them. When he contemplated the horrors of war and the resources of science, he was apt to think that although *Brave New World* revolted *him* it might be the best way out for humanity at large.

Often, however, he followed Mill in avoiding the problem by redefining happiness. The pleasure felt by Huxley's cloned and conditioned creatures was not real happiness – though in his review of *Brave New World* he conceded that it was, and announced 'We Don't Want To Be Happy'. More usually, he held that happiness was more vital, energetic and stressful than what Huxley offered. In his innumerable essays on 'how to be happy' he never suggested that a gramme of the wonder-working soma was the answer. Russell's recipe always involves imagination, individuality, independence of other people's good and bad opinion; happiness is less a matter of pleasure than of experiencing one's own vitality, a doctrine which is defended in *The Conquest of Happiness* in an extended hymn to 'zest'. Viewed this way, the conflict between freedom and happiness dissolves, because the pleasures of conditioned and manipulated creatures are not part of happiness at all. This abandons the attempt to show that freedom is useful as a means to happiness and defends freedom as a good in itself – which is plainly what Russell mostly thought it was. As to whether Russell should have tried more assiduously to *argue* for either the instrumental view or its opposite, we shall see that what underlies his most libertarian essays, such as the *Principles of Social Reconstruction, Political Ideals* and *Roads to Freedom*, is less a moral philosophy in which the claims of different values are carefully weighed than a view of human nature from which it follows at once that freedom is the greatest of social goods.

This sketch of the intellectual bases of liberalism has concentrated on the social and moral face of liberalism, on its moral basis in utilitarianism and on freedom as a social and psychological matter. Although Lord John Russell's claim to fame lay in his campaigns for parliamentary reform, nothing has been said here about the political face of liberalism. The omission is deliberate; I shall now justify it. Russell was an apolitical liberal, perhaps even an anti-political liberal. He was not interested in political institutions in the parliamentary and administrative sense of the term; he was not interested in constitution building (one respect in which he was quite unlike Plato); and when he campaigned for world government during and after the Second World War he concentrated much more on such topics as the educational duties of world government than on the mechanisms through which it would work.[28] The same was true dom-

estically. When he claimed allegiance to the guild socialists at the end of the
First World War, he never shared their fascination with the organizational
details of the various guilds and councils with which they proposed to
replace parliament and the trade unions. This lack of interest in institutional matters had various results, among them an unfortunate casualness
about just how world peace, unilateral disarmament, or equality for the
Black population of the United States might be achieved; but its relevance
here is negative. Russell was not affected by the main anxiety of nineteenth-
century liberals, namely their fears about the advance of democracy.

The central political anxiety of nineteenth-century liberals was the fear
that the working classes would acquire the vote before they acquired the
ability to use it properly. Walter Bagehot opposed the Reform Bill of 1867
because it gave the vote to those who did not understand how the political
system, so elegantly described in *The English Constitution*, actually operated.
Robert Lowe tried to hold up the Bill and, when defeated, announced
gloomily, 'We must educate our masters.' Mill welcomed it just because
of the impetus it gave to such an education. By the time Russell thought
about politics, such concerns were out of date; of course Britain was far
from even 'one *man*, one vote' in 1872 when he was born; and he himself
campaigned to make it 'one person one vote' when he stood as a suffragist
candidate in 1907. All the same, arguments for and against democracy in
the ballot-box sense did not interest him much – he took it for granted
that liberals wanted universal suffrage without distinction of sex. Only in
the 1930s when the fascist dictatorships set themselves to destroy democracy did he set about defending it. And then, it was the spirit of democracy
rather than any particular institutionalization of it which concerned him.[29]

Two further subjects, much debated among nineteenth-century liberals,
are more relevant to Russell. The first was the question of what concessions
had to be made to socialist critics of nineteenth-century capitalism. Russell
was never entirely sure what he thought about this, though he usually
argued that liberal social and political goals implied socialism in industry.
All the same, he did not quite want to call himself a socialist. Radical
liberals like himself had accepted many of the socialist complaints against
capitalism by 1872; conversely, socialists of the kind who would form the
Fabian Society a dozen years later expected to use the Liberal Party to
realize their aims, and had no desire to set up a distinctively working-class
Labour Party. Russell grew up thinking many features of his society
unjust. Most of the wealth was held by people who did not *deserve* it; the
property-less worker was excessively at the mercy of incompetent or
unscrupulous employers; agricultural property was anomalous – tenants

made improvements which put up the value of the land they farmed, but landlords got the capital gains so created. The morality of the whole system left much to be desired; at best employer and employee faced each other in a battle in which they were fairly matched, but generally speaking the employer held the upper hand. To some degree it was already appreciated that what was wrong was not only the poverty of the worker but also his subservient position and the boredom of his work; and it was understood that this was not so much a matter of who *owned* the means of production – as socialists supposed – but of how industry was governed: an issue of power rather than property. It was these views that Russell endorsed.

It is impossible to give a summary account of 'the liberal response' for there was no single such thing.[30] The roots of what historians have called 'the new liberalism' of the years before 1914 – the liberalism of the infant welfare state – go deeper and earlier than many writers have thought. There was always an element in the Liberal Party which held that property was not sacred and that landed property was the source of many abuses. They were happy to see the party act wherever it usefully could in order to secure the liberty of those who would otherwise fall victim to the abuse of private power. Even Gladstone was not unsympathetic to such a view; and a frequent visitor to Pembroke Lodge was John Morley, who had learned such views from Mill. What made such views liberal rather than socialist, and what makes them relevant to Russell's later ideas, is that they are committed to moral individualism. Liberals who held such views still believed that what gave a society its worth was the quality of *individual* existence, not some communal quality, and that what gave individual life its value was the degree of individual choice and responsibility it contained. This made them sceptical of socialist plans to centralize ownership and authority, and hostile to writers who supposed that state ownership and good management formed a recipe for the millennium.[31] The taste for co-operation, municipal ownership and the like which one always finds on the Liberal left has its roots in the conviction that the road to liberty lies through diversity and that an omnicompetent state must be liberticide. Again, it was these views which Russell found congenial.

The second topic is not a question of policy but of philosophical and sociological method. The single most important change in the nineteenth-century intellectual climate could be summed up in the one word 'evolution'.[32] This is not to say that politicians, historians, economists and men of letters spent their days reading *The Origin of the Species* or even had much idea what Darwin's achievement was. Darwin himself was puzzled to know just what he had achieved, and the social and political implications of that achievement are still hotly controversial 140 years later. Yet thinking in developmental terms spread through society throughout the nineteenth century, in whatever subtle and silent ways. The idea that some societies are 'more evolved' than others, that some forms of behaviour are 'atavistic', that races could 'degenerate', all became common-place; the content of such notions is often biologically and politically dubious, but they reinforced the existing belief in progress and existing convictions as to which countries were and which were not in the vanguard of it.

The use of such ideas in politics and in political theory did not wait until Darwin developed his thoughts on differentiation among species of finch. Indeed, Darwin secured so many converts so swiftly just because people were already used to thinking in evolutionary terms in social and political matters and therefore found it easy to do so in matters of biology also. None the less, Darwin's prestige certainly encouraged social scientists to develop grand evolutionary schemas in which the history of technology, science, morals and government would be embraced – the whole having a tendency to culminate in Victorian Britain or Wilhelmine Germany according to the nationality of the writer. Russell did not succumb to anything like that temptation; for one thing, he was taught moral philosophy by Henry Sidgwick, who was a devastating critic of evolutionary ethics.[33] For another, his natural scepticism came into play whenever he contemplated attempts to derive ethics from natural history.[34] All the same, he picked up the thought that progress was manifest, and progressive and unprogressive peoples distinguishable from one another. The ease with which liberals generally accommodated themselves to imperialism owed something to this line of thought; and Russell was no exception to the rule.

In this chapter, I have sketched some of the sources of Russell's later views and ventilated some of the problems he later faced. I have tried to anticipate later chapters no more than was necessary to show the relevance of what was being discussed here. But none of this adds up to even a sketch of nineteenth-century liberalism in its true complexity. Nor does it tell us very much about *how* Russell's background affected him. Nothing could; he was such a voracious reader and so quick to reshape what he read that he often put a new gloss on ideas he might have gleaned from a dozen different books or people. What this chapter has perhaps achieved is a sketch of the intellectual and political climate in which he grew up, accepting all the while that a different man would have made something very different of the same circumstances. And a last *caveat* is in order. Until

1914 Russell was not vitally interested in politics; he was much more interested than is suggested by the romantic picture of his passion for mathematics which he put into circulation. Given his background and his friends, he could never have been uninterested or uninformed. But even when he was speaking in favour of Free Trade or on the hustings campaigning for votes for women, he did not think that what he was doing was the most important thing he could and should be doing. So although his background certainly influenced how he thought about politics and what he thought, we must remember that before 1914 politics was not his ruling passion.

TWO

RELIGION, ETHICS, AND LIBERAL POLITICS

I N a balanced account of Russell's intellectual development, the twenty-four years between October 1890 (when he went up to Trinity College, Cambridge) and August 1914 (when the First World War altered his life for ever) are memorable for his work in logic and the foundations of mathematics. His views on ethics, religion and politics had no similar impact on the subsequent development of analytical philosophy, and in the nature of the case are less strikingly original. They cast much light on the temperament that sustained Russell's passionate search for the ultimate truth about logic and mathematics, but they are not – as Russell himself insisted they were not – in the same intellectual class as that work. In any event, originality in logic is a different matter from originality in ethics or religion; fundamental discoveries may well be made in logic or mathematics, but the very idea of a fundamental discovery in politics or morals is suspect. It was only occasionally, and when excited to it by Lady Ottoline Morrell, that Russell saw himself as the prophet of new religious insights;[1] essays such as his famous essay on 'The Free Man's Worship' were not contributions to revealed religion but speculation on the meaning of life, a subject which allows room for endless discussion but not for proof and not much for prophecy.

If they were not as important to himself or to intellectual history as his views on logic and the foundations of mathematics, Russell's views on religion, morals and politics are still of great interest. Over the twenty-four years Russell changed his mind a good deal; in moral philosophy he began by half-heartedly accepting McTaggart's view that the ultimate good was the universe itself and the intellectual love of the Absolute with which it was imbued, then followed G. E. Moore's 1903 doctrine in *Principia Ethica* that goodness is an objective, but non-natural and un-analysable property of good things, events and actions, and by 1914 had come to think that morality was subjective, and objective moral properties a figment of the imagination.[2] A curiosity of these changes is that they did not correlate with his practical views at all; much of the time he defended a rather brutal utilitarianism in politics, while still committed to the philosophical view that only the detached love which God is said to feel for his creation is really good. His views are interesting, too, as an expression of a frame of mind apparently common among Edwardian intellectuals; this is not wholly easy to describe, but it commonly involved the world-weary reflection that human life is not a great blessing and is for most people a dreary and monotonous progress from the cradle to the grave. On this view, progressive politics cannot do much more than enable more people to be more bored for longer – but, strangely enough, while Russell and his friend Gilbert Murray might say this in letters, they devoted a lot of energy to liberal and humanitarian projects all the same. 'Do you want these people to last forever?' Murray wrote. 'A man selling dead and naked larks outside the Bibl. Lorenziana today had lasted 70 years. And you complain that that is not enough.' Russell often felt much the same, reversing roles to write and say that Murray was a utilitarian, but he, Russell, thought happiness wholly undesirable and misery the sign of moral purity. It seemed to make no difference to his willingness to stand up for liberal good causes.[3] No doubt, nobody ought to be held responsible for tired asides in their private correspondence; yet even Russell's public writing on politics swung between utopian hope for the future and wild irritation with the present; his hankering after some form of mystical insight into what really mattered and the sense that *sub specie aeternitatis* much of human life didn't matter very much is of a piece with that. It evidently does much to explain why he was so easily affected by Wittgenstein, Conrad and Lawrence in spite of finding their moral attachments entirely unacceptable.

Readers of Russell are sometimes puzzled by the seeming discrepancy between his romantic passions and the cool analytical techniques that he introduced to philosophy. Russell himself describes his adolescence as a time when 'I was quite unable to combine into a harmonious total seventeenth-century knowledge, eighteenth-century beliefs and nine-teenth-century enthusiasms'.[4] In fact, there is little real discrepancy, but because Russell's authority as a social and political critic rested on a philosophy which he insisted was irrelevant to his opinions on practical matters, some sense of what that philosophy was is more than useful. Russell published several accounts of his philosophical development; they varied a good deal in seriousness and the degree of detail they went into. However, they all struck a similar note. Russell's first interest in philosophy sprang from a thwarted religious impulse. Certainly, he no longer believed in God. He still wanted to understand the universe at the deepest possible level. As much as Plato, he felt that the truth about reality could not lie on the surface of appearances, but must be sought in some deeper level of reality, to be revealed by mathematics or logic or geometry. When Wittgenstein persuaded him that logic was only 'conventionally' true, and that mathe-matics was therefore not a guide to the structure of the universe but a handy tool for computation, he lost much of his passion for the subject.[5] The driving force behind his concern to explain mathematics in terms of the new formal logic was thus not mere intellectual tidiness. It was, rather, the same desire for an insight into the ultimate nature of things that had driven Leibniz to metaphysical extravagances which Russell was among the first to interpret sympathetically as an attempt to conjure the essence of reality with the tools of formal logic.[6]

Russell was briefly a Hegelian, committed to the view that all relations were internal and therefore logical, that our apparently external and physical dealings with the world were under a proper interpretation really internal, and thus that all 'factual' knowledge was illusion, since reality could only be understood as a whole. By the turn of the century he had been converted by G. E. Moore to the atomistic and analytical views he held for the rest of his life. We did know lots of particular truths about the world, though we might be hard put to it to say just what they meant; but reality was not simply hidden from us, and it was not something other than what empirical sensation and reflection revealed. Russell was an enthusiastic convert: 'Hegel had maintained that all separateness is illusory and that the universe is more like a pot of treacle than a heap of shot. I therefore said, "the universe is exactly like a heap of shot".'[7] This cheerful recollection of a young man's rebellion does not go very deep, but it suggests something that does: good philosophical method, for Russell, was thereafter analytical in character. Readers of his *Problems of Philosophy* were given a course in the application of analysis to traditional problems of metaphysics and the theory of knowledge. On analytical assumptions, philosophical insight can be had only by separating out the elements of knowledge and experience, not by trying to represent them as aspects of some intelligible whole. It is hardly surprising that by the 1930s Russell thought of philosophy as an adjunct of science, nor that the so-called 'philosophy of common sense' which flourished in the 1950s seemed to him to be obscurantist and unwilling to take science seriously. Though it, too, was deeply in his debt for the view that philosophy was analysis, its attachment to common sense was, he thought, an uncritical preference for the metaphysics of the Stone Age.[8]

The techniques of analysis were to be developed from those which the new formal logic had given the philosopher. This is not the place to try to give an account of the way Russell's views on meaning, knowledge, the nature of mind and the physical world developed over a lifetime; Russell was, as C. D. Broad complained, prone to invent a brand new philosophy every five years. But if we cannot go far into the content of his work, an example of the technique in operation will convey the flavour of his philosophy. It is an instance, too, on which Russell draws when explaining why all moral propositions are strictly speaking false.[9] For the logician interested in giving an account of how propositions mean what they do, several sorts of proposition seem particularly awkward. 'This coat is white' seems to be readily analysed: 'this coat' picks out this coat, while 'white' picks out a property which is predicated of it. The proposition is true if this coat *is* white, false if this coat is not. 'The present king of France is bald' presents problems, however. There is no present king of France; but if there is no present king of France, the phrase 'the present king of France' does not pick out anything for us to predicate baldness of. If propositions must be true, false or meaningless, we have a problem on our hands. 'The present king of France is bald' seems to be perfectly meaningful; it is not gibberish in the way 'bald France king present of the is' is gibberish, nor *odd* in the way 'colourless green ideas sleep furiously' is odd. Yet, if there had to be a present king of France before we could say something true or false about him, the proposition could be neither true nor false.

Faced with such puzzles, philosophers had sometimes resorted to heroic ways out. One was to appeal to the idea of 'subsistence'; even in a proposition such as 'the Golden Mountain does not exist', the Golden Mountain must be allowed *sub*sistence so that it could be referred to and its real existence denied. These moves, said Russell, offended against that sense of reality which we ought to preserve even in the most abstract disciplines. Or, as he later put it, if we resort to this sort of notion, we shall end up with a zoo full of ontological monsters.[10] In a famous paper, 'On Denoting', he employed the techniques he and Whitehead had had to use in analysing the foundations of mathematics to clear out the monsters. 'The present king of France is bald' was misleading, because its apparent or merely grammatical form was different from its true logical form. When it was properly transformed to reveal its true structure, the paradoxes vanished. 'The present king of France' was a complex denoting expression, best analysed as 'there is something, X, which is identical with the present king of France, and if there is anything, Y, which is also identical with the present king of France, then Y and X are identical'; it follows that 'the present king of France is bald' is false, because it asserts the existence of a present king of France, and there is no present king of France. Whether this is the right way to analyse such propositions has been disputed ever since, but the validity of the technique of reinterpretation has not.[11]

The method is endlessly applicable; propositions which seem to breed paradoxes are to be cleaned up by being shown to be misleadingly expressed. In epistemology, claims which seem dubious are analysed into less-dubious and more-dubious components; knowledge of our own mental states is immediate and non-inferential, knowledge of the external world inferential and to that degree uncertain. The technique is necessarily reductive and atomistic; existence, meaning and thought are to be reduced to their primitive elements and reconstructed from that basis up. Over a lifetime Russell held many different views about just what the components were and just how they were to be assembled. What gave him such an astonishing intellectual ascendancy was the combination of imagination in inventing and resolving problems and an incisiveness in pressing home difficulties in his own analyses which verged on a talent for intellectual infanticide. What never altered after the turn of the century was the method.

There are two further features of Russell's views which are worth dwelling on briefly, because they illuminate his vision of the point of doing philosophy in the first place, and thus his moral allegiances if not his moral philosophy. Although he often said that the world was only knowable as an inference from our sensations, he always held that the task of philosophy was to discipline thought; all thinking should strive to reflect reality as accurately as possible, yet another reason for thinking that philosophy and science were natural allies. This is what lies behind the other striking feature of his work, which was an extreme antipathy to all forms of pragmatism. The doctrine that truth was 'what it paid to believe' revolted his puritan soul. Much in Russell's moral and political philosophy is reminiscent of much in pragmatism; in particular, Russell's stress on impulse, and on the importance of developing 'compossible' impulses, is very like John Dewey's. None the less, it was not mere pride which led Russell to distinguish his own views so sharply from those of the pragmatists; it was a deep moral revulsion at any philosophy which could play fast and loose with truth.

Russell combined these transcendental interests with political interests of an everyday kind. He did not take a public role in the political controversy over the Boer War, but it forms the main topic of non-geometrical interest in his extended correspondence with the Swiss mathematician and enthusiast for Ido, Louis Couturat. Russell later wrote of him, 'He devoted himself to advocating an international language. Unfortunately international languages are even more numerous than national ones. He did not like Esperanto, which was the general favourite, but preferred Ido. I learned from him that Esperantists (so at least he assured me) were wicked beyond all previous depths of human depravity, but I never examined his evidence.'[12] Sadly, there is no evidence of this in his letters to Russell, though there are a good many shrewd questions about the Boer War. Russell lectured on the virtues of Free Trade during the Tariff controversy of 1903–4; and he stood for Wimbledon as the Suffragist candidate in 1907. There is not much detailed evidence of his views on Free Trade – the lectures seem not to have survived, though one or two essays have done; and there is only one pamphlet of his own beside newspaper reports of the Wimbledon by-election to fill out his views on female suffrage. The pamphlet was provoked by A. V. Dicey's *Letters to a Friend on Votes for Women*, and is a cheerful assault on arguments which he dismisses as 'old friends which have done duty against every reform since the ancient Britons ceased to dye themselves with woad'. Of Russell's own views, little more emerges other than that he thought women should have the vote on the same terms as men.[13] These interventions in day-to-day politics, and his faintly comic attempt to secure selection as the Liberal candidate for Bedford in 1910, are at the lowest estimate entertaining, and not without some intellectual interest.

Before turning to these, a sketch of his life during these years is indispensable. He went up to Trinity College, Cambridge, in October 1890 as a mathematics scholar; he was examined by A. N. Whitehead, who rightly prided himself on seeing the original intellect hidden behind Russell's shyness. Indeed it is said that Whitehead destroyed his original mark sheet to secure Russell's election as a scholar. He spent three years reading mathematics and emerged as Seventh Wrangler; he then decided to stay for a fourth year to read philosophy – 'Moral Sciences' as the tripos was known until the 1970s. Details of his intellectual life are sparse, but he made friendships which lasted for half a century with the Trevelyan brothers, Charles Sanger, the Llewelyn Davieses and, a few years later, with G. E. Moore. He was elected to the Apostles in 1892, a tribute to his personal charm as well as to his cleverness and his aristocratic background, for the society insisted on a wittiness and a freedom from acrimony which would have tested many clever men and Russell himself in later life.

Russell was not a philosophical innocent when he arrived in Cambridge. Not all his knowledge came from books; through his brother Frank he had met the American philosopher George Santayana; his Uncle Rollo had introduced him to the physicist John Tyndall, whose interest in the impact of scientific thought on western religion and other superstitions was as great as Russell's, and in his uncle's house in Hindhead he met George Bernard Shaw, the Comtean positivist Frederic Harrison, Beatrice Potter, soon to be Mrs Beatrice Webb, and Graham Wallas, the Fabian socialist and professor of politics who was to influence Russell by reminding him of the importance of the irrational in politics and of the importance of education both formal and informal.[14]

Russell did not think of making a career out of philosophy, even when he had got a First Class with Distinction in Moral Sciences. The first business he wished to settle was that of his marriage to Alys Pearsall Smith, the sister of Logan Pearsall Smith, a Balliol friend of his brother Frank, through whom he had first met her. His grandmother was fiercely opposed to their marriage – Alys was five years older than he, the Pearsall Smiths were neither well-off nor well connected, and no doubt Countess Russell feared that the marital record of the Amberleys and of Russell's older brother boded ill for whatever a twenty-one-year-old might plunge into. Frank had already turned out to be a source of matrimonial trouble; subsequently he became famous as the last member of the House of Lords to be tried by a jury of his peers. They convicted him of making a bigamous marriage, and he served six months in jail. Countess Russell's tactics were ill-judged – they were cruel but ineffective; she dangled the threat of madness in front of her grandson, reminded him that his Aunt Agatha had never married because she had delusions during her engagement, and that his Uncle William had been in a mental hospital for years. Russell's diary contains a particularly painful entry from this time: 'July 21. 1893. I dreamt last night that I was engaged to be married to Alys, when I discovered that my people had deceived me, that my mother was not dead but in a madhouse: I therefore had of course to give up the thought of ever marrying. This dream haunts me.'[15] During daylight brisk common sense prevailed; he and Alys would not have children. It was her lack of inhibitions which had attracted him to her; if she was prepared to talk about free love, she would not flinch at contraception. None the less, he agreed to put up with a three-month separation from Alys, and to spend the time in the Paris Embassy to see if he ought to enter the diplomatic service. He came back more determined than ever to marry, and with the foundations laid both for his future hatred of the Foreign Office and for his disapproval of the policy of *entente* with France. Since he had inherited enough to live on when he came of age, there was no financial problem about his marriage, and in December 1894 it duly took place.

He was to try for a fellowship at Trinity the next year – the subject he would write on was the foundations of geometry – but he was also tempted by economics. Alys was interested in the condition of women in Germany, and Berlin was as good a place as any to think about geometry and economics, so they filled in time in Berlin. The fellowship was secured in August 1895, and the stay in Berlin provided the material for six lectures at the newly founded London School of Economics (LSE) which were given in the spring of 1896 and emerged in print as *German Social Democracy*.[16]

Russell's first book is neither stale nor out of date even now. It voices the doubts about Marxism which Russell felt all his life; early and late he thought Marxism was an impressive intellectual construction, but a poor guide to action, especially for western countries. He understood from the outset that the attractions of Marxism had nothing to do with the merits of Marx's economic theory. Russell thought the labour theory of value simply wrong, and most of Marx's predictions false, but this, he saw, was neither here nor there. 'For Social Democracy is not a mere political party, nor even a mere economic theory; it is a complete self-contained philosophy of the world and of human development; it is, in a word, a religion and an ethic. To judge the work of Marx, or the aims and beliefs of his followers, from a narrow economic standpoint, is to overlook the whole body and spirit of their greatness.' Bourgeois commentators who thought Marxism would wither away because of its errors were deluded. Sorel described Marxism as 'social poetry'; in somewhat the same way, Russell claimed that the philosophical origins of Marxism were more important than any economic theory. For what Marx produced was a systematic world view with the prestige of science and the emotional qualities of myth.[17] Friends and enemies were set apart as in any religious epic; the bearers of the future and the candidates for the dustbin of history were plainly labelled; the triumph of the good and the confounding of the wicked were assured. The essence of Marxism was the epic account of the class war.[18]

The condensed summary of the *Communist Manifesto*, in which Russell vindicates his claim that 'for terse elegance, for biting wit, and for historical insight, it is one of the best pieces of political literature ever produced', perfectly catches what Russell saw as the religious appeal of the creed.[19] Marx's claim that everything is in flux, in a state of constant upheaval, yet always tending to one ultimate goal possesses just the blend of revolutionary fervour and fatalist assurance that new religions rely on. The combination of the dialectical method and a materialist analysis is a logical confusion but a rhetorical triumph. Logically, it is a confusion because the dialectic, as a process of change through contradiction and the resolution of contradiction, could only characterize the world if the world was ultimately mental or spiritual, embodying ideas which could contradict one another. Hegel had claimed just that, but Marx denied it. But the thought that social change was driven by contradictions and sharp logical oppositions was indispensable to Marx; socialism had to be as inescapable as the conclusion of a valid argument. Conversely, Marx's stress on material factors, on productive forces and technical change, all served to anchor this conviction in the everyday world. This determinism implied that the opponents of the proletariat were not to be blamed for being oppressive and brutal – they had no choice; nor was the proletariat to be led into battle by moral exhortation – it, too, had no choice but to fight. Russell elegantly picks up the crucial point: theories of social evolution usually lead to gradualist politics, because evolution is a process of gradual change. But if you graft a theory of evolution on to a dialectical philosophy which deals in sharp discontinuities, you may argue, as *The German Ideology* says, that social evolution proceeds by means of political revolution.[20] There is no room for utopianism or mindless revolutionism, but no room either for parliamentary and gradualist illusions.

Russell's pleasure in the rhetorical glories of Marxism did not stop him being severe on its political results. He believed that the resources of a radical liberalism had been underrated by the German Left. Moreover, the SPD had built too many hopes on one of Marx's weakest predictions, the prediction of working-class 'immiseration'. Marx had thought that working-class wages would always be kept at a rock-bottom subsistence level; the empirical failure of the prediction was too obvious to be blinked, and Eduard Bernstein based his 'revisionism' on just that point. However, immiseration was a central plank in one variety of Marxism – if capitalism was so oppressive that it could not even keep its workers alive, then they evidently *had* to revolt. To give up this conviction came hard. And it implied, as Russell saw perfectly well, that parliamentary politics might suit the working class better than insurrectionary politics, and that trade-union pressure for better wages and conditions under capitalism might do more good than orthodox Marxism had ever allowed. Indeed, Russell's grasp of the way Marxist politics and economics interacted was impressive. He saw that the image of capitalism as a monolith was essential in inciting the workers to revolt. If there was nothing to be done except work for its destruction, the role of trade unions could only be to encourage solidarity and to sharpen the sense of irreconcilable opposition to the employers. If piecemeal gains were possible, specialized institutions might perform all sorts of specialized tasks; and the question of how to use political and economic opportunities needed discussion rather than dogma – in Germany the great question was whether to fight for the right to organize in trade unions, etc., or whether to campaign for universal suffrage first. In the end the workers had to have both the vote and the right to organize, but which came first was a contingent matter, and the SPD did itself no good by trying to deduce an answer from dogmatic principles.

One reason why wages had risen rather than fallen was the growth of new skills; this, however, created an intermediate stratum of skilled workers whose interests were straightforwardly allied, neither to those of the unskilled workers nor to those of the management. Once again, this blurred the sharp lines on which Marx's prognosis rested; there would be members of the non-propertied classes who would either lose in the transition to socialism or who at any rate might well gain very little, certainly too little to give them any reason to prefer the risky business of revolution to the politics of gradualism.[21] The same moral followed from other aspects of Marx's theory. Russell thought that the 'law' of the increasing concentration of capital was valid in industrial contexts; firms were getting bigger, the amount of capital a given enterprise needed to control was increasing, and in some areas – the railways were an obvious instance – the firm was coextensive with the state.[22] Yet the tendency was not universal; many agricultural holdings became much more efficient when broken up into smaller units; so did some industries. Quite apart from the economics of concentration, the political point was that Marx assimilated industrial and agricultural workers without enough care for the facts; if concentration applied everywhere, there would soon be a homogeneous proletariat facing a homogeneous capitalist enemy – the fact that it did not was part of the explanation of the SPD's inability to broaden its appeal among the peasantry.[23] It hardly needs stressing that the Soviet Union has shown just what damage Marxism's *a priori* approach to the issue has done.

Even in industry Marx had been off-target. Although he had gradually come to terms with the limited liability joint-stock company, he had not revised his first thoughts on concentration. He had failed to consider the extent to which the control of large amounts of capital by one management was compatible with its ownership remaining unconcentrated, or even with its ownership becoming increasingly dispersed. The shareholders of a private company might perform no productive or economic function, but they made a large political difference. They enlarged the class of those who had an interest in the survival of private property and formed an intermediate layer between owners and non-owners. Once more the heightened antagonisms of Marxian theory were not present.[24]

Most of *German Social Democracy* is devoted to a short history of the SPD; it has the verve of his later essays on politics, but less of the urge to shock. As in later essays, it was a history with a moral. Russell argued that the attempts of the old order to rig the constitution of Germany generally, and of Prussia more particularly, in the interests of landed property and its allies would end in civil war. By contrast, British liberal democracy was flourishing and happy. One of Russell's charges against Prussian conservatism was that it would bring about the disasters it feared; excluding the socialists, proscribing trade unions and making government immune to parliamentary control would not hold up the transfer of power so much as ensure that the new world would be governed by embittered and ignorant working-class politicians who lacked all political skills. The SPD could not come out of the ghetto until the government invited it out.

German Social Democracy was well received except by those who thought due deference ought to be paid to all monarchs, even German ones.[25] The book put Russell firmly on the left of the political spectrum – he had no time for inherited power, doubted the legitimacy of landed property, and thought universal adult suffrage the only tolerable basis of political authority; but he was no socialist. He felt no sort of solidarity with working people; and he thought that under any regime differential rewards for differential contributions would be required. Indeed, at the age of twenty-four he was as ambivalent as ever about the demands of justice versus those of personal merit. On the latter he was unabashedly élitist and cheerfully declared that Darwin was worth thirty million ordinary men. On the larger issues on which socialists and liberals disagree, all his life he was torn between thinking that private property was mostly indefensible and the fear that without it society would also lose the independence and initiative which (some) people with private incomes could display. It is unfair and inaccurate to suppose that Russell's views

31

were coloured by the fact that he himself lived on the income from the £20,000 he had inherited at twenty-one. Early and late, he worried about how intelligent and original minds were to be given the freedom and the leisure they required, but, as he wrote in 1896, 'I would wish wealth to be not hereditary, but the perquisite of certain posts of distinction, whether in the service of the State, in art or literature, in Science or Industry, or, in short, in any useful human activity. In this way, we should not be oppressed by that weight of stupidity which usually accompanies the inheritance of wealth from a freebooting ancestry.' He always treated his own money as a social fund, setting up a studentship at the LSE, lavishing it on support for A. N. Whitehead's research, sponsoring Mary Pearsall Smith and Bernhard Berenson when they ran off together and, less romantically, bailing out his mother-in-law.[26] He was not in the least alarmed at the prospect of earning his own living once it was gone.

After *German Social Democracy*, he concentrated on the philosophy of mathematics. His fellowship did not oblige him to live in Cambridge, and he and Alys lived mostly at Fernhurst in Surrey. In 1901, he fell out of love with Alys, or discovered that he was bored by her, perhaps; thereafter they got into the habit of living apart for long periods, he in Cambridge, she elsewhere. Until the complete severing of relations in 1911, things were kept on a footing which avoided scandal and allowed them to campaign together in the Wimbledon by-election of 1907. It was a miserable time for Russell, who felt that he could not work properly so long as he was constrained by his ties to Alys; it was very much worse for her, since she was not merely the rejected party but had to endure a great deal of unkindness from Russell. His aristocratic contempt for the plebeian manners of the Pearsall Smiths was no longer kept under control, and what was worse was his habit of turning it into a matter of moral principle.[27] The miseries of private life did not in fact do much to hinder his work; it was in those years that he and Whitehead wrote *Principia Mathematica*, and in later life he said with some justice that his mind had been at its best in that decade.

Principia Mathematica set out to show how mathematics could be founded on the new formal logic. In part the ambition was to found mathematics on something more certain than itself; as we have seen, Russell's quest for certainty had led him *to* mathematics, but also led him to doubt whether mathematics was certain enough. In part, it was a philosophical enterprise pure and simple, for it was an attempt to found mathematics on what ought in principle to be the simpler and more basic elements of thought. The book itself was so enormous that Russell and Whitehead took it to

Cambridge University Press in a wheelbarrow, and so esoteric that the authors had to contribute towards the cost of its publication. Russell occasionally maintained that no more than half a dozen people had ever read it right through. To logicians it was a quarry of technical problems for the next quarter-century. Its importance to philosophy in general lay, as we saw earlier, in its establishing the analytical approach to philosophical questions as the only intellectually reputable method, a view which dominated ordinary British empiricism, logical positivism and philosophical approaches which are less easily categorized.

If Russell wrote little on politics for most of this time, he was more than casually interested in politics. He was a close friend of the Webbs and on good but not close terms with many other Fabians. One effect of these friendships was to make him, briefly, something of an imperialist. It is not easy to describe either the kind of imperialist Russell sometimes was, nor the kind of imperialist he ceased to be. He certainly welcomed the march of European influence in the non-European world, but never thought that any one country was picked out by destiny to civilize the globe.[28] He disliked the treatment of native populations by their imperialist masters, and disliked even more the effect of militarism and imperialism on the home country. His hatred of German militarism during his stay in Berlin was consistent with a readiness to see Germany colonize large tracts of Africa. Nor was his antipathy to British imperialism part of a general hostility to patriotism; he frequently said, and perfectly truthfully, that love of England was almost the strongest feeling he possessed. Even in 1894, it had been that as much as his pleasure at returning to Alys which made him kneel and kiss the British earth on returning from Paris.

The Boer War revealed the limits of his patriotism. He was in correspondence with Louis Couturat, the Swiss mathematician who was a devoted internationalist and who taxed him with British wickedness. Couturat shared the common European view that the Boer War was simple bullying by a great power. Russell veered off in many directions. First he thought the war had been engineered by Chamberlain at the behest of the financiers who controlled the gold-mines of the Reef – a view which may have owed something to his lifelong passion for conspiracies, but which was quite largely true.[29] Then he came to think that there was a deep-laid plot to undermine British influence throughout the whole of Africa and that the Boer War was a legitimate response, less, however, as a matter of self-defence than because peace and enlightenment would come to Africa only if the continent was sensibly controlled by the imperial powers. It is noticeable that he never flinched at the thought that progress might require imperialism. When Couturat complained of the simple injustice of a rich and powerful people crushing a small, poor people like the Boers, Russell's answer was peremptory: political justice was whatever was demanded by the larger interests of the human race. Russell declared that he would not have expected a philosopher to oppose interest and justice as Couturat had done; there were larger interests and smaller interests, and justice was on the side of the larger interests. The British were on the side of the largest interest of all, that of the '*genre humain*'; British rule meant progress and therefore justice.[30]

Russell has left a dramatic and moving account of his sudden and decisive breach with imperialism.[31] One day in 1901, he returned from a bicycle expedition to find Mrs Whitehead suffering terrible pain from a heart attack; the experience revealed to him the appalling loneliness of suffering and turned him on the instant from a bellicose imperialist into a lover of his fellows who wished them nothing but good. His letters to Couturat reveal that this was a piece of myth-making. The incident of Mrs Whitehead's heart attack undoubtedly made a difference to his life, but it was a personal rather than a political difference. He realized how much he cared for Mrs Whitehead, was perhaps prodded towards a realization that he no longer cared for Alys, and had his already strong sense of isolation reinforced. It is less clear that it altered his political views; some time afterwards, he told Couturat all about Mrs Whitehead's illness and his own distressed reaction to it in a letter in which he reiterated and defended his previous moderate imperialism.[32]

Russell's utilitarian stance on political issues was a recurring feature of his politics. He was always a consequentialist and professedly concerned to calculate consequences in quantitative, even in mathematical, terms. What was unusual about him was his readiness to calculate in global terms and his confidence that he had got the sums right. His conviction that a British victory over the Boers was manifestly in the interests of 'humanity as a whole' and that the costs of imperialism were too small to offset its benefits was a leap beyond any possible evidence.

At the same time his fellow-feeling for the sufferings of those caught up in war was intense. Moreover he had an acute, if unexamined, sense of honour, and was straightforwardly disgusted by the British expedient of herding the Boers' families into concentration camps. Russell's utilitarianism stopped short of fighting wars by killing women and children. All the same, his anti-imperialism was weak enough to let him join the dining club which Sidney Webb set up in 1902 to reflect on the problems of running the Empire along progressive lines. 'The Co-efficients' numbered the future Foreign Secretary, Sir Edward Grey, among its members, but Russell was not a member for long. It is not clear why he left so swiftly. perhaps the feeling that he did not much care whether there was an Empire or not, perhaps his first inkling that war with Germany was the probable upshot of British foreign policy.

Russell later claimed that he had seen all along where Sir Edward Grey's policies would lead. In 1902–3, of course, Grey was out of office, and only became Foreign Secretary with the Liberal landslide of 1906. However, Grey accepted that Lord Lansdowne's policy of *entente* with France was the cornerstone of British policy, and he argued for it at the Co-efficients. In office, he pressed on with making the ties with France even stronger. Russell thought that the policy had two great flaws; first, France was tied to Russia by military treaties which therefore tied Britain to Russia. Liberals loathed Russia as the land of the knout and imperialists feared Russia as a threat to British interests in India and Persia. Alliance with France contradicted any rational foreign policy by giving indirect aid to an autocracy which was itself a direct threat to British interests. Secondly, the French desire to revenge the defeat of 1870 and take back the lost provinces of Alsace and Lorraine heightened the German inclination to make sure of the gains of 1870 by fighting the Franco-Prussian War. A European war of revenge was a certainty in the near future. All this was reason for Britain to steer clear of entanglements. Britain had no vital interests on the continent; and German competition outside Europe could be appeased and contained readily enough. The French alliance would trap Britain into fighting just the kind of war which it had been every statesman's objective to avoid since the end of the Napoleonic Wars almost a century before.[33]

This was quite enough to drive Russell out of the Co-efficients. Even more compelling reasons were provided by the political events of the summer of 1903. In May, Chamberlain launched his campaign for tariff reform. He had many motives; one was to raise revenue, for there was something of a fiscal crisis at the time; another was to cement the Empire by a policy of imperial preference; yet another was the desire to protect British industry against alleged dumping and (perhaps) more efficient competitors. No doubt he also hoped to make the issue so much his own that he would become Prime Minister on it. Russell loathed Chamberlain anyway, and the scheme added to his dislike of the man and his policies. Free trade seemed to Russell the 'one sane element of internationalism', and he at once turned to propaganda on its behalf.[34] At the time he was writing to Elie Halévy, who was then as much a philosopher as a historian, and who was convinced that in an age of imperialism Britain had to renounce free trade. Russell denied it. Every time Halévy produced what purported to be evidence to show how well a country had done under protection, Russell retorted, as orthodox economists did, that it would have done even better without it. The one exception admitted by predecessors such as Mill was the protection of infant industries which would eventually be able to compete without assistance but which needed the help of a (tapering) tariff to get started. Russell was more impressed by the stimulus to inefficiency that tariffs must provide. 'It is possible that, in a few trades, the first effect of Protection might be to stimulate enterprise; but it is at least equally probable that it would cause contentment with ancient methods and antiquated plant.'[35]

Russell's arguments were not very exciting – they were the stock-in-trade of classical economics – and he did not anticipate later ideas about the way governments can affect employment by acting on the demand for domestic goods or shift the terms of trade in their favour if they can impose a tariff without encountering retaliation. In any case, what impressed him was less the economic case than the political one. The fact that it was Chamberlain who had advocated a tariff proved that it was a piece of nationalistic militarism and Russell would have none of it. Anyway, it was foolish: the white dominions would not sacrifice their industries for the sake of Britain, which was what the policy demanded.[36] And the traditional argument against taxes on food was as strong as ever. Tariffs were a tax on 'the people's loaf'; nor could they be defended in Britain as a way of preserving a large farming community, since there was no longer one to preserve. The British working man had become slowly better off precisely because his food had been imported from cheaper and cheaper sources; to reverse this would be mad. It would also be unjust, since taxes on food fall most heavily on those who spend the largest proportion of their incomes on food, that is, on the poor.[37] In the event, Halévy was proved wrong; the British turned away from tariffs, either on principle or because Chamberlain fell ill and could not keep up the pressure. The Liberal landslide in the general election of 1906 put paid to the issue for the immediate future, and it was sixty-five years more before food taxes became part of the economic scene when Britain joined the European Economic Community.

1907 saw the first of Russell's three appearances on the hustings.[38] A by-election at Wimbledon found the local Liberals unable or unwilling to fight a hopeless campaign against an undistinguished but popular Conservative – Henry Chaplin, whose only claim to fame was the ownership of Hermit, one-time winner of the Derby. Russell's decision to stand upset the local Liberals; they did not wish to be associated with a man who stood as the 'Suffragist and Free Trade' candidate, but did not want to look cowardly by endorsing no one. Russell did not endear himself to all shades of feminist opinion either; in supporting the suffra*gists*, or constitutional campaigners for votes for women, he was at odds with the suffra*gettes* who were enthusiasts for direct action. In 1907 Russell was not a defender of direct action, or indeed of anything beyond ordinary electoral politics, though there is some doubt about the basis of his objections to direct action. Later he claimed that they were tactical rather than principled; militant methods would alienate the public and so slow the day when justice would be done. Writing about the by-election in the *Autobiography*, however, he says, 'On pacifist grounds I disliked the Militants and worked always with the Constitutional Party.'[39] The campaign was full of absurd moments which greatly amused the press – rats were let into a hall where Russell was addressing a largely female audience, Alys was struck by an egg hurled by an irate Tory, and so on. Large intellectual issues were not prominent – but Russell did quite decently for a maverick candidate, and the Union of Women's Suffrage Societies, under whose auspices he had fought and who had found £1500 to pay his costs, professed themselves well pleased.[40]

Russell was frequently approached by Liberal associations hoping to secure him as candidate, but he turned them down. In April 1910 he made a serious attempt to secure the nomination at Bedford; the seat was practically a family fief, but internal squabbles had lost it to the Conservatives in the election of January 1910; Russell failed to please the local committee, however; the main counts against him – and the ones he quotes in his own account of the event – were his agnosticism and his unwillingness to attend church services in his constituency for the sake of appearances. His enthusiasm for giving the vote to women cannot have helped his cause either, if only because the Asquith cabinet was still adamantly opposed and was determined not to have a party split on the issue when the party was locked in battle with the Lords over Lloyd George's budget of 1909 and was facing every sort of opposition to its plans for Irish Home Rule. Russell's address to the local association is an interesting document; it shows the extent to which old Radical cries and new welfare measures could blend with each other. Russell spoke up for Lloyd George's budget, for measures to cure the abuses of the drink trade, for measures to restrict the powers of the House of Lords, and, at some length, for a new tax on land values.[41] 'The taxation of Land Values has had my wholehearted support for many years ... The excellence of such taxation is to be measured by the hostility it arouses in landlords.' Taxing increases in the value of land is an old idea which neatly combines the search for justice and the search for efficiency. When land values rise, this is usually nothing to do with the owner's efforts – he simply gets a windfall gain from other people's efforts. Taxes on windfalls are about as painless as taxes can be. Moreover, the imposition of the tax offers to the owner who has to pay the tax an incentive to see that the land is employed as gainfully as possible in order to pay the tax. If a new process allows the iron ore on your land to be used in making steel, a tax on the new value is a way of pressuring you to see that the ore is dug and used. Russell claimed that the tax was part and parcel of the defence of free trade, and so it was, mainly because he thought the only alternative to a land tax was protectionism, but more interestingly because it can be seen as making an imperfect market more nearly perfect.[42]

Between 1910 and the outbreak of war Russell's interest in politics remained strong, but did not result in many very public activities. He continued to lecture on women's suffrage, wrote to newspapers on behalf of mistreated trade unionists, and continued to fulminate publicly and privately about the follies of imperialist competition. But the final collapse of his marriage, his separation from Alys and the beginnings of his prolonged love affair with Lady Ottoline Morrell all preoccupied him too. Nothing in those years prefigured the anti-war crusader of 1914–18. Before we turn to his role in the opposition to the war and its impact on his political ideas, two aspects of his development as a social and political thinker ought to be dealt with. By 1914, Russell had arrived at a view about ethics and a view of religion which were, in outline, to remain constant thereafter. He wrote a great deal about religion after 1914, but what one might call the characteristic tone and the characteristic pattern of argument were established by then; his later writings were essentially essays in the popularization of earlier views. As for ethics (not in the sense of moral advice, but in the philosophical sense of a theory about the intellectual status of moral and political judgement), Russell wrote rather little after 1914. Moral advice, of course, was another matter; that he gave in plenty, as we shall see. Moral philosophy did not much interest him; philosophy was a matter of establishing the truth about the world, but morality, he came to think, has nothing to do with the truth about the world and therefore in the strictest sense nothing to do with philosophy either. He began his discussion in the *Outline of Philosophy* by more or less repudiating the subject altogether. 'Ethics is traditionally a department of philosophy, and that is my reason for discussing it. I hardly think myself that it ought to be included in the domain of philosophy, but to prove this would take as long as to discuss the subject itself . . .' In *The Philosophy of Bertrand Russell*, he added, "The only matter connected with ethics that I can regard as properly belonging to philosophy is the argument that ethical propositions should be expressed in the optative mood, not in the indicative. Where ethics is concerned, I hold that, so far as fundamentals are concerned, it is impossible to produce conclusive intellectual arguments.'[43] What remains of interest is what drove him to think this.

By 1914 Russell was best known outside narrowly philosophical circles as the author of 'A Free Man's Worship' (it began as '*The* Free Man's Worship' but changed articles on reprinting), and the attitudes struck in that essay are very characteristic of one, though only one, side of Russell.[44] It is worth looking at Russell's views on ethics and religion now, and for an obvious reason. Serious political theories must rest on some view or other about the standing of moral judgement, as well as on actual moral judgements, since much political theory is an account of the moral attractions and deficiencies of various courses of political action, backed by what the theorist takes to be compelling arguments. A theorist's view of the intellectual standards which ought to govern moral argument must make a great difference to the arguments he produces and the evidence he thinks relevant. What we in fact see in Russell's case is that it is his intense, though unstable, convictions about 'the human condition' which make most difference to his views and their presentation. Oddly, just as Russell's views about ultimate goodness made little difference to his views about politics, so his philosophical stance on the logic and metaphysics of morals made little difference to the way he presented his views about morality. Critics have complained that Russell presents his views in a casual, 'take it or leave it' fashion; to the extent that Russell thought, as for many years he did, that moral and political allegiances were no more arguable than any other matter of taste, his casualness may seem to be all of a piece with this underlying philosophical view. Yet this cannot be all that explains his casualness and unwillingness to conciliate and disarm his critics and opponents; when Russell espoused the 'objectivist' view of ethics put forward in G. E. Moore's *Principia Ethica* he was just as casual. I shall try to dispel the seeming paradox that subjectivism and objectivism both led to the same result. Russell's views on religion are interesting rather for the light they shed on his view of political psychology. The connection is not absolutely clear-cut or direct, but it is evident that much of the passion that went into Russell's politics had its roots in his interest in religion. He told Ottoline Morrell that the *Principles of Social Reconstruction* were written to reveal 'the spark of the infinite' within each of us. This was entirely consistent with thinking Christianity absurd and institutionalized religion obnoxious. Indeed Russell's sense that trying to catch the spark of the infinite in an institutional framework was grotesque was part of what made him something of a philosophical anarchist; it gave his political writings an oddly anti-political flavour, while lending his attacks on organized religion an almost religious fervour.[45]

The history of Russell's views on moral philosophy is, on the face of it, simple. For a time he accepted G. E. Moore's view that the goodness of actions or states of affairs consisted in their possession of a property named by 'good'; this property was simple, unanalysable and non-natural, that is, a genuine property but not one that scientific investigation could reveal, and although it might accompany other, natural properties it was not susceptible of further explanation or description.[46] With a simple natural property such as redness, all we can do to teach someone what redness is is show them red objects and hope they catch on. Similarly with goodness. Russell defended this objectivist view in his *Philosophical Essays*.[47] He was unsettled by Santayana's teasing discussion in *Winds of Doctrine* which Santayana published in 1913, and moved to thinking that moral judgements were not true or false but were more like commands or statements of desire. The argument for supposing that moral judgements ought to be couched in the optative mood is that 'murder is wicked' does not attribute the property of wickedness to murder but amounts rather to saying 'would that there were no murder' or 'I disapprove of murder'. The first is plainly neither true nor false, the second is true or false, but only of the person whose attitude is expressed, not of the thing disapproved of.[48] This is where matters stood in 1927 with his *Outline of Philosophy*. In 1954, his *Human Society in Ethics and Politics* took up a half-way position between objectivism and subjectivism in as much as he argued that moral judgements were not merely expressions of individual approval and disapproval, though they certainly did not attribute special, non-natural moral properties to states of affairs. He suggested that moral judgements were a disguised sociological judgement about the welfare of society. This did not follow – as Moore's claim about the existence of simple non-natural properties had – from an analysis of the literal meaning of 'good' and the like, but from reflection on the fact that even though there are no ethical properties, there is generally considerable overlap in the judgements made by different members of the same society. This fact invites the thought that what creates the agreement is social pressure and that what lies behind that pressure is consensus on what would benefit people in general.[49] Moral judgements are, in fact, though not as a matter of their logic, rough and ready utilitarian estimates. Russell found this view attractive, and he was in a famous tradition in holding it. What he thought of as wrong-headed moral views could be explained in terms of the false beliefs which underlay them, or in terms of the way powerful people could exert an influence which made people hold such false and socially useless beliefs. Even though moral judgements were neither true nor false, strictly speaking, because moral judgements 'should be enunciated in the optative or imperative mood, not in the indicative', there was the possibility of moral progress to the extent that moral judgements were founded on a more scientific and less superstitious view of the world. We find a some-what similar view in Hume and Mill, and it comes, perhaps, naturally to an empiricist of Russell's persuasion.[50]

Although this skeletal history of Russell's moral philosophy is not wrong (and is, indeed, his own), it leaves out some interesting issues and fails to tackle one important one. It leaves out Russell's earliest views, those he held before accepting the arguments of *Principia Ethica*; it is vague about what drove him to abandon that position; and it says nothing about what he thought as he was abandoning it. The important issue it does not touch at all is why he did not take moral philosophy more seriously as a foundation for his political views. In Kant, Hegel, Hume or Mill, there is a continuous line of argument linking their views on epistemology and morals with their views on such things as the legitimacy of the state, the obligation to obey the law and so on. In Russell there is not. Russell wrote almost nothing on what usually passes for political philosophy – the analysis of rights, law, justice, obligation. There is a good deal about particular sorts of authority and authority in particular states – and about the illegitimacy of states which are a threat to world peace.[51] These, though, are first-order political judgements; they *presuppose* a view about what makes a state legitimate, but they are not arguments for one. Whether Russell was convinced that moral judgements were objectively true or were rather the expression of subjective moral attitudes made no difference. He simply applied his own moral convictions to political issues – which is what his most famous statement of the distinction between his philosophy and his political activism said.[52] His changes of mind about the epistemological standing of moral judgements made no difference at all to his political views.

From the mid-1930s it was a common objection to logical positivism that its analysis of moral judgements as either nonsensical or 'expressive'

41

undermined people's convictions. Faced with the Nazi or Communist conviction that their values were inscribed in history, would not those who thought their values were only their own reactions lose heart and succumb to confident authoritarianism?[53] Russell never much minded this objection. His view of morality when he followed Moore and thought it 'objective' made it quite as little a subject for rational argument as it was on his 'subjectivist' analysis. Even before he accepted Moore's claim that goodness was a simple, non-natural property, and still held McTaggart's view of the ultimate good, he thought that the ultimate good was so remote from everyday politics that it was absurd to judge politics as more or less productive of ultimate good.[54] It is in this sense that Russell was not a political philosopher of an orthodox kind, though everything he wrote was, of course, marked by a distinctively philosophical approach.

Russell's first excursions into moral philosophy were unpublished.[55] They were the essays he wrote for himself or the Apostles in the 1890s. Russell shared what seems to have been the common view in his circle, that McTaggart's claim that the ultimate good was the intellectual love which God felt for his universe was intellectually compelling but could provide no guide to everyday choice. It was an image of ethical perfection, like Spinoza's account of the free man who is not tossed this way and that by his passions but shares in the calm intellectual pleasure which God takes in his creation, and as such provides a vision of individual happiness or blessedness. Knowing this, however, will not help a man decide whether to be a conscientious objector, whether to wed or 'live in sin' and so on. This Spinozistic picture is in the usual sense hardly a moral ideal at all, but it powerfully influenced Russell, throughout his life, as one can see in his first essays, in 'The Free Man's Worship' and in innumerable other places.

What, then, of the morality of everyday life? Russell was tempted by utilitarianism, but saw that it could not provide an answer to every dilemma; the obvious difficulty of combining the principle of maximizing happiness with the injunction to spread it as widely as possible was merely the first of many problems. The indeterminacy of the notion of happiness was another. When he did decide in favour of consequentialism, the goal to be attained embraced knowledge and a civilized love of humanity rather than pleasure. Such goals would yield happiness, but it was not for that reason that they were to be valued. As for the utilitarian attempt to reduce happiness to the surplus of pleasure over pain, Russell could never quite believe that pleasures only differed in a quantitative way; some pleasures were simply better than others. Arguing with Couturat, he was ready to declare himself a utilitarian, but that was a way of insisting that coarser-grained considerations operate in politics than in the rest of life. Always, too, the Spinozistic goal of a calm acceptance of the world led him towards the idea that individuals should aim to render their own desires 'compossible' or mutually supportive, and that social ethics should adopt the same principle on a larger scale. For everyday morality he often fell back on common sense, not because he thought common sense embodied the wisdom of the ages, but because there was nothing else to fall back on, and mankind would not be *argued* into a morality which parted too drastically from common sense.[56]

A belief in common sense led Russell to abandon McTaggart's Hegelianism and then led him to accept Moore's analysis of goodness. Many critics find it hard to believe that common sense could teach us that beauty, goodness and truth are objective properties, but there is much to be said for the claim that Moore's analysis follows common sense. When we call something good, we must mean to say that it possesses a certain property, since if we wanted to say no more than that we liked or approved of whatever it was, we could have said that instead. Yet we do not think that goodness is on all fours with redness and hardness; all of which suggests that common sense does subscribe to the idea that it is a non-natural property. The philosophical climate has been for so long hostile to the idea that we possess a moral sense by means of which we detect the moral properties of actions and events that it is enough to gesture towards the thought that such properties need a special sense to detect them in order to discredit the whole idea. However, claims about the existence of moral properties can be detached from claims about how we perceive them. One can be agnostic about how we perceive them while still accepting Moore's claim that they are real properties of states of affairs; that at least seems to have been Russell's position. 'When we say that a thing is good in itself, and not merely as a means, we attribute to the thing a property which it either has or does not have, quite independently of our opinion upon the subject, or of our wishes or other people's.'[57]

In his *Philosophical Essays* of 1910, Russell tackled a wide range of issues in ethics – the indefinability of good, the distinction between the subjective and objective rightness of actions, the irrelevance of determinism to ethics, egoism, and the way to discover what is good in itself. Though, as he says, the discussion is doctrinally in Moore's debt, it could not be more different in tone. All memoirs of Moore point out that the impact of his views on what became known as 'Bloomsbury' was not philosophical, but the result of Moore's extraordinary sweetness of character and the long

43

discussion in the second half of *Principia Ethica* of the absolute value of beauty and friendship.[58] Russell, however, simply declined to give any account of what was in fact intrinsically good: other people could see it as well as he could, and if they couldn't, argument would not convert them. 'The making of such judgements we did not undertake; for if the reader agrees, he could make them himself, and if he disagrees without falling into any of the possible confusions, there is no way of altering his opinion.'[59] Russell's briskness is infinitely unlike Moore's patient advance on the truth – free will, for instance, is dealt with in a famous couple of sentences: 'People never do, as a matter of fact, believe that any one else's actions are not determined by motives, however much they may think *themselves* free. Bradshaw consists entirely of predictions as to the actions of engine-drivers, but no one doubts Bradshaw on the grounds that the volitions of engine-drivers are not determined by motives.'[60] And Russell's taste for the engaging paradox which will madden the virtuous is well to the fore when he argues that 'a man who, in exceptional circumstances, acts contrary to a received and generally true moral rule, is more likely to be right if he will be thought to be wrong, for then his action will have less tendency to weaken the authority of the rule'.[61]

Russell's arguments for the objectivity of goodness are now standard arguments. 'Good' cannot be reduced to anything subjective since that would remove the possibility of genuine evaluative disagreement. 'I like chicken' said by me is entirely consistent with 'I dislike chicken' said by you; 'murder is wrong' or 'fidelity is good' is flatly inconsistent with 'murder is good' and 'fidelity is wicked', no matter who says it. We evidently mean to attribute value to states of affairs, modes of conduct and the rest; we may partially resolve this value into natural properties – 'fidelity is good' may mean 'fidelity encourages friendship and security, and *they* are good' – but all such translation involves an implicit reference to what is good in its own right and not as a means to something else. Russell offers Moore's proof that the property of goodness is simple, unanalysable and non-natural: a person who says 'pleasure is good' is making a judgement, not offering a definition, as is shown by the fact that it makes perfect sense to deny the judgement but no sense to 'deny' a definition.[62]

Russell's discussion of rightness as distinct from goodness is less assured than the rest of his section on 'the elements of ethics'. He has (the traditional) problems with balancing goodness of motive and goodness of outcome as elements in judging an action right or wrong. To insist that only the action which in fact has the best possible consequences is *right* is impossibly rigorous; but to say that any action which the agent sincerely believes right *is* right allows through much that we rightly disapprove. Russell first suggests that there is 'one sense in which a man does right when he does what will probably have the best consequences, and another in which he does right when he follows the dictates of his conscience, whatever the probable consequences may be'.[63] But he does not stick to this view. The man who tries to do what is right does what his conscience tells him only because he thinks his conscience tells him what is right – not merely what it approves of. The objective sense of right is primary, therefore. Objectively, the right action is the one with the probable best consequences. Happily, conscience is largely determined by training in the rules of our society, and its rules have largely been evolved for their good consequences; feelings of obligation and objective rightness will therefore coincide pretty well.[64] The *de facto* best action Russell felicitously names 'the most fortunate action'.[65]

We can be obliged to do only what it is possible for us to do – we ought to do what is right, and 'ought implies can'. This raises the problem of determinism, for if determinism is true, then whatever we in fact do is the only thing we can do and moral judgement appears redundant. Russell's reply is the standard empiricist answer. The sense in which we can do what we do not do is not merely consistent with determinism but requires it. In a deterministic universe, we act as a result of our choices and choose as the result of our deliberations; if our actions were not caused by such processes, argument and exhortation would be pointless and indeed unintelligible. There are impossibilities which rule out praise and blame; I cannot be blamed for not preventing an accident by stopping a runaway train with my bare hands, and I cannot be encouraged to jump thirty feet into the air. These are not, however, impossibilities on a par with acting in the absence of appropriate causal antecedents. Russell comes close to following Moore's view that a person can 'act otherwise' if it is true that he *would act otherwise if he chose*. This analysis shows how the usual distinction between sane choosers and madmen incapable of choice survives determinism. The madman would not act differently, no matter what arguments were levelled at him; the sane man would.

The theory of 'psychological egoism' poses another threat to the view that we ought to do what is right by claiming that all we *can* do is pursue our own good. Russell neatly turns the point by distinguishing between the truth that I must have some reason for what I do and in that sense do it as part of my own projects, and the falsehood that the only project I can have is my own advantage. And Russell distinguishes between the true proposition that a man who does not do what he thinks he ought will be made unhappy by his lapse and the falsehood that he does what he thinks he ought only in order to make himself happy. Thus there is no philosophical difficulty about the common-sense view that we ought to do what is right, and that what is right is what will probably have the best consequences.

How are we to estimate what they are? This is what Russell refuses to tell us, for the reasons we have seen. He does, however, attempt to defuse the objection to his theory which rests on the fact that different people have very different ideas about what is or is not good. First, he points out that very few judgements are pure judgements of ultimate goodness; most are consequentialist judgements in which factual and evaluative claims are intermingled. When the factual disputes are resolved, evaluative agreement is almost invariably reached. Second, some bad things contain good elements and vice versa, so we have to be clear whether we are judging something as part of a whole or as it would be on its own. Thus, compassion is a good, but it requires the existence of someone else's misfortune, so it is debatable whether the world is better for its existence or not. The great defect of moralists and philosophers, on this analysis, is their desire to reduce everything to one or two simple principles, and to leave out of account all the factual complexities which make moral life difficult in reality. Moreover, they become over-attached to means and myopic about ends, with the result that they become obsessed with laying down rules and forgetful of their purpose.

Russell was not so much persuaded as mocked out of this view by Santayana's *Winds of Doctrine*. Santayana did not direct his irony at Russell's arguments for the objectivist theory of the good. What he did was more effective than that; in essence he raised one sceptical eyebrow as if to remind Russell that he had once objected to writers like Meinong because they offended his 'sense of reality'. Did Russell want to clutter the universe with 'non-natural' properties? Russell did not. After the war, he wrote but never published a little paper, 'Is there an absolute good?', which contains the gist of a theory he never explored but which would have served him very well. The paper distinguishes between the literal meaning of terms such as 'good' and the truth about the world. Russell sees the force of his old argument that the proposition that a thing is good and the proposition that it is bad really do contradict one another. The *grammar* of a proposition like 'piety is good' is certainly a matter of ascribing a property to piety. Russell now says that there is no such property and the proposition is therefore literally false. All evaluative

46

propositions purport to attribute to states of affairs properties which do not actually exist. The question which this raises is why we fall into the error of supposing that there are such qualities. Russell's reply is something like an appeal to Hume's claim that the mind is disposed to spread itself upon its objects. We project on to the things themselves the approval and disapproval which is really a matter of our own psyches. So, says Russell, we approve of a, b, c, etc., and therefore *call* them good. But 'good' does not *mean* 'I approve'; the connection between approval and the meaning of good is genetic, not logical. The literal meaning of 'piety is good' is thus 'piety has the same quality as truthfulness, friendship ...', but the only fact in the case is our approval of all these things – there is no such quality.

This 'error' theory explains something which Moore and Russell had never tried to explain, but which Russell now sees as a virtue in the theory. This is the connection between calling something good and our positive feelings for it. If goodness was a property on all fours with redness or hardness, it would be possible to agree with someone else about the goodness of something but disagree about its desirability – but 'I dislike hard apples' or 'I dislike red cars' are intelligible in a way that 'I dislike good apples' or 'I dislike good cars' are not entirely. Russell realized that 'goodness' had to be 'attractive'; adding yet another peculiarity to non-naturalness was philosophically implausible. If, however, the attribution of goodness to something *expresses* approval under the misleading guise of attributing a property to it, the connection between calling it good and inclining in its favour is simply explained. Russell concludes triumphantly that his theory does justice to all the facts without importing strange properties into our ontology. This little essay is perhaps the best thing he ever wrote on moral philosophy in the strict sense – that is, as an exercise in analysis rather than moral persuasion. It is brisk, original, clever and yet leaves all the room one could want for the creation of a substantial moral theory.[66] Russell's failure to follow it up is one of the many intellectual disappointments of his career in the 1920s and 1930s.

Russell's final views were set out in an accessible shape in *Human Society in Ethics and Politics* which was published in 1954. The chapters on ethics, which occupy the first quarter of the book, were written in 1946 as a conclusion to *Human Knowledge: Its Scope and Limits* but were omitted, because he was – as he had so often said – quite unsure whether ethics was in any sense a branch of knowledge. Russell's theory is not easy to characterize, and is in any case rather cluttered by his excursions into further discussions of the epistemological standing of ethics. However, it

47

is plausible to call the moral theory he produces a form of naturalism and up to a point a form of utilitarianism; it is not fully fledged utilitarianism because it does not assert that the *summum bonum* is happiness or pleasure, but the satisfaction of desires and impulses, and these as Russell had always said were not invariably directed towards happiness or pleasure. It is Russell's anxieties about the sense in which ethics was a matter of knowledge which cause difficulties. He begins by saying that the data of ethics are emotions. This must not be taken in the sense in which they would provide the data of a sociology of morals; it is not the fact that we *have* emotions which provides the starting point but the emotions themselves. This, however, is quite obscure, and Russell's gloss does not help. He considers the suggestion that 'murder is wrong' has a truth value, because it *means* 'most people who consider murder disapprove of it' – though that turns it into a sociological rather than a moral truth. He also tries to disarm the thought that approval and disapproval are 'only subjective' by pointing out that so are judgements about colour which, like moral judgements, only work because there is a *de facto* consensus about when to say what. But more fruitfully he turns to the view that the grammatical form of moral judgements is misleading. 'Murder is wrong' is a disguised imperative or optative, better read as 'let there be no murder' or 'would that there were no murder'.[67]

These analytical issues are not Russell's main concern, however. His concern is to offer a persuasive definition of 'good' in terms of the satisfaction of desire. This is a somewhat misleading way of putting it, although the concept of persuasive definition was a popular one in its day; for what we are asked to do is not to attach a meaning to 'good' but to accept a standard of goodness.[68] Russell's proffered standard is desire satisfaction; if accepted, it turns moral issues into factual ones, for the question we ask in contemplating actions, social customs, rules, laws and government policies is whether they will or will not lead to the satisfaction of as many desires as possible. Needless to say, there will be no very exact answer on many occasions. More problematically, it is a standard which can produce anomalous results; people's desires are often coloured by their existing moral views – are we to count these 'coloured' desires or not? If we do, we may reach the paradoxical result that in a society where many people loathe homosexuals, homosexuality is bad because it upsets so many people, whereas it would be perfectly all right in a society where such loathing did not exist. Russell seems inclined to swallow this degree of relativism, though not without anxiety.

Other issues cause more heart-searching. Given what Russell called a 'democracy not of persons but of desires', all desires are equal; bad ones are only bad in virtue of their consequences. The Nazi's desire to kill Jews is bad only because it is inconsistent with the satisfaction of the Jews' desire to go on living. Russell does not much like this conclusion but sees no ready way out – what he wishes to avoid at all costs is the chaos of contending appeals to moral intuition. Unfortunately, he does not work his way through enough examples to test his own intuitions about what outcomes are acceptable. Most of us think that sometimes the view that desire is bad only consequentially is justified and sometimes not. Russell offers us the example of the madman who is made happy by the (false) belief that his enemy is suffering torments; but here we concede that he might as well be made happy by the thought partly because it is false, and partly because he is mad and not responsible for his desires.[69] The Nazi is a different matter; he is, we think, sane and responsible for his desires. What he has is a desire he ought to wish himself rid of, just as we try to quell, say, daydreams of the misfortunes of our rivals. Bad desires are symptoms of a bad character, not free-floating events for which nobody is responsible. Russell's atomism led him to treat them as free-floating events, and the result is not happy. Compared with, say, Dewey, who tried to develop a more extended account of an ethics based on 'compossibility of desire', Russell's scheme is sketchy and undeveloped. The explanation is not discreditable, however. Once he had drawn the initial sharp line between genuinely philosophical inquiries and the realm of advocacy and persuasion, he was so unsure that there was anything worth saying about moral philosophy, and so passionate in innumerable good causes, that he turned away from philosophical ethics to a lifetime of advocacy and persuasion, though with some residual increase.[70]

In that advocacy he employs a rhetorical style and appeals to psychological considerations which have made many commentators regard him as a 'religious' thinker. Even those who see him as in some sense a 'saint of rationalism' and a figure in the humanist pantheon often treat him as a lay, secular visionary in the same line of descent as more traditional religious visionaries. It will be apparent by now that I am sceptical about this approach and think the rhetorical style of 'The Free Man's Worship' and of unpublished essays like 'Prisons' unconvincing in itself and something which Russell himself was right to dislike in retrospect. Like all of us, he was capable of self-deception and all the more so when he was particularly unhappy; it is hardly an accident that his most florid writing occurs when he is most miserable about the collapse of his first marriage and when he was most deeply embroiled with Lady Ottoline Morrell.[71]

Russell was an agnostic. As a consistent empiricist, he did not deny that God *might* exist; he simply thought it overwhelmingly unlikely. He was often asked what he would say when he got to heaven and had to justify himself before the Almighty; he invariably replied that he would ask God why he had provided such insufficient evidence of his existence. Against Pascal, who had urged us to bet on the existence of God because if we were right the pay-off was infinitely valuable, Russell retorted that God would want us to use our brains and would therefore approve of unbelievers who shared his view that the evidence was against God's existence. Russell's scepticism proceeds by negation in the sense that he denied the validity of all the traditional attempts to prove God's existence, though he did so so casually that he gives the impression that his disbelief is unshakeable. On the other hand, his arguments are cogent enough.[72]

He was not exactly indifferent to the existence of God and had very strong views about organized religion. At one level, he seems to have felt that the world would be made less bearable by the existence of God; the old 'argument from evil' weighed heavily with him – that is, the claim that the existence of evil was incompatible with the existence of a benevolent and omnipotent God. For any entity to have willed the existence of a world containing so much misery and folly would have been bad enough; for such an entity to claim to be perfectly good would have been utterly intolerable. As for the Christian churches, all of them were a conspiracy against truth, integrity and happiness. His assaults on Christianity are commonly conducted at the level of knockabout – a characteristic specimen being his reiterated complaint that Sabbatarianism starts from God's injunction not to work on Saturday and somehow derives the conclusion that we should have no fun on Sunday. His indignation at Catholic interdictions of birth control, however, was simply savage; insisting that children should be brought into the world when we know they will be ill, under-nourished, exploited and brutalized is a piece of cruelty on a level with the Conquistadores' practice of baptizing Indian babies and immediately beating their brains out in order that they should die in grace.[73] Rhetorically, all this suffers from the same defect that afflicted his writing on nuclear warfare – he cannot resist insulting his opponents. He is never content to say that they are wrong; he cannot resist adding that they are monsters of iniquity and sadists who have hardened their hearts to the sufferings of defenceless children. The example of people such as Mother Teresa who, however misguidedly, is desperately opposed to artificial birth control and abortion but devotes herself with entire unselfishness to the care of the sick and the dying in the hideous slums of

Calcutta shows that things cannot be so simple.

His purely intellectual quarrel with Christianity centred on the feeble arguments which pass for 'natural theology'. The First Cause argument is self-destructive – if *everything* has to have a cause, so does the First Cause. The argument from design is no better; there are many things with their own purposes in the world, but no sign of an overall purpose. Indeed, Russell was rather gloomily impressed by the implication of the second law of thermodynamics that the universe as a whole is running down, going, in the very long run, nowhere at all. 'Only within the scaffolding of these truths, only on the firm foundation of unyielding despair, can the soul's habitation henceforth be safely built.'[74] The moral argument for God is savaged; Kant held that there had to be a God to restore the balance between doing good (to others) and doing well (oneself) since it was so obvious that here below the virtuous were not particularly likely to be happy. This, says Russell, is like inferring the existence of good oranges at the bottom of a crate from the presence of bad ones at the top; the rational inference is that we've got a dud consignment. The theological implications of the analogy are not lost on Russell either.[75]

Unlike many free-thinkers, Russell was not impressed by the personality of Christ himself. He thought him much inferior in sweetness of character to Buddha and greatly inferior to Socrates in both character and intellect. His belief that he would return from the dead within the lifetime of his disciples was absurd, and his miracles reflect strangely on his wisdom – Russell followed John Locke in wondering why Christ should blast a fig-tree which was hardly acting strangely in not supplying figs out of season.[76] Moreover, there was a vindictive streak in the way he threatened his enemies with hell-fire and tried to persuade us into virtue as an insurance against the worm that never dies and the fire that never fades. Good-natured Christians try to persuade their twentieth-century readers that this is all to be taken metaphorically, but Russell will have none of it. So long as it was respectable to believe in the literal truth of such dire warnings, Christians believed in them. Only when humanitarians made Christians ashamed of their bloodthirstiness did they start saying that it was all a matter of metaphor.[77]

This leaves unexplained Russell's own rhetorical style, which certainly has streaks of the religiose in it. Russell emulated the traditional preacher in one way at least; he invariably painted the existing world in the blackest possible colours in order to contrast it with the heaven to which we might aspire if only we cast off sin – or, in Russell's version, if we cast away fear and superstition. What Russell most objects to in traditional religion is that it trades in fear; fear of death is doubtless the worst of the fears it relies on, but fear of ourselves and of public opinion figures largely, too. 'The Free Man's Worship' is rightly thought of by many people as an epitome of Russell's response. It is in essence a piece of pure self-assertion, a flat refusal to be frightened by metaphysical terrors. Certainly the universe cares nothing for us; it has no purposes of its own and is indifferent to ours; if we look for comfort, it offers none. The free man is the man who is undaunted by all this, who scorns comforting illusions and values love, beauty and intelligence for their own sake, 'who remains undismayed by the empire of chance ... proudly defiant of the irresistible forces that tolerate, for a moment, his knowledge and his condemnation ...'[78] Russell worked his way towards this view in a paper he gave to the Apostles in 1899. 'Seems, Madam, Nay It Is' burned his Hegelian boats, when it denounced the Hegelian doctrine that the 'real is the rational and the rational is the real'. Against McTaggart, he argued that any philosophy which distinguishes between appearance and reality and goes on to claim that reality is rational, perfect, infinitely good or whatever hits an insoluble difficulty. Either reality makes contact with appearance at some point in the future or it does not; if not, the perfections of reality are no consolation whatever for the miseries of the world of appearance in which we live. If reality and appearance do make contact, either we already have some experience of that perfection – which amounts to an implausible claim that the world isn't as bad as it seems – or we are asked to cross our fingers and believe that it will all be all right when reality and appearance do coincide. This last claim is just traditional religion in philosophical disguise. In short, if philosophy tries to console us, it becomes intellectually disreputable, as religion is; if it remains reputable, it offers no consolations beyond the satisfaction of intellectual curiosity.[79] From this view Russell never budged.

Many conventionally pious people played into Russell's hands by letting his knockabout atheism upset them. They got their revenge in 1940, when they managed to prevent him from taking up the chair he had been offered at the City University of New York on the grounds that he was a danger to the religion and morals of his students. The more serious complaint against him is that he chronically misrepresented the nature of religion and offered as a replacement for it only some rather self-indulgent aesthetics. Apart from his own later doubts about the florid style of 'The Free Man's Worship' there is something unsatisfactory about the claim that we can defeat a cold and purposeless universe merely by announcing that we are undefeated. The essay suggests no practical means of staying unde-

depicted in colours appropriate to Lady Ottoline Morrell's tastes, and this colouring reappeared on occasion in later years. Whether Russell found it a relief to express this side of his nature or whether there was no such side to be expressed is a mystery. Happily, it is a mystery we can set aside in estimating Russell's standing as a social and political theorist.

What we cannot set aside is what we began with – what we may loosely call the religious tone of his social and political writings. He was always prone to contrast the utopian possibilities of the world we might build with the desperate misery of the world we have built, and he was vulnerable to the thought that there *ought* to be some point to the universe; there is even some hint that the point of the universe's having *no* point is to tell us we are on our own. He has the preacher's conviction of the sinfulness of mankind – supposing the notion of sin to have been purged of any hint of the Decalogue – and the preacher's voice in reprobating it. Nothing very simple or straightforward follows from this, though it is surely plausible that a man to whom this tone comes naturally will tend to lose patience with the minutiae of political life, will find the politics of the grand gesture more attractive than the politics of gradual amelioration, will not take to compromise, and will not deal kindly with the motives of opponents. One thing such a frame of mind will certainly sustain is an ability to defend unpopular causes without flinching; 'thou shalt not follow a multitude to do evil' was an injunction Russell found easy to follow. The outbreak of the First World War provided the first occasion when he was called on to do so.

result none the less. It reinforced Russell's conviction that social theory
had to be based on a psychology which was not afraid of the instincts.
Russell had half learned this already from reading William James, and he
had accepted James's idea that civilizations needed activities which were
the 'moral equivalents of war', but who were not destructive and destructive. Then he discovered Russell's buried or half incoherent ways the
same bloodthirsty passions he criticized in others, a silly charge but one
which showed Russell he could not just invite everyone to behave better
in the interests of averting war. By 1914 he had already lost his conviction
that ethical values were objective. He was now a convinced subjectivist.
This made him much more anxious about the basis of people's moral
attachments and persuaded him he needed an account of a society in which
people's energies were employed at full stretch in creative rather than
destructive ways. Russell began his lectures on *The Principles of Social
Reconstruction* in an almost religious mood, writing to Ottoline Morrell
that he hoped to show 'the spark of the infinite' in each of us; by the time
he showed the draft lectures to Lawrence he was more sober. Lawrence
hated them; they were bloodless appeals for full-blooded emotion, written
in bad faith.[9] The lectures occupied Russell's energies in the summer and
autumn of 1915; he gave them in London from January to March 1916.
They were a great success, but they cost more effort to write and deliver
than their brevity and relaxed prose would suggest. He was already under
some pressure from the authorities, although they did not ban him from
'restricted areas' until September 1916 (supposedly because he might
communicate with the enemy, but really because he might incite dis-
affection among munitions workers). He had in any case abandoned the
idea of setting up in London as an independent lecturer as soon as he had
given his lectures on social reconstruction; he turned instead to work for
the NCF.

His connections with the No-Conscription Fellowship went back to the
beginning of the war. One of its founders was Fenner Brockway, the
editor of *Labour Leader* who had published Russell's articles after *The
Nation* was closed to him. It was founded in anticipation of conscription,
and Russell became active when conscription was introduced in January
1916. The government's bill made all men from eighteen to forty liable
to military service; as well as exemption for work of military importance,
there was provision for conscientious objection to the bearing of arms.
In 1916 the provision was unusual, and was real evidence of Asquith's
liberal scruples about conscription. The provisions for exemption were in
themselves generous. Conscience was not identified with religion, and the

This difference of ultimate purpose did not show up in the internal politics of the NCF, however. The solidarity of the NCF was more immediately threatened by the question whether it should help COs who were willing to do alternative forms of national service. The 'absolutists' argued that undertaking alternative service released someone else to go and do the killing, so that only absolute exemption was acceptable, and only those taking that stance ought to be helped. Russell would have been an 'absolutist' had he been called up. But he saw that the more absolute the position adopted by the NCF the fewer allies it would gain and the smaller its basis would be. To exercise any political influence, the NCF needed to hold up the absolutist position as a moral aspiration but also to assist all sorts of objectors. Allen reached the same catholic conclusion by a different route. He was himself an absolutist, but since he objected so strongly to the way government trampled on the consciences of the COs he was unwilling to press his own moral views on those who felt they could not share them. Their different outlooks resulted in a happy though unexpected harmony.[11]

Russell's troubles with Trinity began in the first few weeks. A CO named Ernest Everett had been called up, court-martialled when he refused to wear uniform, and received two years hard labour. Russell wrote a pamphlet called *Two Years Hard Labour for not Disobeying the Dictates of Conscience*. It appeared in April 1916; in May, he found that the police were harassing its distributors. So he wrote a short letter to *The Times* – '*Adsum qui feci*' – in which he announced his authorship and wondered if the authorities were willing to prosecute the person mainly responsible for the pamphlet. The authorities evidently wondered the same thing; it took them two weeks to make up their mind.

The Home Office might have discouraged prosecution, but Russell planned to visit the United States and hoped to meet President Wilson. The Foreign Office needed an excuse to refuse him a passport, and a conviction under DORA (the Defence of the Realm Act) would provide one. Whether the law was on their side is a moot point. It was an offence under DORA to 'hinder recruitment', but advocating the repeal of conscription was only dubiously an attempt to hinder recruitment. Russell did not seek acquittal. He wanted publicity; ideally, a heavy-handed and incompetent prosecution, followed by a biased and oppressive judgement. The magistrate was rather too fair-minded and good-natured for his purposes, but the prosecutor, A. H. Bodkin, was quite sufficiently humourless and inept.

Russell was fined £100, refused to pay, had his chattels distrained for sale by auction, but found them back in his rooms when his friends bought them before they could be auctioned. He found all this exhilarating; but he was distressed by Trinity's subsequent action in dismissing him from his lecturership. In fairness to Trinity it must be said that it was the small governing council which dismissed him, and the junior fellows almost all bitterly deplored their action – even those who were fighting in France. In spite of this comfort, the event rankled almost more than the government's actions; on 7 June he was denied a passport and on 1 September banned from entering 'restricted areas'.

Outside the day-to-day work of the NCF, Russell was embroiled in the campaign for a negotiated peace. He never ceased to hope that sense might eventually break in on the warring governments; at the end of 1916, the combatant powers began to wonder whether the war might really be interminable, and there was some prospect that American mediation might bring about a negotiated peace. For Britain that prospect was extinguished when Lloyd George replaced Asquith on 7 December 1916 at the head of a cabinet committed to unconditional surrender. Even so, there was a further month of diplomatic flurry after the German note of 12 December inviting the allied powers to discuss peace terms. In the hope of swaying American opinion Russell wrote the first of his famous letters to world leaders – though this one had none of the impact of his cables during the Cuban missile crisis of 1962. He wrote an open letter to President Wilson which he had smuggled into America and which was read to Wilson. The romantic circumstances secured wide publicity for the letter, and it was printed in most major newspapers on 23 December. Wilson was polite but aloof and, three months later, the United States settled the outcome of the war, not by sponsoring negotiation, but by entering the war on the allied side. Russell's response was gloomy. It would shorten the war, and that was good; but he was certain that victory would make America militaristic and greedy and that the only beneficiaries of an American victory would be J. P. Morgan and Standard Oil.[12]

Increasingly, Russell felt he had no more to contribute to the NCF and the anti-war movement. At the end of 1917 he resigned from the committee. It was all the more absurd that almost the last thing he did for the NCF finally landed him in prison. In January 1918, he wrote an article for the *Tribunal* on the German offers of peace with the Bolsheviks; in passing, he mentioned that one horror to be expected if peace was delayed until all the European powers were exhausted was an American occupation of France and Britain. The point of this would be to prevent insurrection from the working classes, and intimidate them back to work. The American army had done it for years at home. Russell readily – if charitably – admitted that it may not have been in the government's mind to use American troops to put down the English working class, but that was only because there was nothing whatever in the government's mind. This jibe did not cause much offence; the remark about the American soldiers did. Once more Russell was hauled into court, and this time got six months imprisonment for 'insulting an ally'. The sentence was universally agreed to be out of all proportion to the offence, and even politicians who supported the war joined in the petition to have it reduced, but the best that could be achieved on appeal was to have the sentence changed from six months in the second division to six months in the first division. The change was important; second-division prisoners sewed mailbags, got a poor diet and no privacy. In the first division, Russell could have a larger cell, and a prisoner to clean it for sixpence a day; decent food could be sent in for him; he could have three visitors a week, and unlimited reading matter. It was prison, but it was more comfortable than the environment in which Russell's predecessors worked in medieval Cambridge. He read 200 books and wrote two. When he was released in September 1918 the war was visibly drawing to a close, and if neither his own future nor that of the world at large looked very secure, he could at least look away from the immediate horrors of the war.

Most of what Russell wrote during the war he wrote in response to particular events, particularly the fifty-five articles for the *Tribunal*, and those he contributed to the *Labour Leader*. Looking for the 'philosophical' basis of Russell's opposition to the war presents the familiar problem of distinguishing the wood from the trees. Still, it does not unduly distort Russell's outlook to concentrate on two issues. The first is his view of the causes and the ethics of war, and the second, his account of the unsatisfactory nature of modern industrial society (an important element in the causes of war, on his account), and what might replace it.

The characteristic style of Russell's political writings is very visible in his preface to *Justice in Wartime*. He describes commentators as divided over the question of the natural bellicosity of the ordinary man, some holding that he is naturally pacific, others that he is naturally warlike. He judiciously suggests that mankind has some natural tendency to fight, but this 'might remain completely latent' unless aroused by 'the machinations of warmongers'.[13] The causes of war have to be looked for both in the human psyche and in the plots of those who want war for pride or profit. Russell was criticized towards the end of his life for his readiness to see conspiracies behind all important events. The habit was an old one, and often enough there were conspiracies. More objectionable, then and later, were the lavish accusations of malice, ill-will, or a blind attachment to evil for evil's sake he hurled at politicians. Sir Edward Grey may have been culpably inefficient and more to blame than anyone else for the policies which led to war, but to describe him as a 'warmonger' imputes to him a positive desire to see large numbers killed and injured which he plainly never felt.

Russell's defence was neither wholly convincing nor wholly unfair. What he claimed in 1915 (and in 1965) was that intelligent men must be presumed to intend the consequences of their actions. Men who utter threats must be ready to carry out those threats; and they must be sincere in claiming that it would be worse to yield to the enemy than to carry out their threats. Anyone who supported a foreign policy likely to lead to war must have been willing to fight, and must have thought that the slaughter on the battlefield was a lesser evil than the success of German foreign policy.[14] To Russell it was simply incredible that anyone should think so, once the issue was put clearly. It followed that the war was either a matter of pride or mere self-assertion, or had some more sinister basis. At times he came close to suggesting what one of Wilfred Owen's most famous war poems says explicitly – that the war was an expression of intergenerational rivalry with the old men at home sending out the young men to be murdered.

All the same, when Russell wrote his extended criticism of the foreign policy of the Allies, he took pains to claim that while Gilbert Murray's pamphlet, *The Foreign Policy of Sir E. Grey, 1906–15*, instantly resorted to personalities by describing Russell and Brailsford as 'pro-German' he was going to avoid all such 'sensationalism'. Russell agreed that much, or most, of the blame for the war fell on the aggressive foreign policy pursued by the German government, and on the militarism with which Prussia had long been infected. But this did not mean that British foreign policy had been of 'immaculate sinlessness' nor that the war was worth fighting. One of Russell's more controversial views was that self-defence was not a sufficient reason for fighting a war – or indeed for fighting at all – and another was that the criminal behaviour of our enemies is not a sufficient reason for fighting them. He admitted that the German invasion of Belgium was dishonourable and a breach of international law; but he denied that this obliged Britain to go to war. Readers from a later generation find Russell's views unsurprising and unshocking. Russell denied that he was 'pro-German' and always said that he was passionately patriotic. He was right – he excused the Germans their follies only on the grounds that Germany was an arriviste and resentful power which was bound to behave badly, and attacked his own government on the grounds that an established, liberal power like Britain could have conciliated Germany and made the French and Russians behave better too. The charge against Sir Edward Grey was that his foreign policy had not been liberal but identical with the policy of his Tory predecessor, Lord Lansdowne.

The ulterior point of demolishing the government claim that Britain had reluctantly gone to war for the sake of a high moral principle was revealed in a simple conclusion. 'Stripped of parliamentary verbiage, the fundamental fact about the European situation is that all the Great Powers of Europe have precisely the same objects: territory, trade and prestige. In pursuit of these objects, no one of the Great Powers shrinks from wanton aggression, war and chicanery. But owing to the geographical position of Germany and her naval supremacy, England can achieve all its purposes by wars outside Europe, whereas English and Russian policy has shown that Germany cannot achieve its aims except by a European war. We have made small wars because small wars were what suited our purposes; Germany has made a great war because a great war was what suited Germany's purpose.'[15] The bulk of *The Entente Policy 1904–1915* is devoted to showing that in Morocco, in Persia, and generally through the operation of the *entente*, France, Britain and Russia consistently excited German fears of losing out in the race for colonies and markets, in a way which dispelled any claim that their policies were motivated by something more high-minded than greed.

Russell's view of what was at stake between Britain and Germany never altered. In 1914 and 1918 he argued the same case; no real difference of economic interest separated them, and the war was purely a matter of national pride. He was an appeaser; that is, he thought that Germany's failure to get much out of the colonial carve-up – owing to her late entry into the race – was an understandable cause of German anger. The fears of the British were much less understandable. As a free trader Russell thought that colonies were generally an expensive mistake and the search for closed markets an error; handing over some of these mistakes to Germany was no disaster. Rational governments would have little difficulty in reconciling their differences once they were brought to think in terms of negotiable self-interest rather than national pride. Russell thought that part of the explanation for the universal reign of folly was the fact that foreign ministries throughout Europe were an upper-class preserve. Rational calculation of interests was alien to the aristocratic mind; calculation looked commercial and middle class, so common sense was despised.

Russell's radicalism was limited. He had no general objection to imperialism. When he offers examples of the ease with which friendly nations can reconcile disagreements – the way Russia and Britain settled their disputes in Afghanistan is one of them – he never suggests that there is anything wrong with great powers disposing of the affairs of small and primitive countries in this way. What is wrong with imperialism is that competitive imperialisms threaten to destroy European civilization because of war between European states. There is no suggestion that imperialism as such is an outrage on colonized peoples. Where Russell waxes indignant over Persia, it is because Persia is on the way to what Russell recognized as civilization. The Russians in Persia had murdered the leaders of movements towards liberalism and parliamentary government.

Russell's view that cool self-interest would have averted war is somewhat at odds with his utopian account of how war was to be prevented in future. Russell's account of the economic and imperialist rivalries behind the way the war broke out could be accepted by someone who shared none of Russell's beliefs about the possibility of a better society. For them, the war would be a disastrous mistake of the sort to which nation states are inherently likely to fall prey.[16] Russell held that society might be so reconstituted that governments were no longer motivated in the way the realist takes for granted. A nation's vital interests would be exceedingly different if we were all persuaded by *The Principles of Social Reconstruction*. It is also difficult to reconcile the realism of *The Entente Policy* with Russell's view of the ethics of war. Russell argued the extremely anti-realist view that there is no such thing as a right to resort to war in self-defence, and if he never suggested that an absolute prohibition on war made political or ethical sense, he emphatically rejected the realist view that nations both do, and should, fight for their own interests. This is not strictly a contradiction; we may be realists about what motives do drive states into war, and as utopian as we like about what motives ought to activate their policies. Still, it is pragmatically self-defeating to write ethical tracts which could have no chance of a hearing from people whose existing attitudes were what Russell supposed.

Russell's views on the ethics of war are interesting and peculiar, and wholly consistent with his general moral outlook. Russell's moral theory was utilitarian in holding that the justification of moral rules and principles lies in the contribution they make to the general happiness; but it was unlike any other utilitarian theory in the special place it gave to a particular kind of happiness. The only happiness worth promoting was that of enlightened people whose sympathies lay with the development of the whole human race, with great causes transcending themselves and their own immediate welfare.[17] Russell's emphasis on these impersonal and ideal goals makes it almost misleading to call him a utilitarian. The great good, by which all lesser goods are to be judged, is the expansion of the ideals of European civilization, which can hardly be summed up as 'happiness'. Russell's theory implied that the justification of all violence, both official violence in warfare and internal policing, and unofficial in individual resistance to assault or theft, rests on its impact on the wider welfare. There is no right to self-defence, and violence can never be justified by appealing to such a right. Russell could be an all-out opponent of the war without describing himself as an absolute pacifist because he was a consequentialist; *if* the results of war were good enough, war was justified. However, the consequences he took into account were such as to make it unlikely that war ever would be justified.

Russell acknowledges that he and common sense are at odds. If a robber demands my wallet I am not automatically entitled to refuse and defend myself with force if I can; maybe more good is done by his having the money than by my having it, maybe more good is done by his having it and nobody being killed. Russell thinks I would be justified in killing my assailant if I had discovered an important mathematical theorem which increased the sum of important truths in the world and I could not reveal it otherwise. By analogy, wars of colonization, if not justified in advance, commonly turn out to be justified after the event. For it is by such wars that civilization has been spread all over the globe. Russell shrinks from saying that it was all right to destroy the culture and society of the American Red Indian or the Australian Aborigine, but he takes it for granted that we do not retrospectively regret it. What is not justified is the sort of war which usually takes place for the interests of one state at the expense of another or in defence of national pride or prestige.

Russell sets nation states the same standards. Nations, like individuals, have no general right of self-defence. The question is always whether greater good would be done by fighting than by non-resistance. So he thought that Belgian resistance to Germany ought not to have been encouraged; Belgium was manifestly in the right, but that was no reason for Britain and France to fight. *If* a system of collective security meant that a police operation of a straightforward kind could be mounted, then it would be possible to claim that a general principle was being upheld, and it would be worth fighting. Since Russell had shown (to his own satisfaction at least) that the war was the unwanted result of competition among imperialist powers, and was sustained by nothing more than national pride and self-assertion, there was no such justification on this occasion. War as a policing operation requires a recognized international authority to instruct the police; in its absence any claim to be acting as a quasi-policeman is special pleading.

What can a nation do if threatened with invasion or with intolerable economic demands or whatever? This question haunted Russell from 1915 onwards. It was inescapable during the 1930s when he wrote *Which Way to Peace?* and after 1945 when atomic weapons raised the question more acutely than ever. Russell always insisted that he was not an absolute pacifist – he did not believe in the sanctity of life and thought that killing large numbers of people was defensible if the good achieved was sufficient. He was utterly uninterested in the questions which exercised traditional exponents of 'just war' doctrines, such as the degree of guilt required for a non-combatant to be treated as anything other than an innocent bystander. The mass bombing of civilian targets in the Second World War did not raise for him the issues it raised for Catholic thinkers who held that the innocent were never to be used as mere means to other ends. Yet, since one of the chief values of European civilization is the individual character, and the evil of war the damage it does to the individual character, it is not surprising that he advocated passive non-cooperation as the best way to deal with aggressors.

He undoubtedly overestimated the readiness with which most people would passively resist their oppressors at the cost of death and injury to themselves or, more importantly, to their family and their friends. In 1915 he underestimated the ingenuity with which invaders would set about the task of making people cooperate against their will; justified scepticism about the tales of German atrocities in Belgium and an unjustified faith in the civilized character of European nations even when they were at war hid from him the possibilities which Hitler's rise to power belatedly revealed. What Russell was right about, of course, was that a government which invaded another for the sake of pure economic gain would be baffled by consistent non-cooperation. It would be mad for any Soviet planner to suppose that the imposition of Soviet rule on the United States would yield sudden riches, since the effect of the imposition would plainly be to reduce American prosperity so dramatically that what was left would not pay the costs of seizing it. As regards the German invasion of Belgium, Russell was proposing that the civilian population should ignore all orders issued by the invaders, and this was asking more than was reasonable of civilian morale and self-confidence.

This does not settle the issue. It is often argued, and plausibly, that if we were to devote the same energy to cultivating courage in passive disobedience that we devote to inculcating bravery in warfare, we should have a population which *could* adopt a non-military defence; we could be sure that, given time enough, we could grind down the invaders and make them go home. But this is not an argument which we need explore here, for Russell's obsession with the qualities of *individual* character meant that he never paid any attention to what one might call long-term social training in passive disobedience. He wrote as if the solidarity required for it to work was a spontaneous gift rather than something ordinary people might work at over a long period.

His critics mostly met him on the ground of German guilt; when they did not, they raised obvious ethical issues about conscientious objection. Even when Russell's opponents were philosophers – as W. R. Sorley was – they fought him on this ground rather than on more philosophical ground. The one exception was T. E. Hulme who, writing under the pseudonym of 'North Staffs' (he was a lieutenant in the North Staffordshire Regiment and was killed in the summer of 1916), wrote several short articles in the *Cambridge Magazine* between January and March 1916 attacking Russell's view of what was at stake between Britain and Germany, in particular criticizing Russell's lectures on *The Principles of Social Reconstruction*. Even Hulme came down from the high ground of philosophical objection to the empirical question of what German success in the war would mean for Britain.[18] He thought that Russell and his friends were absurdly over-optimistic about the compatibility of German victory and everyday British freedom. The German aim was European hegemony, and the technique was brute force. Hulme was eager to remind his opponents that 'Force does settle things, does create facts' and that a German victory would be the end of everything Britain had taken for granted over the past hundred years.

There was a philosophical gulf between Russell and Hulme, but it bulked larger in Hulme's mind than in Russell's, and Russell would not have subscribed to Hulme's account of what the difference was. Hulme was not an academically sophisticated philosopher; he was a passionate disciple of Bergson and shortly before the war he had translated Sorel's *Reflections on Violence*, which evidently made a great impact on him. He shared Sorel's contempt for hedonism and individualism, and his admiration for the heroic values revealed only in conflict. Like Sorel, he was contemptuous of the view that progress was 'natural' or 'inevitable' (whence the title of one of his squibs). Liberals were chronically deluded. They thought, like Rousseau, that man was naturally good and would inevitably develop into a free and rational creature if he wasn't hindered by reactionaries. He accused Russell of 'faded Rousseauism', and added for good measure that Russell had 'an entirely false conception of the nature of man, and of the true hierarchy of values' which stemmed from 'an uncritical acceptance of the romantic tradition'.[19] He went on to defend the anti-romantic and pessimistic ethics of Sorel, and evidently felt that Sorel was right to think of societies as more than collections of individuals; it was a sloppy *petit-bourgeois* habit of mind to think of them as made up of individuals and amenable to change by rational tinkering. The British were fighting for liberty, but their liberty was not a matter of a law here and a law there, or a few more civil servants here and a few less there. Britain embodied a conception of freedom, and to fail to fight for it would have been to abandon what gave Britain life. Germany embodied a bureaucratic and authoritarian view of the world which, if it triumphed, would be the death of freedom. There was no room for compromise, only for struggle.

Hulme took Russell as his target for several reasons. One was that Russell had always been hostile to Bergson. He wrote a mocking review of *Le rire*,[20] and a long-prepared, wholesale attack in *The Monist* in 1912.[21] By 1916, Russell had been cured of his infatuation with D. H. Lawrence, and would have had less patience with Bergson's notion of the *élan vital* than before. Hulme mistakenly still thought of Russell as an ally in the fight against subjectivism and hedonism, and was the more outraged when Russell failed to share his conception of the ends of life. He certainly understood Russell's distance from the pessimism which Sorel preached in *Reflections on Violence*, and accused Russell of employing the language of heroic values while emptying it of all meaning. He skated impatiently over the question whether objectivism was necessarily anti-hedonistic and anti-individualistic, but he was quite sure that different ethical theories led to different hierarchies of values.

Hulme's pessimism enabled him to put up a compelling case for the 1914 war.[22] He was convinced (wrongly) that Russell believed in the naturalness of progress and therefore the inevitability of the peaceful triumph of his ideals; against this he argued that evil was quite as much 'in the nature of things' as was progress. Indeed, deterioration was the law of nature. So there was nothing surprising about the need to defend Britain from German aggression. This did not mean that the war would achieve anything positive; all that could be said for it was that it would ward off a real evil and that nothing else would do it. Russell, said Hulme, believed that *no* war could be justified, and therefore that his task was only to explain what madness had brought people to launch the present war, so he defended this particular war as a rational response to a real evil. It was easy for Russell to point out that he had never believed in the inevitability of progress or in any natural tendency to improvement, and that Hulme was attacking a straw man. A real difference between them, however, was that Russell was prone to think that only a great positive good could justify war, whereas Hulme was clear that the choice was only of the lesser evil.

In a series of essays which began with a review of Russell's London lectures on *The Principles of Social Reconstruction*,[23] Hulme denounced Russell's capitulation to hedonism and subjectivism. His first complaint was that Russell's account of 'impulse' treated his opponents as slaves of unconscious motives, and their ethical positions as mere rationalization. This was such a travesty of his views that Russell replied that he supposed 'North Staffs' must have been the man at the back of the room who read the *Daily Express* throughout the proceedings. But as the argument proceeded, Hulme could develop his own picture of the contrast between utilitarian and heroic values. Utilitarian values were necessarily pacifist, because they took life as the highest good and the boundary of all value. But heroic values were 'beyond life'. Death in battle was by no means the ultimate misfortune that it must appear to hedonists and individualists.

Hulme's biographers have dismissed his attack on Russell as an outburst by a philosophical incompetent who resorted to vulgar abuse and came badly out of the exchange.[24] That is not fair. An odd aspect of the exchange is that Russell remained good-humoured and courteous throughout, and was not disturbed by Hulme's hectoring tone. There was good reason for this. Hulme was much easier to deal with than Lawrence; he was aggressive, but very much less abusive. More importantly, Russell sympathized with Hulme's attack on hedonism; although Russell's *Principles of Social Reconstruction* was concerned with making mankind too happy to fight, it was not concerned with the pursuit of pleasure. Hulme's defence of heroic values struck a chord in Russell; he, too, thought that everyday life offered too few opportunities for the strenuous pursuit of great ends, and admired the heroic temper. So he was anxious not to be misunderstood and, instead of responding with his habitual sharpness, he pointed out that the difference between them was not about heroic values, which Russell agreed were in a sense 'beyond life'. The difference was that

Russell held that such values had to be realized *in* life, not in mutual destruction. Because values were human values, human life had to continue in order to give the values any sense; mutual destruction in an age of mechanized warfare would not be an expression of heroic values but the end of civilization. As to subjectivism, Russell was glad to recant his former adherence to Moore's brand of ethical objectivism. In 1913 Santayana had persuaded him that his belief in the existence of objective values cluttered up the universe with entities that performed no explanatory function. Russell now held that values were essentially subjective; moral judgements expressed our evaluations of the world. That was not to say that all we could value was our own feelings or other subjective states; we might value mathematical truth and the beauty of the starlit heavens more highly than anything in the world – and Russell often thought that he did. None the less, it was *our* evaluation of them which introduced value into the world.

Hulme came off the worse if we think of the encounter as a philosophical dialogue; it remains interesting how much he and Russell shared, and that Hulme – uniquely – induced Russell to respond non-polemically, and to explain himself without preaching. For all that, Russell's *Autobiography* ignores the episode completely.

Russell's writings on the war all contain a latent theory of the relationship between individual psychology and social and political events. The main monument to that theory is Russell's *Principles*, the most sustained and original political writing in all Russell's enormous output. Its basis is Russell's claim that we have neglected the role of instinct in human affairs and overestimated the role of rational calculation. Russell draws a line between *impulse* on the one hand and *desire* on the other. Impulses simply push their owners towards whatever satisfies them; desires allow room for conscious calculation of the best way to satisfy them. It was to assist the satisfaction of desires that Bentham and the utilitarians were so eager to provide a hedonic calculus. About the impulses that just demanded satisfaction, regardless of consequences, they had nothing to say.[25]

Like Hume and Mill before him, Russell thought that reason was powerless against both impulse and desire. Reason can work out the consequences of different courses of action, and can work out the most effective means to any goal we may contemplate. But unless we *want* to take some notice of the calculations, we do not have to do so and shall not do so. In the realm of desire, however, it is easy to make use of reason if we wish to do so. We desire something not yet present, and in this interval between the desire and its satisfaction we work out how best to satisfy our desire and implement the results of our calculation. Impulses, on the other hand, we simply gratify without reflection. We boast even when we know that no good will come of it, because we are impelled by an impulse to self-assertion. Less alarmingly, we struggle to solve a mathematical problem not for the sake of a remoter goal but simply out of the impulse of curiosity. It is characteristic of impulses that when they are satisfied we do not relax and enjoy what we have achieved but become bored with it and start on a new project. A poet may be glad to have the money he has been paid for writing poetry, but if he writes out of the impulse to create, he doesn't stop once he has got the money: he loses interest in the poetry he has written already and strives to write new and better poetry in future.

Impulse is not uncontrollable. We commonly repress the impulse to kick an irritating child or colleague, for instance. All the same, it is impulse which supplies the driving force for the emotional life; too much control and too much discipline produce boredom and a sense that life is pointless. Life would be impossible if all impulses were allowed free reign, for adult anger would cause great damage. But suppression is less useful than redirection; we must think how to divert impulse into non-destructive and life-enhancing paths. In essence, *The Principles of Social Reconstruction* is an essay on the nurturing of benign impulses. Two preliminary points are worth noticing, however. First, Russell's emphasis on the resistance of impulse to anything other than the indirect sway of reason is important to his explanation of the origins of the war. German aggression and diplomatic error were part of the explanation; but they only provided the spark which exploded the powder-keg. The powder-keg itself was the boredom and frustration which so many of the members of the combatant powers experienced in peacetime, and the mischievous socialization and education to which they had been subjected and which had encouraged their aggressive and anti-social impulses rather than their creative and sociable ones. It is because everyday life is so unsatisfying that states can rally their citizens behind policies which defend national prestige and nothing more useful. That explains why so many young men were ready to go and fight. It was not that they enjoyed killing other people, let alone that they had any great enthusiasm for being blown to bits themselves. They needed to exert themselves strenuously in some important task, and if they could not do so in peace they were ready to go off to find a purpose in life at the front. Russell's 'depth psychology' is not quite that of either Freud or Adler (though he knew of their work), for he did not believe either in the 'death wish' suggested by Freud or in the will to power uncovered by Adler. None the less, it plainly has something in common with their appeal to the pressures of the unconscious on conscious behaviour.

Secondly, the aim of appealing to the psychological sub-structure of social life was to provide foundations for a better political theory than old-fashioned rationalist liberalism. Whether Russell achieved this, and quite what he thought would replace old-fashioned liberalism, it is not easy to say. What is clear, though, is that Russell thinks that old-fashioned liberalism exaggerated the role of reason in human affairs and overstated the desire to be happy. It is no good telling people that it is a mistake to fight and that war will not make them prosperous or happy; they will not listen; they will go off to fight, not happy in the usual sense, but exultant and fulfilled. If Russell extends traditional liberalism it is because he makes the need for freedom a matter of deep underlying impulse, and not a rather implausible means to prosperity and peace.[26]

Russell distinguishes two kinds of impulse, the possessive and the creative; he does not, however, do very much to press our ordinary classification of our impulses into these two theoretical compartments. When discussing the causes of and cure for war, he talks much more loosely of impulses of liking and disliking, pride and fear and the rest of it. But the distinction is important. On it his hopes for a near-utopian future have to rest. Instincts of a possessive kind are those which set people at odds, create conflicts of interest, and conflicts of pure pride. Creative impulses lead us to do things and make things where there is no question of individuals monopolizing the results and where we can all share in the results without anyone losing out. Possessiveness leads first to divisiveness, then to conflict, and ultimately to death; creativity leads to cooperation and life. We cannot wish impulses into existence or out of existence, but social training will foster the life-enhancing impulses and channel our energies into creative rather than destructive outlets.

Russell's *Principles* tackles most of the subjects that were to preoccupy him for the rest of his life, and a great many of the usual issues of political philosophy: the nature of authority, the power of the state, the need to abolish capitalism without substituting an equally oppressive form of socialism, the prospects of an international authority to prevent war, the role of education in the modern world, the duties of parents and the future of marriage and the family. The book is marked by something which is very characteristic of all Russell's work, namely a combination of a brisk rationalism together with the claim that what mankind needs is something like a new religious *Weltanschauung*.

The *Principles* reflects the conditions under which Russell wrote. Since the book began as anti-war lectures, much of it is coloured by the conviction that the need to prevent war is the greatest of all needs. But many topics – property and the organization of industry is the most striking instance – do not particularly lend themselves to discussion in these terms, and what we get instead is a neat, lucid and persuasive account of the ills of industrial society and of the only partial plausibility of socialist remedies for them. The central theme, however, runs through this discussion as through all the rest: how to preserve life and liveliness against narrowness, oppression, debility and death. Like his liberal predecessors, Russell is fearful of asking the state to do too much. His discussion of the state's potential for oppression is firmly in the tradition of *Liberty* and *Democracy in America*. The state is necessary, since civilization depends upon adequate policing of social relations; but this is far from suggesting that states do all they ought, let alone that they can be expected to be benign. Like Mill, Russell thinks education so vital that the state must take responsibility for it; but, like Mill again, he thinks that there is such a danger of the state fostering dullness and orthodoxy that it must promote research only at arm's length, and must ensure that children are properly educated without taking direct control of the education system. Like de Tocqueville, he thinks that a major source of unfreedom in modern society lies in the individual's sense of powerlessness in the face of the impersonal machinery of administration. States are so large that individuals cannot much affect what happens, and individuals feel lost in the crowd. One debilitating effect of this is to make people hanker after demagogic leaders whose orders they can obey without question.

Where he goes beyond the tradition is in linking this internal oppressiveness to the state's external relations and in looking to something like guild socialism as a remedy. Mill and de Tocqueville largely blamed the lifelessness of modern society on the fact that it was a 'mass' society – anonymous, egalitarian, commercially minded, with few local or class attachments to break up the oppressive mass. Russell was more concerned with the state's disposition to impose sanctions on individual attempts at non-conformity, and the explanation he sought for the state's hostility to variety and non-conformism was that states which were constantly preparing to fight their neighbours inevitably tried to achieve a degree of internal unity which was simply liberticide. The view that obedience is the supreme virtue is a thought that comes naturally to a state which sees itself as an armed force in which the willingness of everyone to obey orders is vital to survival. Unless international peace can be guaranteed, internal liberty is precarious. This was a view which Russell never abandoned. In later life he often said that 1914 had been a watershed; before that, countries such as Britain and France were slowly becoming freer, but afterwards the demands of security cost them all the gains in freedom they had earlier made.

If one condition of liberty under the law is external peace, the other is to confine the state to the tasks it is suited to and to prevent it interfering in what it is not suited to. This is the argument for arm's length control mentioned above, supplemented by a sketch of the case for letting voluntary organizations perform many of the functions which states would otherwise perform. Russell's sketch is no more than that, but he suggests that much of economic life could be controlled by the representatives of productive and distributive enterprises, supervised by central government only to the extent that government would back agreements which commended themselves to everyone as equitable. It is noticeable that Russell takes no interest in the creation of legal obstacles to government misbehaviour; he does not suggest a Bill of Rights, for instance. On the whole, Russell assumes throughout that what checks government is the power of social groups rather than the provisions of the legal system, and that what gives social groups their power is the strength of opinion among their members. Only voluntary associations whose morale is strong enough to resist government bullying can really limit the power of governments; that such groups exist is clear enough – the Welsh miners took on Lloyd George in the middle of a war and won.

The underlying argument for Russell's pluralism is that variety and conflict (of opinion) are healthy phenomena; individual growth can come about only in a bracing environment. This argument sustains Russell's account of industrial organization and the reform of property rights. There, too, his concern is not with ownership in the legal sense, but with industrial morale. The great aim of industry is not to maximize production: to suppose that is to suppose that the great aim of life in general is to consume as much as possible. But people do not really want to be passive consumers on an ever increasing scale. The aim of industry is to produce what contributes to an expansive existence without wearing ourselves out in the process. That this aim is truer to human nature than the maximization of consumption is shown by the behaviour of large capitalists who expend great efforts in making money, not in order to join the *idle* rich, but in order to stamp their mark on the world. They compete with each other out of pride rather than greed. Vitality should decide the merits of schemes of industrial reorganization. What matters above all else is to eliminate drudgery and spread the opportunity to exercise initiative. State ownership would be worse than capitalism if all it achieved was the arrival of government-appointed managers to run industry in the same way as their capitalist predecessors had done. Something close to cooperative ownership ought to exist where it is feasible – and where it is not, as in the case of the railways, say, some other form of internal workers' democracy must be looked for.

Lest this make Russell sound too much like a sensible guild socialist, rational, energetic and reformist, it is worth stressing that the *Principles* contains a lot that is truer to Russell's more romantic and less matter-of-fact self. When discussing education, he insists that the quality a teacher most needs is *reverence*. Merely to like children and want them to grow up to earn a decent living is not enough, even if it is a great deal better than wanting to turn out cannon-fodder. Reverence is not a very matter-of-fact quality: Russell says that even its possessor is more likely to be able to recognize it than understand it. Nor does he know quite what it is about children which inspires the sensation, though it evidently has to do with the combination of dependence and potential for growth which all children possess. An analogy to it is the sympathy we feel for a plant striving dumbly to reach the light, and what it calls out in us is the desire to be part of the process by which the striving reaches its fulfilment. When Russell insists that something like a religious transformation is needed if people are to cultivate the creative impulses and divert their aggression into useful channels, what he means is best understood in terms of this reverence. To some extent it may be a feeling founded on an illusion – the belief that these strivings are the real point of the universe's existence – or it may be the inevitable result of the way the imagination projects our own concerns on to the natural world. But whatever the explanation, learning to see the spark of the infinite in what lies around us is what Russell holds to be an essential part of any serious commitment to a better world.

Russell stood by the views expressed in his *Principles* almost all his life. Like J. S. Mill before him, he stood by the liberal view that a tolerable democracy must reconcile majority rule with the liberties of the minority, and with the exception of one post-war essay on direct action and his very much later career with CND and the Committee of 100, he remained a liberal of a very recognizable kind.[27] Certainly, he thought that parliamentary democracy was generally a sham, but he had no great enthusiasm for the politics of insurgency. Even when he changed his mind, it was not so much a change of mind about underlying principles as one impelled by the sense that the desperate times demanded a politics uncon-strained by old inhibitions. What is novel in the *Principles* is their attach-ment to Russell's 'impulse theory' of human psychology, their utopianism about a possible future, and their concentration on the causes of, and the cure for, war. Russell intended to give a briefer version of the *Principles* as lectures in the autumn of 1916; it was these that his banning order prevented him from delivering. It made no difference, however; Russell gave one in Manchester, the miners' leader Robert Smillie gave another in Glasgow, where Russell could not go; the banning order ensured large audiences, and they were published in America in 1917.[28] They concentrate more directly on political issues – on the scope and limits of democracy, on the need to replace capitalism with socialism, and on the need for a form of world government with a monopoly of military force – but otherwise they are simply an abbreviated version of the *Principles*.

Before leaving Russell's reactions to the war, two critical points need to be made. Russell invoked imperialism as one of the causes of the outbreak of the First World War, but with little of the subtlety of the best Marxists; he did not see the war as an 'imperialist' war in the sense of a war which monopoly capitalism forced upon the warring powers. He was no Lenin or Rosa Luxemburg. It was certainly an imperialist war in another sense; as we have seen, Russell explained its outbreak as the result of Germany envy of British success in acquiring an empire. But Russell's appeal to envy shows how un-Marxist his explanation was; he treated the issue as a matter of national psychology and the psychological state of national leaders. It is thus all the harder to see why Russell insisted that only if capitalism were abolished would there be a chance for peace. For the connection between capitalism and war is obscure. Certainly some capitalists were in armaments and had a direct interest in war, and Russell made much of this; but as Sorley kept on pointing out, many capitalists do not flourish in wartime, and shareholders will probably find themselves on average worse off in wartime than in peace. Why should capitalists generally – as opposed to arms manufacturers in particular – be a force for war? To this Russell gives no straightforward answer. One might suppose that the aggressiveness of captains of industry is part of the explanation; Russell thought of them as natural imperialists propelled by an urge for power rather than wealth. What they wanted was primarily to control what happened. This, however, has little to do with capitalism; it suggests rather what Russell emphasized later in his essay on *Power* – that many leaders, whether of industry or armies or nations, simply want to accumulate power. If that is a fact about human nature, changing the ownership of industry will hardly alter it. The other face of the argument is simpler, though indirect. Capitalism leads to war through its effect on the motivation of the rest of the population. The working class, faced with a lifetime of dreary and repetitive work, are bored to death by useful activities and therefore vulnerable to the charms of excitement, even when it is a lethal form of excitement. Russell always claimed to have seen cheering crowds on the day war broke out – his critics said there were no crowds and the general mood was gloomy – and the only thing that could account for their cheerfulness was the prospect of shuffling off dull routine for something more exciting.

The other obvious target for complaint is Russell's extreme vagueness about the form of world government that he imagines we may set up. This vagueness persisted all his life; the only thing he was ever clear about was that the likely first stage of the process of creating it would have to be the despotism of the United States over the rest of the world. What Russell never explains is why the powers that were willing to fight to the last drop of their soldiers' blood during the first war would be able to reconcile themselves to the existence of this despotism or the subsequent world authority. G. D. H. Cole complained to Russell that he was too Platonic, too much the philosopher-king inventing solutions to impose on the average man, and it is perfectly true that Russell was prone to the Platonic temptation to push all practical difficulties aside by mere *fiat* – as if to say, 'Let there be an omnipotent world authority,' was the first step in the argument, when its possibility was really what was at stake. And even if Russell may be excused the sketchiness of his account of what it would be like and how it might be created, he surely cannot be excused his optimism about how it would work.

Russell argued that the possession of absolute authority is very corrupting; this was an argument for always being cautious about giving power to governments, and in favour of checks upon our rulers. Yet he proposed to entrust absolute power to a world government and never wondered whether those who became its executive could be trusted with such power. Why, if every other government was a tangle of conflicting ambitions, should this one be different? Why should we expect such a government to keep world peace, rather than to reinvent world war in the guise of internal civil war? If the heads of armed forces in nation states could not entirely be trusted to do what their civilian chiefs told them, why should we expect the leaders of the world government's forces to be immune to the temptation to launch a *coup*? This is not to say that there are no answers to such questions; it is to complain that Russell hardly seemed to see the need for answers. It is as if Russell had read Hobbes's *Leviathan* and been carried away by Hobbes's argument that the state of nature and the war of all against all was so dreadful that any rational man would fly to absolute monarchy for protection. Russell generalizes Hobbes's argument to the international sphere, but fails to ask how men who get themselves into a 'war of all against all' can be expected to get themselves out again, and fails to show how they have done more than exchange the frying pan for the fire.

The wonderful briskness and flair with which Russell writes, and the entertaining invective with which he laces his work, perhaps disguised from both his audience and himself a curious thinness in his argument. That thinness is not exactly philosophical, though it defies other labels; the problem is that he moves too quickly from asserting basic truths about human nature to employing those few truths in explanation and employing them as the basis of his prescriptions for a brave new world. Neither institutions nor situations seem to play enough of a role in explanation – where Russell treats us as the playthings of a few psychological pressures; yet they seem to be omnipotent in prescription – where Russell thinks that changing the framework in which we act will bring out good impulses and divert bad ones. It is altogether too quick and too glib. Russell's critics said so for half a century, and the strange thing was that Russell never seemed to see what they were complaining about.

FOUR

AN AMBIVALENT SOCIALIST

RUSSELL was never an unequivocal socialist. When he joined the Independent Labour Party (ILP), he took care to explain that he was not really a socialist. In fact he remained a member of the Labour Party until he tore up his party card in 1965 as a gesture of protest at the Labour government's subservience to America over Vietnam; but at the theoretical level it is perfectly true that he was at best a hesitant and anxious socialist. Practically speaking, he would have made a difficult member of either the parliamentary party or a Labour government – whereas his older brother Frank redeemed his misspent middle age by serving as Under-Secretary for India in the first Labour government. Bertrand Russell fought two elections – in 1922 and 1923 – as a Labour candidate, taking care to fight the unwinnable seat of Chelsea. Had a miracle given him victory he would have been horrified. All the same, it was in the books and essays of the years between 1918 and 1925 that he committed himself most energetically to the view that socialism in some form was the only thing that could save industrial civilization. The case he makes will not surprise readers of *The Principles of Social Reconstruction*; the argument for socialism was a pacifist one: 'you cannot make a silk purse out of a sow's ear, and you cannot make peace and freedom out of capitalism'. Only socialism could avert another world war.

Roads to Freedom, commissioned in 1916 but not finished until near the end of the war, systematically explored the attractions of rival socialisms – Marxist state socialism, anarcho-syndicalism, and guild socialism – coming down in favour of the last. It showed Russell, not only as a socialist, but as the heir to the anxieties of de Tocqueville and Mill, alarmed by the difficulty of reconciling socialist egalitarianism with the freedom needed by the artistic and intellectual élite. Russell took it for granted that all progress is the work of men who are both unintelligible to and unappreciated by the great majority, as his estimate that Darwin was worth thirty million 'ordinary men' revealed. Since socialism is the culmination of democracy, it is vulnerable to a democratic unconcern for imagination, initiative and intellect.[1]

Russell had made up his mind about Marx in 1894. All the same, his first reaction to the Bolshevik revolution of October 1917 was unmitigated enthusiasm. He had welcomed the liberal revolution of March 1917, but had been disillusioned by the way in which first Miliukov and then Kerensky wished to prosecute the war against Germany with greater efficiency – rather than abandon it altogether.[2] The Bolsheviks' policy of getting out of the war at once, no matter what the cost to the Allies, met with his whole-hearted approval. Their boldness excited him, and he readily forgave Lenin's first dictatorial steps when he sent the Constituent Assembly packing.[3] Russell followed his liberal grandfather in accepting compulsory enlightenment, and Lenin seemed only to be following in Napoleon's footsteps. When he went to Russia in the early summer of 1920, Russell changed his mind. The physical conditions were horrific. Astrakan was 'more like hell than anything I had ever imagined', malaria was rife and starvation imminent; the people were demoralized, and the mathematicians of Petrograd more abject than any tramp in England, while intellectuals were cowed into talking what they knew to be nonsense. Nor was this merely a side-effect of war and revolution; the country, he told Ottoline Morrell, was run by 'Americanized Jews' and ideologues who would rather starve in a dialectically correct manner than live sensibly.[4]

All the old reasons for thinking Marxist revolutions not worth the price struck him with renewed force. These doubts set him at odds with the young woman who soon afterwards became his second wife. He had met Dora Black, at that time a Fellow of Girton, during 1916; their relationship had ripened after he was released from prison. By the end of 1919 she played a more important part in his life than either Lady Ottoline Morrell or Lady Constance Malleson. Though she had not been particularly interested in politics when they first met, she had become a passionate socialist. She went to Russia independently, at almost the same time as he did, after a ferocious row about whether she should risk going at all. His doubts also set him at odds with some, though by no means all, of his travelling companions; they saw what was supposedly being built, he saw what it was costing in life and liberty. Nor did he ever change his mind. He was an unwavering critic of the Soviet Union until the end of his life. Unlike H. G. Wells and the Webbs, who believed that they were seeing a new society in the making, he saw old-fashioned Asiatic brutality, tsarist inefficiency and an attitude to Marxism which blended superstition and hypocrisy. We must not exaggerate Russell's prescience; in 1920 he was no better able than anyone else to guess that Stalin would succeed Lenin and would launch a second revolution from above. Like Trotsky in his pessimistic moods, Russell thought the demands of the peasantry would lead to a semi-capitalist economy in which Russia would remain permanently indebted to foreign capital and her socialism be only such as was acceptable to foreign creditors. However, he was prepared to admit that Bolshevism might suit the Russians, so long as nobody suggested that it was a model for the West, for all industrialisation was more or less a forced march.[5] Even so, the idea that anyone would be mad enough to impose forced collectivization and industrialization in the way Stalin did in the 1930s never occurred to him.

The journey bore fruit in *The Practice and Theory of Bolshevism*, a book which his friends on the Left denounced as treason, but which, as usual, upset the Right even more. If he was hard on the Bolsheviks, he was ferocious about the stupidity and cruelty of allied intervention: '... there is no depth of cruelty, perfidy or brutality from which the present holders of power will shrink when they feel themselves threatened'. By arming the enemies of the Soviet government and trying to starve out the regime, the British government would not kill the revolution; but they would kill innumerable children and harden the Reds' hatred of the West. That would doubtless aid the Bolsheviks in securing their grip on Russia, and in so doing help neither Russia nor the West.

Soon after, Russell and Dora went on an extended visit to China. They were away from August 1920 to August 1921. Dora's account of the visit in her autobiography is extremely engaging and conjures up a vivid picture of an ancient society dominated by the twin figures of the trader and the missionary – with military missions and a good deal of imperialist hardware none too invisible in the background.[6] As always, Russell's political allegiances caused various difficulties; the Foreign Office was convinced he was a Bolshevik agitator, and the silliness of the reports sent back from China make his most extravagant abuse of the diplomatic service look like the musings of a moderate man. He lectured on philosophy in Peking for several months, and more briefly in Japan. In March 1921 he suffered a near-fatal attack of pneumonia, and was saved partly by the technology of the despised Americans – a new serum produced by the American Hospital cleared the infection – and partly by the devoted attention of a Christian nurse who later admitted to him that she had wondered whether her Christian duty wasn't to let him die; happily, professionalism triumphed over piety. It was a near thing, though, and at one stage the press believed he had died – giving him the pleasure of reading some hostile but premature obituaries. One result of the journey was *The Problem of China*, a long and careful consideration of how China might survive the attentions of competing imperialisms. Russell evidently also lectured on the problem of transplanting liberal democracy into Chinese soil, for Mao Tse-tung noted that he had heard him and was unconvinced by the recipe.[7]

Although it is an accurate enough description of his political interests to say that what agitated Russell in much of his political writing was the double question of what kind of socialism best suited advanced countries and what arrangements would deflate their conflicts over the exploitable colonial world, it does not catch the distinctive tone of his essays. They were a curious mixture of utopianism and *Realpolitik*. Both were present in his insistence that international authority had to be able to get the better of individual nation states by brute force, if necessary, and his speculations about how such an authority might be created. *Realpolitik* persuaded him that the pre-war scramble for Africa would be followed by a contest between Japan and the United States for mastery of the Pacific basin; utopianism recurred in his habit of appealing to immensely exalted considerations as the first premises of the politics of change – as if governments were to be estimated by their success in promoting that sense of communion with an impersonal god that Spinoza called freedom or blessedness. The two things went together; governments as they were were intolerably wicked, and only a dramatic change of heart could save mankind. Russell was much more insistent on matters of principle and morale than on matters of institutional detail. He did not propose formulae for a colonialist peace treaty or constitutions for the socialist republic of Great Britain. He insisted that an international authority needed to be able to impose its will on nation states and that socialism would not work without a change of heart, but left it to others to fill in the details.

This was all the more odd, given the distinctive framework within which Russell thought about politics. To borrow the title of one of his best and most famous books, he was obsessed with the relationship between freedom and organization.[8] Moreover, he thought that the currency of politics was power – not, like most socialists, the ownership of property, though property certainly mattered.[9] Russell thought that the basis of power in civilized societies was opinion – partly because anyone wanting to achieve changes of any kind depends upon knowledge of the necessary techniques to do so, partly because getting the cooperation of others depends on persuasion, which is directly a matter of opinion, or on coercion, which depends on opinion, though less directly, to the degree that it requires people to believe that cooperation is in their interests and non-cooperation is not.[10] The role of knowledge also encouraged him to place the discussion of socialism in the context of the impact of science on society – to refer to yet another of his books.[11] *The Prospects of Industrial Civilization*, written with Dora in 1924, argued that thus far mankind had been wonderfully efficient in applying science in controlling nature but atrociously ineffectual in applying science to self-control and social control. As a rationalist and an empiricist, Russell took it for granted that what we need above all is a calm and accurate view of our own natures if we are to devise unsuperstitious forms of social organization better suited to them and more likely to allow us to survive the effects of our mechanical cleverness. In short, the foundation of politics is education, and the basis of education is an adequate psychology.

In 1921, Russell became a father; six years later, his interest in education became direct and very practical when he and Dora became the owners and managers and a substantial part of the teaching staff of Beacon Hill School. Russell's views on education and the family occupy Chapter Five; but we should recall that Russell had much on his mind besides politics before 1927. He had wanted to leave the NCF and return to his work on the philosophy of mathematics and the application of his analytical techniques to questions in epistemology and metaphysics even before the war was over. In prison he was allowed to write only on non-political topics and there completed his *Introduction to Mathematical Philosophy* and drafts of *The Analysis of Mind*. He was at the same time anxious about how he was to make a living thereafter; he had given away what he had inherited and was now obliged to support himself. Writing philosophy would not keep body and soul together; journalism and lecturing would, but would consume the time he needed for reflection. There were the usual difficulties: the people most eager to help were those he had fallen out with over the war, though in the end Gilbert Murray was instrumental in setting up a lecturership for him, and Trinity also asked him back.[12]

His emotional life, which at the best of times gave him little rest, was particularly turbulent. He had embarked on a love affair with Lady Constance Malleson in 1916, more or less with the blessing of Ottoline Morrell; his American lover Helen Dudley remained in England until the end of the war and he had to keep relations with her discreet; after the war, he rattled around a good deal, swinging from exhilaration to despair according to whether he felt much loved or grossly neglected. In 1919 he fell in love with Dora Black, a young Fellow of Girton. She was even more hostile to marriage than his other lovers; unlike them, she was not committed to husbands and families elsewhere, and if she hated the thought of marriage she longed for children as much as he did. Since he never relinquished any relationship if he could help it, he had to engage in some complex manoeuvres to secure the blessing of both Constance Malleson and Ottoline Morrell for this new love. All was safely accomplished in the end, and just as Alys had written a chapter on the woman question in Germany for Russell's first book, so Dora contributed a chapter on women under Bolshevik rule to *The Practice and Theory of Bolshevism.*[13]

When he and Dora returned from China in 1921, she was already pregnant, and they hastened to marry. There is some evidence that they would not have married if she had not been pregnant. She said that she was ashamed at having given in and produced a legitimate child, but this may have been bravado, high spirits or post-natal depression, though her hatred of marriage was intense. The long-suffering Alys, who had already bitten on the bullet and sued him for divorce, bit on it once more and hastened the decree absolute so that the future fourth earl would be born legitimate. The bearing of all this on Russell's political views is less direct than its bearing on his day-to-day life; from 1921 he was a man with family responsibilities, and from 1927 part-proprietor of a financially non-viable school. He began to spend a lot of time on the American lecture circuit, which brought in a substantial income in itself and from the subsequent sale of his lectures as magazine articles. The vices complained of by Russell's critics were exacerbated by the demands of this career – the habit of making out that all his opponents are knaves or fools or both at once, the subordination of literal truth to the telling phrase, and the pretence that very simple solutions will cope with very complex problems. The literary charm of what he writes is irresistible even when the subject is of the slightest; the pot-boiling pieces he wrote for the Hearst newspaper chain at the end of the decade on such topics as 'Should Socialists Smoke Good Cigars?' or 'Who May Wear Lipstick?' are classics of their kind, even if the kind is not elevated.[14] Perhaps the slickness they required infected his politics, but we ought not to underestimate the effects of age and impatience. Russell turned fifty in 1922; we know that he was barely half-way through his life, but *he* did not. The urgency which in the 1960s justified casualness in analysis and stridency in exhortation was not something he felt for the first time then.

Russell's preoccupation with love and marriage, and with the more casual promptings of the flesh, does something to explain his lack of interest in practical politics. It is possible to combine a career as a philanderer with a career in politics; Lloyd George is only the most famous of many who have done so. Russell could not have done so. His obsession with solitude and his emphasis on the unsocial and unpolitical aspect of creativity was temperamental as much as doctrinal, but either way offered a shaky basis for a career in radical politics. As we have seen, much of his politics is straightforwardly utilitarian: capitalism makes too many people work too hard at boring work in order to enrich the few; war does vast physical and spiritual damage for little compensating good; imperialism exploits defenceless populations for the benefit of overfed speculators. His most distinctive contribution was less utilitarian, however; his vision of the free creative self owes much to Spinoza, perhaps even more to Shelley, and nothing whatever to the tidily bureaucratic politics of the Fabians. When he cried out for solidarity in the face of human loneliness, it was not of a kind politics can readily provide.

His friendships provided no basis for political activity. Women often felt they were being exploited. Many men found him unbearable at close quarters; he was censorious and prickly, quick to dismiss others as unperceptive and insensitive. No doubt, the NCF had simply exhausted his ability to serve on committees – a view he sometimes expressed. In any case, his sense of his own uniqueness, and his feeling that in a non-religious sense he was 'called' to bring to the world the philosophical intuitions he alone possessed, would always have made him an alarming colleague. All his close friendships were based on emotional empathy; but politics demands an ability to cooperate on practical matters, and to form partnerships on the basis of hard work and political agreement. A common project can do without friendship, and may allow friendship to grow, if at all, from something other than emotional affinity, but Russell would have none of such thoughts.

The friendships formed in the NCF began to cool. He and Clifford Allen briefly shared a flat and went on the Russian expedition together, but Russell's censoriousness began to irritate Allen and they quarrelled (though non-terminally) over the rent.[15] Russell remained a political 'loner', particularly after the Russian trip. He was and remained torn between his attachment to socialism as a cure for the horrors of war and a replacement for imperialist capitalism and his sense that the individualist, aristocratic values to which he was most deeply attached were only loosely attached to socialism in theory and might well fare badly under socialism in practice.

None the less Russell joined the ILP and declared himself a democratic socialist, then and thereafter. He kept up an active career as a reviewer and political controversialist and became an expert in the varieties of socialist thinking. It was in *The Guildsman* for September 1919 that he declared himself a guild socialist, and in 1920 he published in the *English Review* a lecture given to the National Guilds League in February of that year, in which he declared that liberal values would be safe only in a socialist world.[16] Many Labour Party voters support the party because it does not take its socialism too seriously – its constitution commits it to public ownership, but in practice it is a party of moderate, liberal reformism. The Liberal Party had ceased to be such, so its progressive wing went into exile in the Labour Party. Russell was not of their number. He held that relatively old-fashioned liberal values demanded changes which were more drastic than anything the Labour Party had proposed. Far from asserting socialist values but being content with liberal policies, he thought capitalism endangered both peace and liberty, and that its abolition was a priority for the sake of bare survival. Moreover, by this time he accepted that controversial methods of protest or of gaining power might be needed. He had nearly fallen out with the Quaker wing of the NCF over his unabashed support for violent revolution in Russia, and as a consistent utilitarian about institutions he was by no means an 'absolutist' about the constitutional proprieties. In 'Democracy and Direct Action' he raised the question whether workers should engage in political strikes. This was a very live issue at the time, for after the war there was a good deal of talk of 'the political general strike' which featured so prominently in syndicalist theory; some workers and almost all employers thought the time might be ripe for an unconstitutional push for socialism.[17]

Russell was writing for a guild socialist audience; in essence he argued that workers would be justified in striking to bring about industrial self-government – *if* it would work. There was no reason in principle why they should not employ the strike weapon to replace the property rights of existing owners by rights which would-be managers would have to earn by election. In practice, they should be cautious: it was imprudent to outrage the community at large. Socialists could influence the government if they had public opinion on their side, but it was immoral to misuse whatever power they had to exploit or bully the rest of the community. To take an example dear to the intellectual, printers might occasionally make their employers print their non-capitalist view of the world to redress the balance, but to use their power to impose a censorship of their own was simply intolerable. Russell deftly incorporated a defence of democracy, nationality and group autonomy into a vision of a world in which power is normally and naturally devolved as far as possible; to strike to bring that about was hardly to espouse the red terror. If he gives the impression that, once we have agreed on his principles, we shall be able to implement them within a few weeks or months, that touch of glibness hardly detracts from the impressively coherent case for controlled disobedience as a way of preserving the good constitution.

Oddly, this coherence is missing from the longer treatment of *Roads to Freedom*, in which he discusses Marxism, anarchism and guild socialism.[18] Russell argues that although Marx's views are false, state socialism is practicable but unattractive; conversely, Bakuninist anarchy is attractive, though equally intellectually flawed; however, it is simply not practicable. Guild socialism is a practicable compromise; it avoids the rigid centralization of state socialist theories but demands enough discipline to make cooperation possible. The two main contenders having eliminated each other, the compromise survives. Real guild socialists, who thought their creed something other and better than a compromise, could hardly be satisfied with that.

Russell tackles his subject in his usual way – the history of Marxism, anarchism and syndicalism first, then their capacity to deal with current problems, finally the decision that non-revolutionary, non-anarchist syndicalism is the most acceptable form of organization of industrial society. Marx is treated more lightly than in *German Social Democracy*; his economics is pushed to one side and Marx the revolutionary brought centre stage. Russell points out what its forbidding bulk prevents many readers discovering – that *Capital* contains rather little economics but a great deal of history and contemporary description. Richly textured description and denunciation here, as in the *Manifesto*, is the essence of Marx. The economics is a reflection of Marx's desire for intellectual respectability and not essential to Marxism as a fighting creed.

Russell is, however, more concerned for the fate of freedom under a Marxist government. The answer is that there would be little of it. Marxists would establish state socialism; the state would not 'wither away', and Marxists who used the coercive apparatus of government to 'expropriate the expropriators' would continue to use it to run society thereafter. Russell wrote this before Lenin's *State and Revolution* appeared in the West, and so had nothing to say about his claim that when the proletariat seized power they smashed the 'bourgeois' state and thereafter ruled through machinery which became less like a traditional state. Soon afterwards, Russell had much to say about what the 'dictatorship of the proletariat' looked like in practice. He observed that Marxists claimed that 'dictatorship' was not to be taken in its usual sense, but 'proletariat' was, and that they were instituting an expanded form of democracy; but, he said, it was really the other way about, 'dictatorship' was to be taken literally, but 'proletariat' was not, and what was achieved was the dictatorship of the *apparatchiki*.[19] In *Roads to Freedom*, Russell notes but does not analyse Marx's enigmatic claim that administrative functions would 'lose their political character'. What this means is quite unclear, though it must mean that there would be fewer laws, no policemen and no 'officials' with lifetime jobs in government service. What would replace them Marx left to the future. Russell does not press the matter. He notes that Marx's views are obscure, but insists on the crucial difference between Marx and Bakunin – that Marxists are firmly committed to *political* as well as *industrial* action, in which they differ from the syndicalists, and are prepared to use the machinery of the state for the foreseeable future, in which they differ from the anarchists.

Russell was quite clear that Marxism had been falsified by events; immiseration had not occurred, and the concentration of capital had not diminished the number of capitalists. Rather, the separation of ownership and management and the creation of huge limited-liability companies had vastly increased the numbers with an interest in the capitalist system. Marxism had been unable to explain or predict the continued impact of nationalism, and no doctrine could be taken seriously which failed to take nationalism seriously. None the less, Marxism was intrinsically realistic. Anarchism was more attractive in principle, but no anarchist society would last more than a few months. The state, once abolished, would reappear either to defend the society against foreign attack or after defeat.

Russell spends little time on the more obvious problems of how society can secure cooperation without any form of coercion whatever just because they are so obvious. He was more eager to praise Peter Kropotkin – whom he rightly regarded as much the most distinguished anarchist thinker and the man who brought order into the chaotic jumble of Bakunin's hopes and fears. Kropotkin had tackled seriously the question of how people were to be induced to work if they were not forced to do so by coercion or the threat of starvation. His answer was that necessary work would occupy us for less time than most people supposed – four hours a day would suffice, and this could be achieved by appealing to people's public spirit and their desire to feel useful. Russell doubted this, but felt that Kropotkin was quite right about the evils of the present; the working day was far too long, and men were kept at work against their will only by the fear of starvation. 'There is no reason why work should remain the dreary drudgery in horrible conditions that most of it is now. If men had to be tempted to work instead of driven to it, the obvious interest of the community would be to make work pleasant.'[20]

Russell borrows from G. D. H. Cole's *Self-Government in Industry* for his picture of his preferred form of socialism. Cole had argued that what was wrong with capitalism was not poverty but slavery; workers were devoid of rights in the workplace and their poverty was an effect of that, not an independent evil. Guild socialism, says Russell, amounts to a happy British compromise between impractical anarchism and rigid bureaucratic state socialism. If we place the control of industry in the hands of the producers, retain a minimal state to repress crimes of violence and to make sure that industrial and commercial organizations stick to the rules they have agreed, we can disperse power, limit coercion and avoid the horrors of bureaucracy while retaining the benefits of socialism.[21]

In the preface to a new edition thirty years later, Russell stood by his denunciation of state socialism and observed that 'what has happened in Russia only confirms the justice of these warnings'. Guild socialism had fared badly in the interim, 'but still seems to me an admirable project, and I could wish to see advocacy of it revived'. The horrors of Nazism and Stalinist communism had, however, made him less happy about anarchism because they had led him 'to take a blacker view as to what men are likely to become if there is no forcible control over their tyrannical impulses'. The problem of reconciling economic justice with political liberty remained.[22] Looking back, Russell thought his hopes had been utopian. They were certainly dashed by the 1920s and '30s. Still, they were very much his own. Russell fitted awkwardly into the socialist tradition because he never bothered himself with its economic anxieties; fixing prices and production he thought of as a technical matter to be resolved by trial and error. What he sought was freedom, two kinds of freedom above all. The first was freedom from war and imperialism; this would not only benefit the exploited inhabitants of colonial countries but the developed world, too. It would free them from fear of each other, and from the bullying, lying and political malpractice of militarist politicians. The other was the large emotional and intellectual freedom which is most easily described by contrasting it with the anxious narrow-mindedness to which, thought Russell, existing industrial societies mostly consigned their victims.

To achieve either would not be easy. Capitalism was *a* cause of war but by no means the only cause of war. He thought, as J. A. Hobson and other radicals had done, that capitalism had to expand or perish and that national capitalisms would always come into conflict over new markets.[23] However, nationalism and elemental racial antagonisms were quite enough to cause wars where no economic interest was at stake, and he saw no reason why a socialist state should refrain from exploiting undeveloped areas and peoples if it could do so.[24] The British working class already benefited from imperialism; merely abolishing capitalists would not stop that. To stop it demanded a definite political decision; it was not an automatic gift of socialism. Nor would internal freedom necessarily follow from the abolition of the private ownership of the means of production. The market was a mixture of tyranny and liberty; socialism might result in tyranny pure and simple. The virtue of socialism would be that the talented would not need private means or an acquiescent patron; the danger would be that the unorthodox would have no means of pursuing their own goals. The more bureaucratic the system, the more likely that conformism would result. He sets out some simple rules for avoiding disaster – no censorship, room to publish anything its producers are willing to pay to have published if neither the state nor the guilds will pay for it – but relies most heavily on the idea that an audience with a passion for freedom ought to be created by offering education to everyone on a take-it-or-leave-it basis up to the age of twenty-one. Sixty years later, Russell's advocacy of an expanded educational system is surprising not for its utopianism but for its conservatism; he takes it for granted that most people ought to have technical training rather than a liberal education after the age of fourteen – just the sort of thought which many educators hope we shall leave behind.[25]

The Practice and Theory of Bolshevism showed that his visit to Russia and his encounters with Bolshevik rule had confirmed in practice his doubts about Marx's theory. The book was thirty years ahead of its time. Apart from Russell, it was largely anarchists such as Victor Serge, Emma Goldmann and Louis Berkman who realized that a new tyranny was in the making. Writers such as Malcolm Muggeridge, who pride themselves on their percipience in recognizing the horrors of Soviet communism in the early 1930s, fail to give credit to Russell for seeing it a dozen years earlier. Only after the Second World War when his old hatred of Russia had again become politically respectable did Russell receive his due.[26] He was at odds with Dora over the Soviet Union; she complained that he lectured the Bolsheviks like an old-fashioned liberal. This is not *wholly* unfair; he certainly recoiled from the collective personality of the Bolsheviks: Lenin was cruel, Trotsky vain and flashy; and he thought the savagery of Bolshevism brought it no political advantage, which was doubtless an old-fashioned liberal thing to think. The book was very much more than a liberal lecture, however. Russell was even-handed in his anger; the yellow press seized on every atrocity as an excuse to lie about socialism, just as the British Left closed its eyes to Russian realities. Moreover many, perhaps most, of the horrors of Russia had nothing to do with Bolshevism; they were the product of centuries of brutality, incompetence and superstition, and were peculiarly Russian, not peculiarly Marxist. The message of the book is that Bolshevism is no recipe for western socialists to follow. In Russia one might excuse the excesses on the grounds that able and determined men were working against appalling odds; the West had the luxury of being able to launch socialism against a background of developed industries, secure government and domestic peace.[27] Russell preached the message of *The Principles of Social Reconstruction*: Marxism was a bad predictor of events, a bad guide to the human psyche, and an incitement to hatred which we could do without. 'In the principles of Bolshevism, there is more desire to destroy ancient evils than to build up new goods; it is for this reason that success in destruction has been so much greater than in construction. The desire to destroy is inspired with hatred, which is not a constructive principle ... It is only out of a quite different mentality that a happier world can be created.'[28] It was both old-fashioned liberalism and new-fangled utopianism which he opposed to the Bolsheviks.

As we have seen, Russell observed that the so-called dictatorship of the proletariat had already turned out to be the dictatorship of spies, bureaucrats and the 'extraordinary commission' or Cheka which was the forerunner of the OGPU, NKVD and KGB. What struck him most, however, was the wholesale incompetence and chaos. Industry had been destroyed in the war; there was a blockade. None the less, that did not explain why industrial growth failed to resume. The chief cause, he thought, was the lack of skilled manpower. There had always been a very thin stratum of skilled workers and professionals, and the combination of the war and the Bolshevik suspicion of 'bourgeois' figures had wiped that stratum out. It was not merely a matter of material shortages; it was also a matter of there being no accountants or managers to check what was produced and where it went. Episodic brutality was no substitute for skilled workers and management.[29]

Russell was grimly prescient about the reaction of the peasants. Lenin was right to claim that the peasants were eating better than ever before, and Russell thought Lenin was right to let the peasants claim the land as their own, though there was something odd about a socialist government creating private property on a vast scale. None the less, the peasants were not flocking to the communist banner in gratitude for Lenin's concessions. Out in the country, they traded in tsarist roubles, went to church and bitterly resented any disturbance. Naturally they ate well; the towns produced nothing they wanted in exchange for the food they grew, so they might as well eat it themselves.[30]

Russell did not anticipate Stalin; nobody did. He toyed with various possible futures: perhaps a reversion to 'Asiatic' despotism, in the form of a modified tsarism or a government like the British government of India, perhaps an Allied triumph and the restoration of a client regime, but most likely of all a diminution of revolutionary ardour and a moderate regime which would sacrifice ideology to production and would make its peace with whichever industrialized nations were willing to help in the work of reconstruction.[31] He was quite wrong; but it was a very near miss. Had Bukharin and his friends succeeded in place of Stalin, he would have been quite right. Still, his main aim was not prediction but warning. Whatever happened in Russia, Bolshevik methods were an intolerably expensive way of achieving something which was very far from socialism. Short of the aftermath of war, there was no situation in which the industrial workers of a western country could swallow Bolshevism. Marx had never been right that workers had nothing but their chains to lose, and they could see with half an eye that whatever chains they shed would be replaced by new ones chosen for them by the party leadership.[32] For all this Russell received no thanks. The Right hated his pacifism and socialism and could not praise his condemnation of Bolshevism while he maintained that no sane person could defend capitalism instead; the Left, which took him more seriously, was shocked at the betrayal of an ally. Trotsky observed that the British working class neither needed nor would heed the advice of a 'moth-eaten old aristocrat', which was doubtless true but had consequences other than Trotsky supposed.[33]

Russell and Dora argued a good deal about their very different experiences of Russia, an argument which later culminated in their writing the *Prospects*. More immediately, they prepared to go to China and Japan. When they got back he set about *The Problem of China*. It is a curious book, more expressive than many of a familiar tension. Russell sometimes described himself as the last of the Whigs, and the picture of China which Russell provides in *The Problem of China* somewhat resembles the picture of China to be found in the essayists of the French Enlightenment. In general terms, Russell sympathized with the 'modernizers', wanted to see the imperialist exploiters thrown out, wanted to see the peasants literate; but he could not help wishing that it could happen without the arrival of the factory whistle and the foreman. As an intellectual, he found the Chinese reverence for learning and contempt for worldliness very much to his taste, too.

The Problem of China – with a chapter on the increasingly militaristic politics of Japan – is cast in the mould which Russell made his own. It provides a skeleton history of China's relations with the West, an account of the contemporary political scene, and some advice on future policy on the part of both the Chinese and western governments. Russell almost had the opportunity to put his advice into effect, for after his return the first Labour government, led by Ramsay MacDonald, set up the Phillimore Committee to consider British policy towards China and in particular to consider how to spend Britain's share of the indemnity extorted after the Boxer Rising, and Russell was to have been on it. When MacDonald's government fell after only ten months in office, the incoming Tory government threw him off.

The world Russell was writing about is now very remote. So much has happened to China since 1920 that it is hard to cast one's mind back to the days of arguments over the 'Open Door' – the principle that trading concessions given to one great power must be given to all, which all countries other than the United States regarded as a mere screen for American domination of Chinese trade and banking.[34]

Two things remain interesting, however. In the realms of political theory, the book displays Russell's habit of writing about nations as if they are individuals writ large. The Chinese and Japanese characters intrigue him because politics is so largely the expression of national character. Western nations are discussed in terms which suggest that 'the English' and 'the Americans' act internationally as their national characters prompt them to. Of course Russell knew national character was not innate but the result of social training; more importantly, he was often astute about the way a country's political stance might reflect something very subterranean about the character of its politicians and people.[35] The whole book hangs none the less on the contrast between the western and the Chinese (and to a lesser extent the Japanese) character, for *The Problem of China* is a moralizing tract, urging the Chinese to emulate the good and avoid the bad aspects of the European temperament, and lamenting that the Japanese had done exactly the reverse.

The other interesting aspect of the book is the moral Russell drew from the recent history of China and Japan. As he did in *The Foreign Policy of the Entente*, Russell gave a blistering account of the actions of the major imperialist powers. He was especially savage, not only because the western powers had been so blatantly greedy and dictatorial, but because he thought that even when they acted in a relatively altruistic fashion they had nothing to offer the Chinese. Early in the book he quoted the famous answer which the Chinese emperor returned to George III's proposal of diplomatic and trading relations – the emperor could understand that the British, living far from civilization in their scruffy little islands, would wish to share the felicities of the celestial empire, but, alas, they could offer the Chinese nothing in return, so there was no point in establishing a connection.[36] Russell wrote, 'what I want to suggest is that no one understands China until this document has ceased to seem absurd'. Indeed, China had suffered nothing but damage from the West. The Chinese had a calmly epicurean view of the world; they cultivated politeness, intelligence and innumerable small pleasures. He was very much taken with the Chinese capacity for happiness and the way the Chinese bubbled with a sly humour which their western oppressors mostly failed to catch. He was impressed by the Chinese ability to think in the very long term, to deflect and absorb their conquerors over centuries rather than decades, let alone years. The Japanese by contrast had merely acquired the most narrowly utilitarian qualities of their American infiltrators; they valued the arts of war and money-making, and their brutally undemocratic politics was adequate to nothing more. Like pre-war Germany, they were making up for lost time in the imperialist scramble, and war was the inevitable result of these efforts.[37]

Russell did not write off the Japanese as mere imitators. The Japanese despised the rest of the world; they wished to defeat the Americans, not just to catch them up. It took no great skill as a political soothsayer to see that the rivalry between America and Japan would dominate the Pacific basin in coming decades. What Russell saw – which many commentators failed to – was that the Japanese were likely to discount America as a military power and might well delude themselves that they could establish their hegemony in the Pacific by quick and decisive action against an American army and navy which they believed to be inefficient and lacking in warrior spirit. If they tried, they would be destroyed – a view which many Japanese strategists held in 1941 even while the attack on Pearl Harbor was being planned. It might take a long time for America fully to rouse herself, but even if it took ten years Japan would be crushed.[38]

The one thing that does not emerge from *The Problem of China* is what 'the' problem was. Russell was surprisingly insouciant about the most obvious problem, the near-anarchy of Chinese politics. Since China was larger and more populous than all Europe, it might be expected to divide into semi-autonomous areas. The civil war was low-key and bloodless because it was fought by mercenaries who had the sense to run away rather than get killed for the sake of a principle. Whether the average peasant was quite so sanguine we may doubt. Perhaps 'the' problem was one posed by Russell, rather than by the Chinese – could China come to terms with the industrial age without suffering all the horrors of the industrialized western nations? He thought it was possible if everyone left the Chinese alone; but his own analysis of Japanese foreign policy made it incredible that the Chinese should be so lucky. The eventual outcome – Chiang Kai-shek's nationalism followed by Mao Tse-tung's communism – he did not foresee. He thought Bolshevism appealed to no more than a few young intellectuals; the example of Russia was a deterrent, and in any case Russia was doomed to slip back towards capitalism merely to survive. Moreover, China could only be governed federally and loosely, but Bolshevism was a centralizing creed. Perhaps we should not conclude that Russell was simply mistaken; Mao himself said that it was still too soon to judge whether the French Revolution of 1789 had been a success, and we might well apply the same caution to his achievements. Still, there is no denying that Russell's views do not touch the late-twentieth-century concerns of China, which are essentially bound up with the long-run prospects of the local brand of communism.[39]

The Problem of China marked the end of an epoch in Russell's life. Marriage and fatherhood now imposed on him the need for an adequate income. Until the campaigns for nuclear disarmament and world peace in the 1950s and '60s, he was henceforth obliged to write for money; this is not to say that he wrote much that he did not believe or that he was anything but serious in what he wrote. If the style was 'racy', the content was generally sober, frequently sombre. There was a good deal of lay preaching; but there, too, the content reflected the usual curious mixture of sombre reflection and ecstatic hankering. However, from now on he was pressed for time and pressed for material; the same ideas and often the same phrases are a good deal recycled; more importantly, he had too little time for reconsideration and reflection and too little to find the aptest expression of his ideas. He was a very great success as a popular writer, but anyone who today sat down to read *all* his popular essays would soon find themselves skipping.

The Prospects of Industrial Civilization which he and Dora co-authored was the last fruit of the journey to China, and was heavily dependent on newspaper articles he had written during and just after the trip. It served to reconcile them after their violent arguments over Russia. It had looked as if her almost mystical enthusiasm for the strivings of the Russian people had clashed head-on with his scepticism and distaste for the crude illiberalism of the regime. Though their arguments lasted well into the journey to China, they were not as serious as they seemed. Her romanticism was hardly greater than his, though doubtless she found handsome Red Army soldiers a more convincing argument for communism than her husband did.[40] Her initial belief that nothing mattered except immediate industrialization gave way to the more sober thought that if freedom depended crucially upon being able to hand over drudgery and back-breaking toil to machines rather than people, it depended on much else, and it was fatal to neglect civil and political rights.[41]

The Prospects of Industrial Civilization, written in the first person singular but advertised as 'by Bertrand Russell with the cooperation of Dora Russell', represents their agreed position. It divides into analysis and prescription, and in both areas induces a mixture of admiration and irritation. Russell begins, as so often, by declaring that the great pressures on the modern world are nationalism and industrialization; their import-ance is impossible to exaggerate, for together they have vastly increased mankind's capacity for mutual destruction and the willingness to use the means of destruction thus provided. The essence of industrialization is organization. Russell never alluded to sociologists other than Marx; if he had, he might have declared that in making organization rather than capital central, he was siding with Durkheim and Weber (and most later-twentieth-century sociologists) rather than Marx. Industry demands the mobilization of great quantities of labour and fixed equipment; it is at the opposite pole from the hand-to-mouth existence of simpler societies, for men must produce capital equipment which is not itself consumable and does not directly produce consumable goods. The emblem of indus-trialization is a railway – we can eat neither the rolling-stock nor the services it provides, and it demands detailed division of labour and fixed hierarchical management. The London Midland and Scottish railway is at the opposite extreme from the loosely structured hunter-gatherer clan.[42] So plausible is this view, and so well did it serve Russell's purposes, that it re-mained the basis of his defences of democratic socialism until the end of his life.

What he does not pause to consider is the claim which is at the heart of Marx's analysis, that private capitalism was an indispensable condition of industrialization in the first place, though it had now become a fetter on the forces of production. He would probably have thought it irrelevant. The crux was that there was no necessary connection between industrialism and capitalism now. The important connection was between industrialism and powerful government; industrial society was more 'organic' than previous societies, that is, the division of labour was more minute and production was more vulnerable to disruption if any element in the process failed to perform properly. This, added to the characterstically long wait between investment and effort on the one hand and increased consumption on the other, made strong government essential.[43] Again, it is strange that Russell's historical curiosity did not lead him to speculate that the rise of strong, centralized, national governments in the sixteenth and seventeenth centuries was the decisive factor in the rise of industrial society. What he does, and again he very much resembles Durkheim in so doing, is to emphasize the contrast between industrial society as it now exists and all other forms of society. This is hardly surprising, since the emphasis on function and organization fits his guild socialism as neatly as Durkheim's emphasis on the organic division of labour fits Durkheim's emphasis on 'secondary institutions' such as trade unions and employers' organizations.[44] Russell once again points out how far events are from fulfilling Marx's predictions; but as energetically as any Marxist he also insists that under capitalism large corporations own the state. If the state is not the executive committee of the bourgeoisie, it is certainly the servant of J. P. Morgan and Standard Oil.[45]

Russell cannot decide whether this is wholly intolerable or merely somewhat unpleasant. If the world were rationally organized to suit Standard Oil, it might be a peaceful and prosperous plutocracy, and it is easy to think of many worse outcomes. Two things made him think it was more likely to be intolerable. The first was that capitalists were unlikely to be able to keep the peace. As much as the rest of the population, they were vulnerable to irrational outbreaks of patriotic sentiment; the steeliest banker might begin by siding with war or peace on selfish economic grounds, but would end by succumbing to patriotic fervour once his homeland was under attack. Even if they had been reliably pacifist, it was impossible for the capitalists to exercise *independent* power; the ability to control events depended on public opinion and, if the public ceased to think them indispensable and public-spirited, they could not stand out against public sentiment. If they were thus not much of a barrier to chaos, they were domestically liberticide. The main domestic concern of the big trusts was a docile, non-socialist workforce. They would try to get it by a combination of force and propaganda – not that they were wholly distinct, seeing the way American capitalists secured a pro-capitalist educational system by sacking the dissident, hiring the compliant and bullying education officials over syllabuses. Russell had, of course, served six months in jail for saying much the same in early 1918, but jail had not persuaded him he was wrong.[46]

As for what could be achieved instead, Russell again insisted that socialism as usually construed would not make any difference. Rats were astonishingly self-sacrificing for members of the same rat-pack and hideously vicious in their treatment of non-members; humans were much the same, unless persuaded out of it. A socialist state which had undergone no change of heart would exploit other countries, like any capitalist state, and Russell took plesaure in showing that Trotsky's defence of the Soviet conquest of Georgia was a long-winded way of saying that the Bolsheviks wanted the Georgian oilfields: 'what he calls "capitalist greed and piracy" is to be succeeded by proletarian greed and piracy. He does not say in what way this constitutes an advance.'[47] British capitalists hated German capitalists; Russian socialists might well hate Chinese socialists.

One of the shrewdest chapters tackles the question whether underdeveloped countries could industrialize under socialism without suffering the horrors of capitalist industrialization. It amounts to an obituary of 'war communism' as practised in the Russian civil war. Russell makes a more general point, however; forced industrialization is wildly inefficient, because national fervour is the only alternative to draconian coercion on the one hand or the profit motive on the other, and national fervour simply will not last long enough to sustain the sacrifices and change of long-entrenched habits which industrialization demands. Lenin had learned the lesson and seemed ready to allow small businesses to flourish alongside state capitalism. Anything else would have collapsed in incompetence and corruption – a view which the subsequent history of the Soviet Union and post-war China does nothing to refute.[48]

Most of the *Prospects* is devoted to the other great passion of Russell's life, the need for world government as a means of enforcing world peace. Although nothing he wrote was ever dull, his speculations on the way the world might be carved up between the Russian, American and British empires before finally falling under one world government are dated. Their dated content makes more obvious two vices which always weakened his writings on the subject. The first is a habit of oversimplifying the factors involved in an argument which is then pressed to implausible extremes. So here, in the course of pointing out, what very few people were inclined to dispute, that America had finished the First World War as the most powerful of western nations, he argues that America can always get her own way over matters in dispute because she could bring Britain to her knees by imposing an embargo on grain and cotton. This ignores the fact that Americans whose trade was thus destroyed would put pressure on the American government not to do any such thing, just as it ignores the fact that embargoes are notoriously leaky. In an all-out war things are different, but that is precisely the case he is not envisaging; what he is unable to imagine is that American superiority in wealth and power need not and perhaps could not express itself in a series of threats of increasing ferocity.[49]

The other vice is a too ready assumption that politics between states obeys just the same rules as disputes between individuals. It is true, as Hobbes's *Leviathan* argued three centuries ago, that we resort to government to escape the state of nature and its risk of 'sudden and violent death'.[50] But not all societies need a state and not all societies have one; villages where peace is kept by a combination of moral pressure and the knowledge that any injury done to an individual will be avenged by his clansmen do not need a state. It is unprotected individuals who are vulnerable to violence which they cannot themselves deter who need the protection of the state. Whole nations are not much like such individuals; they do not die in the instantaneous way individuals do; they have allies; they can cause enough trouble to aggressors to make the effort of overrunning them seem a bad bargain. Russell's assumption that general obliteration was the only alternative to omnicompetent world government was never correct, then or later.

None of that means that the socialist commonwealth which he and Dora wished to see in the place of competing capitalist states was anything but attractive. Its attractions need no describing, however, for they are precisely those of *The Principles of Social Reconstruction* and induce in most readers the same combination of acceptance and unease. To the extent that such a transformation of society depends on remodelling the education of our children, we shall shortly see what Russell proposed in that area. We can conclude this chapter with some general reflections on the strengths and weaknesses of Russell's political sociology. His strength is that he makes power and organization central issues of social analysis, not property and social class. This saves him from expecting too much from socialism, from wondering why the Soviet experiment failed or why the working class keeps on refusing to revolt in the way Marxists expect it to. It leads in turn to a dilemma on which everything turns after the *Prospects*, namely how to secure sufficient organization to restrain mankind from self-destruction and to enable us to live comfortably and well without creating so many constraints that we end up cramped and anxious, incapable of spontaneous happiness. This is exactly the dilemma that any libertarian socialist must take seriously; it is to Russell's credit that he does so, and to the discredit of most Marxists that they either ignore it, equivocate about the nature of freedom, or relegate its achievement to some far distant date. This side of Russell's work is, to my mind, admirable. It is his vision of 'human nature' which is more equivocal in its effects. Because he ascribed so much to instinct, he wrote very compellingly of what we tend to think of as the instinctual sources of happiness and about the way they are blotted out by anxiety and an excess of deferred gratification. Conversely, his sense of all this lurking beneath everyday life often induced a degree of political naïvety. He too often said that things went badly only because stupid and wicked men were in power, and that paradise might be regained if the virtuous and intelligent took over. This in turn led to a certain amount of lurching between an élitist vision of what philosopher-kings might do if armed with unlimited power and a straightforward populism which appeals to the good-heartedness of the uncorrupted plain man; it made friendly critics like G. D. H. Cole anxious in 1918, and made many of us sceptical about his views on Vietnam half a century later. One must not exaggerate; there are many wicked rulers and many stupid ones; power does corrupt and the thickening of the skin which politics demands is not very attractive. All the same, it is implausible to think that the *only* reason we have not built the earthly paradise is that criminal idiots have stopped us – and the sociologically minded Russell knew it. Though he wriggled a good deal when reminded of it, it was one of his many virtues that he so readily admitted that there was a large gap between his cooler analysis and his more heated advocacy. He excused himself on the grounds that there was a world to be saved or lost.[51] If anyone was entitled to excuse himself on such grounds, Russell was.

FIVE
EDUCATION FOR UTOPIA

BETWEEN 1927 and the collapse of his second marriage in 1933, Russell was deeply involved with education. He owned, and had to manage the finances of, Beacon Hill, the school he and Dora founded and installed at Telegraph House, high on the South Downs. In the American lecture tours which paid the school's bills and in the magazine articles which were a spin-off of the tours, education was the subject to which he continually returned. In those years he was (and remained until the end of the Second World War) less politically active than he had been during the First World War and was again to be in extreme old age. He was extremely fond of his young children, just as he was later extremely fond of the son born to his third marriage. He was less happy as a husband. He and Dora had perhaps been too optimistic about the prospects of an 'open' marriage or insufficiently careful about contemplating all the possible threats to it; as it was, they accepted one another's affairs with relative equanimity, but eventually came to grief when Dora had a child by Griffin Barry, who was less a lover than a permanent fixture in her life. Russell's private life is a matter of public interest less because it was spectacular than because he himself drew on it for evidence of the soundness of his ideas about love, marriage and family life, and because he was sometimes tempted to adjust his advice to other people in order to justify his own conduct. So *Marriage and Morals* recommends that husbands and wives tolerate infidelities but holds that wives who produce their lovers' children give their husbands grounds for divorce. Dora Russell's autobiography says, no doubt truthfully enough, that she had no idea that that was where he proposed to draw the line; and Russell himself seems entirely unaware that his readers might think that to draw the line there was either arbitrary or was calculated to give the husband – who could not, after all, suffer an illicit pregnancy himself – all the benefits of openness and none of the duties. Nor do Russell's arguments wholly convince: ' ... if the marriage persists, the husband is faced with the necessity of having another man's child brought up with his own, and (if scandal is to be avoided) even as his own. This goes against the biological basis of marriage, and will also involve an almost intolerable instinctive strain.'[1] One might wonder how the man who inveighed so eloquently against the possessive and exclusive impulses could be so unselfconsciously proprietorial about children.

When present, he was generally a successful father; he was, however, sometimes obtuse. His daughter tells a wholly believable tale of woe about her and her brother's lives at Beacon Hill School. Since mother and father were also the heads of the school, Russell treated his own children with the same distant friendliness with which he dealt with all the other children; the result was that they felt abandoned and miserable for much of their schooldays. Again, one might think these private failures irrelevant to the merits of his public utterances were it not that he appealed to his own practice in support of the advice he offered in *On Education* and in the many articles he wrote about Beacon Hill and its virtues. The most awful tale of all is perhaps the most familiar; *On Education* explains, rather engagingly, how Russell persuaded his son to take heights seriously – John had been impressed by the way plates smashed, and was equally impressed by being told he would smash like a plate if he fell over the cliff. Russell's recipe for curing fear reversed the process; John was terrified of waves, so his father simply plunged him into them until he ceased to struggle. According to Russell, this cured John's fears; according to the children, it made every visit to the beach thereafter very hard work as John forced himself to put on a bold front to avoid his father's scorn. Russell came to understand this, too, by the time he wrote his *Autobiography*.[2] Nor did less tangible fears vanish.

The successes and failures of Beacon Hill School are a contentious subject which we may decently avoid here; Russell gives the impression that it was pretty disastrous, but Dora Russell gives an equally persuasive account of the virtues that enabled it to survive the departure of her husband and most of its income, and to last out until the middle of the war. It is not so much that the truth lies somewhere in between as that they had very different ambitions for it; she had much less interest in conventional intellectual excellence than he and was more readily engaged by almost any flicker of creativity in children; her ability cheerfully to struggle on through mess and chaos, both physical, emotional and financial, was much greater than his – and she was twenty-two years younger than her husband, too. He must often have seen the school as a terrible machine for swallowing up his time, his energy and his money, a device for making him give pot-boiling lectures to stupid audiences and write

silly little articles for American newspapers. That the school was something
of a dumping ground for eccentric children whose parents could not stand
them, or for the children of parents themselves too eccentric to cope, only
added to his gloom about it; so far as one can tell from her autobiography,
Dora was both wonderfully immune to such resentments and wonderfully
self-deceived about how well the children were doing.[3]

Liberals have always been obsessed with education. Liberals want
reform, not revolution; revolution is costly, inefficient, violent and nasty;
education offers progress without the horrors of violent change. Where
revolutions are undone by the slow pace at which mankind changes its
habits and beliefs, education works on just those habits and beliefs which
most resist forcible alteration. This is not to say that all liberals believe
that '*l'éducation peut tout*', as Helvetius said and Robert Owen reiterated
after him. Russell, for one, believed in something like original sin, at least
to the extent of believing that a certain amount of greed, anger and bloody-
mindedness is built into all of us; and in his more reflective moments, he
was cautious about putting too much trust in any scheme of social
improvement. 'Education' in this sense is more than the three Rs or the
formal syllabuses of schools and colleges; on those subjects Russell wrote
next to nothing, just as he was silent on classroom technique. When he
wrote about the place of science in education or the place of history in
education, he was concerned with what one might call the spiritual benefits
of abstract thought or of a concentration on the concrete fact, not with
potential A-level syllabuses.[4]

Education in Russell's extended sense was a matter of bringing up
children so that they would not repeat the mistakes of their parents'
generation; most of this education took place at home rather than in
school. In writing about it Russell emphasized the role of a scientific
understanding of human nature. He was persuaded neither by Freud nor
by behaviourism, though he was influenced by both; the one thing to
which he was wholly hostile was turning psychology into an instrument
for producing what governments regarded as good citizens.[5] Since families
consist of more than parents and children or, rather, since family relationships involve more than parent–child relationships, the education of
children demanded that relations between parents be in good shape.
Marriage and Morals cost Russell his professorship at the City University
of New York in 1940 and ten years later secured him a Nobel Prize for
Literature. Fifty-five years later we may wonder why Russell's defence of
premarital sex, companionate marriage, sex education in schools and
public support of birth control should cause so much fuss; but this is

partly because Russell himself did such a good job of propaganda and partly because innumerable social and economic forces have had the kind of effect he expected. In defending the cause of sexual liberation he was both bold and mischievous; he suffered a good deal of abuse and some financial loss, but very much enjoyed teasing the righteous.[6]

The framework of Russell's essays in this area was the view of impulse he had adopted in the *Principles*, and the goals he put forward were the mixture of utilitarian and idealistic ends he put forward elsewhere. One aim in education was to equip people to be happy in everyday ways – to make them friendly, unanxious, tolerant, lively and interested in the world; another was to equip them with rational social and political opinions – to make them prefer peace to prestige, contentment to profit, cooperation to power; yet another was to give those who could benefit the resources to explore the peaks of human achievement: the pure sciences, mathematics, philosophy and great literature. In later terms, Russell was a 'child-centred' educator, but not passionately so. He believed that children had a right to happiness, and that children were something other than inadequate adults; but he was sure that the point of education was to teach children what they could not find out for themselves and that the process demanded a good deal of old-fashioned discipline.

As an element in education, science bulked large. Like Spinoza whom he admired and Kant whom he detested, Russell thought the impersonal knowledge produced by science one of the glories of mankind. That knowledge was the nearest thing to the Godlike element in man. Science as a social force was another matter. It was simultaneously liberating and constricting; on the one hand it gave us more power over nature, allowed us to eat, clothe and house ourselves without backbreaking toil; on the other hand it made war more terrible than ever and raised the spectre of social manipulation. In depressed moments, Russell found it hard to decide whether education should be more than a process of benign manipulation; if science could teach us how to condition ourselves into benign peace-ableness, ought we not to sacrifice free will to tranquillity? Or was the price too high, and would we be better off as dangerously self-destructive *men* than as placid sheep? Mill had asked himself the question and had unhesitatingly settled for liberty with danger; but Mill had not seen a generation slaughtered in war.

Russell gave only limited attention to secondary schools and universities. On the whole, he was concerned to open higher education to those otherwise prevented from enjoying it through shortage of funds, and had little to say about what they might study or how. The same was true of access to a decent secondary education. He disliked the public schools, regarding them with some justice as places where militaristic and xeno- phobic attitudes were inculcated in the young men who would be called on for leadership in the next war. Their outdated teaching methods and antiquated curricula did not worry him as one might have supposed they would; nor did he launch the sort of diatribe against the celibacy and homosexuality of single-sex boarding schools which one might have thought the advocate of sexual freedom and a guilt-free upbringing would have launched. His views were orthodox, middle-of-the-road Labour Party views; what was wicked was handing out education on the basis of privilege rather than ability, less the details of the syllabus as such. He thought, of course, that there should be less classics and more science in secondary schools, but the two chief offences of public school education were its class character and its attachment to nationalism and militarism. It is not wholly surprising that Russell thought this: he had not been to school at all, and had experienced the transition between Pembroke Lodge and Cambridge as an ascent from Purgatory to Paradise.[7]

The main reason why Russell did not spend much time on the organ- ization of secondary schools and universities was because he believed that almost all the good and harm done by educators was done in the child's first decade. He had conventional views about the distinction between the more and less gifted child; and he thought schools should select rigorously to choose the best. If they were to do so, it was essential that all children got the best possible start. This was a matter for parents and primary schools but above all for parents. *On Education* came out in 1926; Russell told the American philosopher John Dewey, at that time perhaps the best- known educational theorist in the western world, that it was not a contribution to educational theory but was 'written from the standpoint of common sense'. It was aimed at parents worried about how much or how little attention to devote to their children's education, and drew a good deal on the experience of looking after John and Kate. None the less, Russell was far from an amateur. With his usual facility he had read and accepted Maria Montessori's ideas, read and rejected Rousseau's *Emile*, and had got J. B. Watson's ideas sufficiently under control to be able to debate behaviourism with him on American lecture platforms. Dora Russell remarks that they had together read Freud's disciple and critic, Wilhelm Adler, but it would seem that Russell's conviction, that the 'will to power' was even more fundamental than the sexual drive, antedated his acquaintance with Adler.[8] The crucial effect of an interest in depth psychology was that Russell differed from traditional empiricists who had thought the child came into the world as a *tabula rasa* on which the teacher might inscribe anything; on the contrary, children arrived with innumerable potentialities and tendencies, which parents and teachers might develop or thwart. Education was more akin to gardening than it was to engineering, and demanded something of the same affection for variety and difficulty.

Reading *On Education* six decades later, some readers find it old hat and obvious; in its day it was anything but. We still find it difficult to treat children with quite the mixture of attention and insouciance that Russell recommends, but, as an ideal, doing so has become much more popular than it was when he advocated it. Moreover, Russell's ideals are rather more contentious than they seem at first sight. The degree of fearlessness we want our children to possess, to take but one example, is less agreed than one might think. Certainly we do not want children to be neurotic cowards, reduced to abject terror by things that pose no real threat, just as we do not want them to be madly rash or to hurl themselves on genuine dangers. Whether we all want them to be fearless in Russell's sense is quite another question; many people think that the bloody-minded intellectual boldness which he warmed to is in actuality a crass inability to see the value of traditional ways of thinking, and that he vastly overestimates the originality and courage of most children, who would be better off following authority than making their own pointless mistakes.

If his values are more debatable than they seem at first blush, so are his methods. He stresses the need for calm and stability in the first year of the child's life; but it is not at all obvious that children are anything like as dominated by *habit* as he supposed. Later, he came to think that he had had rather a brutal attitude to very young children, but even with rather older ones there are passages in the book which make one wince. He borrowed from Madame Montessori the suggestion that disruptive or ill-behaved children ought to be isolated from their fellows as if they are ill until they behave better, but one may doubt whether this is a way of teaching *self*-discipline, let alone whether it is entirely consistent with an enthusiasm for fearlessness and an ability to stand up to hostile opinion. In short, far from being old hat, Russell's views are distinctively part of the 'modern movement in education', both as to aims and as to method.[9]

With his usual tidiness, he begins *On Education* by asserting that the aims of education are the production of 'vitality', courage, sensitiveness and intelligence, in the highest degree'; a community of people with such traits would be Utopia. The gap between this Utopia and the world we live in casts no doubt on either the goals or the methods of attaining them; it merely demonstrates that we have not thus far been sufficiently radical in our efforts. The goals of *On Education* are self-assertive; whether they are at odds with Russell's earlier advocacy of a degree of humility and self-abnegation in the face of a mysterious universe is matter for dispute. It is, however, not hard to see that Russell would himself have thought that a decent intellectual humility was far from implying any lack of self-respect and infinitely far from demanding any deference to human authority. What is clear is that *On Education* is avowedly un- or even anti-Christian. Pagan self-assertion scores highly, Christian humility scores poorly; in the 1920s the role of religion was still strong, many writers still thought that schools ought to teach social deference according to the principles of the well known hymn:

> 'The rich man in his castle
> The poor man at his gate,
> God made them high and lowly
> And ordered their estate.'

Russell thoroughly irritated everyone who subscribed to that sort of view. Even the utterly impious, however, might complain of an excess of individualism. Ought not the Russell who wrote *The Principles of Social Reconstruction* to have placed the ability to cooperate with others nearer the centre of his scheme of valued goals? What has to happened to his advocacy of worker cooperatives and guild socialism? Russell does not object to cooperation, even at his most individualistic; nobody could, other than Max Stirner and Nietzsche perhaps. Moreover, he insists on the importance of the company of other children in any programme. He recalls that he lacked it and became 'an angular prig'. All the same, there is something to the complaint that Russell's image of cooperation was too much modelled on the marriage of exalted spirits he and Lady Ottoline Morrell had cherished, and too little on an extrapolation from the patient efforts of the branch secretary of the Gasworkers' Union.[10]

In spelling out how to attain vitality, courage, sensitiveness and intelligence, Russell was practical, sensible, and sometimes old-fashioned even in 1926. Vitality does not get much attention; it does not need cultivating, since in the absence of ill-health and excessive anxiety it appears automatically.[11] This explains why Beacon Hill was so committed to physical health as well as mental alertness, but it could not have been written by someone who had experienced the spontaneous lethargy which so often afflicts teenage children. In another sense, vitality is the central feature of the whole book, as it is of every piece of advice on 'how to be happy' that

Russell ever laid before the public. Intellectual and emotional liveliness is the largest part of intelligence; and the 'get up and go' that stops its possessor hanging about feeling frightened does much to allow its possessor freedom to be curious about and sensitive to what is going on around him or her. It would be odd if this were not a central part of Russell's argument, given his emphasis on the place of impulse in the *Principles*.[12]

Russell begins with the new-born baby. His advice is very straightforward, though it will fail to carry conviction with half those who read it: establish a routine and stick to it. Babies need no more than a regular timetable of eating and sleeping to get started. Whether he would have thought it quite so easy to feed baby on a timetable or leave baby to cry himself or herself to sleep if his own children had not had a nurse is a question on which cynical speculation is possible. At all events, he writes in a thoroughly 'pre-Spockian' fashion about the first months. Even then, his eye for dilemmas and his enthusiasm for spontaneity are well to the fore.[13] Babies, he says, have so much energy and such a capacity for absorbing new experiences that parents need only provide opportunities for learning, but parents who know this are just the sort who may well worry about their children's welfare; the urge to protect the child from harm is constantly in conflict with the knowledge that the child needs to explore. Whether the advice to 'hide your anxiety very carefully, lest it pass to the child by suggestion' much advances the problem is another question.[14]

The great aim of education is the creation of character; so much of the book is about 'moral education' in the broadest sense. This is largely a job for parents, with help from other children, but Russell insists on the merits of a spell in a good nursery school. The loneliness and oppressiveness of Pembroke Lodge seems to lie behind the emphasis on play, fantasy and the development of the constructive impulses. He was certainly convinced that the Victorian attempt to curb the energies of small boys and make them think of the distant future was an error; it achieved nothing but guilt and world-weariness. How all this is to be stopped and cheerfulness maintained is explained in familiar fashion; fear and anxiety are not instinctive in higher mammals, so neurotic anxieties in children must be caught from the adults they come in contact with. It is in explaining how parents can reduce irrational fears and instil rational ones that he adduces his own treatment of his son. Though he adopted a very simple picture of how children acquire and lose emotional reactions, he did not think that they were in any obvious sense 'mechanisms'. In American debates and lectures he steered a careful line between Freudian theories which credited tiny children with an elaborate and sophisticated set of guilts and anxieties and behaviourist theories which treated them as if they had no inner lives at all.[15] His insistence on the individuality of each child made him an essentially 'child-centred' thinker; but he redressed the emphasis a little in reminding parents that they ought not to martyr themselves for their children's sakes.[16]

Where Russell hits his most engaging and characteristic note is in his insistence that learning is itself liberating and an enemy to irrational fear. Spinoza's vision of the free man as a man with literally universal interests, who was not imprisoned in anxieties about his own narrow concerns, had always attracted him. Russell saw clearly enough that techniques which cured a groundless fear of waves were not applicable to a child's fear of death; here Spinoza has to step in. Children can only be told that people fall into a sleep from which they never wake, and that it will not happen to them for a very long time. More crucially, they need to be encouraged to acquire so many interests outside themselves that they cease to brood upon their own fates. 'The man whose hopes and fears are all centred upon himself can hardly view death with equanimity, since it extinguishes his whole emotional universe ... every interest in something outside a man's own body makes his life to that degree impersonal. For this reason, paradoxical as it may seem, a man of wide and vivid interests finds less difficulty in leaving life than is experienced by some miserable hypochondriac whose interests are bounded by his own ailments.' In that frame of mind, they will see the difference between rational measures of self-defence and the groundless anxieties of housemaids.[17]

It is not clear how far one can go in persuading the unconvinced about the merits of Russell's recipes. To my mind, his emphasis on a concern for the outside world as the surest remedy for pointless fear is absolutely right; but many people find themselves unable to apply the remedy and can hardly be argued into success.

On the conventional virtues such as truthfulness, generosity and friendship, Russell writes impeccable sense. We must not become so anxious about every departure from truth that we stamp out imagination – the small child who says he has just seen a lion in the garden is not *lying*. A regard for the truth is best inculcated by telling it oneself wherever possible. Generosity is not inculcated in children who are forced to part with their favourite possessions; they are more likely to become greedy and suspicious. They have to be lured into it by seeing that the generous are better liked and end up happier than the mean and grasping. The optimistic theory behind all this is that happy children will spontaneously behave truthfully, generously and in a friendly fashion. This perhaps does not allow enough room for the possibility that they will behave decently within a limited circle and badly outside it. It is not uncommon in criminal circles to find great affection within the family circle and complete unscrupulousness outside it.[18] Many Nazis were loyal in a bad cause.

On the intellectual virtues he is tougher and more persuasive, particularly where it is a question of inculcating concentration. Punishment other than merely expressing disapproval of idleness and disorganization is not needed and not effective. The knack is to get children to see that work is more interesting than idleness; in the schoolroom the obvious way to achieve that is to see that while lessons are voluntary the alternative to them is literally doing nothing, sitting somewhere empty and dull. This may strike some readers as altogether less libertarian than they expected from Russell, but the truth is that Russell thought that there was one and one only form of legitimate discipline, and that was the discipline imposed by a subject. It was not punishment that was needed or obedience to some particular person, but practice at working steadily in the way a particular problem or discipline required. Russell's willingness to lean on children quite heavily for the sake of inculcating such habits of self-control rested heavily on his belief that, once such habits were acquired, they were liberating rather than constraining, since they made it possible to explore the intellectual universe in a way that was otherwise impossible.[19]

What shocked readers in the 1920s was his breezily secular attitude to sexual education for children. It was this which provoked innumerable stories about Beacon Hill, all of them false, though some were at least *ben trovato*. There never was a visiting vicar who exclaimed, 'Good God!' on meeting a naked child on the doorstep, only to be told, 'There is no God,' though it seems a pity that it never happened. What scandalous behaviour there was took place between the proprietors and their good-looking staff and seems to have gone unnoticed by the children. *On Education* nowadays seems oddly timid about sex and excessively cautious about the whole subject. Russell is readier to believe that masturbation is bad for children than anyone is today, and much too eager to insist that if only people stopped fussing, sex would be simple. One might, after all, believe that it will always cause trouble and rather rejoice in the fact; he doesn't.[20] On the other hand, his views on what one might call 'formal' sex education are sane and have by now been incorporated into most successful sex education programmes. The great aim is to avoid children panicking or acquiring a sense of guilt about their bodies; this entails giving sex education before puberty – by puberty children will have heard terrible tales from other children and will be too excited by their own sexual desires to take in information calmly. What is needed is dispassionate instruction on the mechanics, given before sexuality rears its head and given as and when curiosity demands it.[21]

If Russell's views on the ordinary school syllabus are unexciting, what comes through very clearly is his love for the nursery school programmes of Madame Montessori and Margaret McMillan. His usual scepticism vanished in face of their vision of a race of stunningly healthy, happy and intelligent children they were rearing. What were essentially optimistic prospectuses were taken as flatly literal descriptions of what they had achieved – though if they had, it is hard to see why this race of gods in human form has not been the saving of humanity over the past sixty years. It is what emerges between the lines which induces anxiety: Russell's entirely unselfconscious conviction that parents were sure to be much better off when they followed the findings of 'science', his belief that the children of the towns were uniformly sickly, and that his own children, educated in the fresh air and on the beach, were sure to be mentally and physically healthier than the offspring of shopkeepers – assumed, on no evidence whatever, to be the victims of unsuitable food, late nights, and an excess of adult company.[22] What many readers will find a more sinister note is struck by the suggestion that this educational programme ought to be backed up by a eugenic programme to ensure good raw material for a more rational upbringing.

Formal schooling hardly seems to interest Russell very much.[23] He takes the conventional view that children should read by five, and ought to begin on a couple of languages, since an early start makes for real fluency. Arithmetic needs some drilling and the most liberal instructor must not flinch from it; imaginative literature will not strike a chord until the age of twelve or so, but children enjoy learning poetry and performing plays, and that instils a useful sense of accuracy in them – which Russell astutely links to the aesthetics of literature by insisting that one good effect of a concern for accuracy is that children come to understand why the accurate version of a text is better than the mangled version.[24] As the child gets older, Russell's interest visibly diminishes, perhaps because his own were very young; specialization is swallowed without demur – children ought to try classics, history, mathematics and science and specialize in what they do best. To a reader who has grown up on the thought that it is the teaching which tends to close off options and that students of the humanities would often benefit from a training in science and vice versa, it all looks very rigid. On universities, his views are thin to vanishing;

rightly, he says that universities ought not to be places where the idle children of the rich go to finishing school; more debatably, he denies entirely the utility of lecturing and formal instruction – leaving us to wonder how it is that American and German universities remain so distinguished.[25]

The fundamental message is not much obscured by these small prejudices and omissions; what education demands is love plus science. Ignorant love will make mistakes; science deals in means not ends, and, guided by hatred, greed or the love of power, it will achieve untold horrors. The same techniques can instil bigotry or enlightenment, narrow patriotism or a sense of world citizenship. The familiar polemical oversimplification reappears when he suggests that quarrels in education are simply between those who are motivated by love and those whose views are veneers for hatred. Oversimplification as such is not entirely to be complained of in such a short and brisk piece of work; but the proposition that all social struggles lie between goodness, light and love on the one hand, and evil, narrowness and hatred on the other, is too deeply incredible to be worth scrutiny. Polemically, it is self-defeating, both because it leaves it mysterious why a world in which everyone hungers for love and cooperation should so consistently be in the hands of the greedy and the selfish, and because if one's opponents are described as the incarnation of evil it makes it impossible to deal with them save in the terms of a Holy War.[26]

The ease with which pessimism got the upper hand of his utopian hopes emerges much more clearly in *Education and the Social Order* which he wrote in 1931. It reveals the side of Russell which was so alarmed by the dangers of war and social strife that he was prepared to accept a great deal of indoctrination and thought control to escape these horrors, and to envisage a world government of tyrannical powers rather than endure the dangers of international conflict. This is what one might call the Platonic aspect of Russell's social theory, the conviction that if individuals are left to themselves they will run amok, and that it is the task of the social theorist to invent a social order which will stop them doing so.[27] Matters are even grimmer in Russell's universe than they are in Plato's. Plato thought his republic mirrored a natural order in which everyone had a proper place; Russell is perfectly clear that nature does not divide men into rulers and ruled, philosopher-kings and artisans. Such order as could be achieved would have to be imposed rather than discovered.[28]

The intellectual shift between *On Education* and *Education and the Social Order* is of some interest. Russell now claims that his former theory is only one of three plausible views – it is what he calls the 'negative theory of education', which holds that we ought to provide opportunities and remove handicaps but otherwise leave the child to blossom in his or her own way. To this he opposes two further 'positive' theories, the first that education ought to instil into children as much culture as possible, the other that education ought to turn out useful citizens.[29] He still maintains that the negative theory holds more truth than its rivals, but it is not the whole truth. Five years of a school in which the Bigs were prone to bully the Middles, who then took it out on the Littles, had reinforced his belief in original sin, and he concluded that positive instruction in how to get on with others was required and that children were not just 'born inapt for society' as Hobbes had remarked – they needed a good deal of pushing into sociability. The greater realism of his theorizing went along with a much sourer argumentative tone. The sunny optimism which had come from contemplating a world in which children were taught by Maria Montessori and Margaret McMillan had given way to the gloomy conviction that they would fall into the hands of priests and politicians who would try to keep them brutal, ignorant and unhappy. As to why our spiritual and temporal rulers should do so, Russell fell back on his old belief that superstitious and powerful men are chronically unhappy, and being both unhappy and half mad tend to seize on the very things that do them no good – power over others in particular – and try to get more and more of them.[30] As always, it is impossible to deny that this is sometimes true, but equally impossible to believe it is the whole truth.

The political background to the book was growing bleaker and more miserable by the minute. All over the world, competing nationalism seemed likely to bring about economic ruin and global military catastrophe. So Russell wrote *Education and the Social Order* more firmly than ever in the grip of the melancholy conviction that human beings were the victims of an irrational herd-instinct which underlay playground bullying, just as it underlay anti-semitism, and ordinary patriotism. It was not always a force for evil; unaggressive love of one's own country is a valuable emotion, but is always liable to result in a determination to force everyone to belong to our group or be trampled on. The expression of the herd-instinct in nationalism was by no means the only misery of the modern world. Another was the increasing domination of domestic politics by the bureaucrat; here was the other face of Russell's insistence that organization was the essence of industrial society. Properly handled, the need for organization was a simple fact about complex societies; as it was, the rise of the bureaucrat was the rise of a soulless tidy-mindedness and an inability to make fine but non-practical judgements. Whether his accession to the peerage on the death of his brother Frank in 1931 made him more tolerant of aristocracies we may well doubt; however, he points out that if the world needs bureaucrats and no longer needs aristocrats, the latter are a great deal more interesting figures.[31]

Almost every social pressure on education is denounced with a gloomy relish. Religion inevitably provides one target; religious education destroys intellectual independence because it demands that children take propositions on trust and not on the evidence. Liberal-minded people are no longer Christians, but professed agnostics are never appointed to teaching posts; so teachers have to be either stupid or hypocritical. Cheerfulness is in short supply throughout. Sex education is to be welcomed, not as introducing the young to harmless pleasure, but because it will take their minds off sex when they ought to be working. He is as censorious as any elderly usher in denouncing the resort to masturbation and homosexuality which public schools supposedly impose on their pupils, but it is quite unclear why. One hardly supposes that he thought chastity an improvement and, aside from the claim that sex is a distraction from hard work, he has no arguments except his own adolescence against the view that, under the conditions, the young are almost bound to take whatever sexual opportunities remain open to them.[32]

The real target in any case is not so much education as the evils of nationalism and the need for a world authority to keep the peace. It is this that explains an otherwise extraordinary excursus into the prospects of education under communism. He was certainly opposed to the educational system which he thought typical of capitalism, but given his conviction that the Soviet Union was run by Russian chauvinists who believed in Marx's doctrines with the blindness of religious fanatics, he could hardly have been looking to the Soviet example as the way forward. Indeed, he was not. He mocks the way Marxism turns into fixed dogma, sides with Henry George's attack on monopoly rather than Marx's attack on capitalism, and presciently argues that 'if the Marxian dogma remains as virulent as at present, it must in time become a great obstacle to intellectual progress'. Lysenko was merely one case which showed how right he was.[33] However, he goes on to say that the triumph of communism, after a war or by some other means, would be wholly acceptable to the educator. He did not mean that bigotry was acceptable; what he meant was that Soviet domination of the world would be an improvement on competing nationalisms, and only in that sense a tolerable educational environment. The one absolutely intolerable outcome was the continued division of the world into warring states bent on refighting the battles of the First World War for equally insubstantial goals. Any non-competitive solution was better than that. If communism were to triumph world-wide, it would abandon competition, class-conflict and competing nationalisms; even in saying that, he did not mean to go back on what he had always said about the consistency of nationalism and socialism. What he visualizes is world-wide Soviet hegemony, not independent socialist states. Whether such an outcome would lead to the replacement of propaganda by education and reduce a generally 'religious' attitude to social creeds is another question. Russell, writing in the last lull before the Stalinist storm of collectivization, thought that if Soviet communism triumphed world-wide, it would become less messianic, leaving nothing worse than the standing hazard of the modern world, bureaucratic organization and a proneness to pointless uniformity. This was not an absurd view. It was more nearly absurd in 1936 to write *Which Way to Peace?* and argue that the Nazi domination of Europe, too, would be a lesser evil than a general European war.[34] But it is not hard to see what lay behind his readiness to accept various serfdoms rather than universal extermination, and what therefore dominated much of what he wrote during the 1930s.

The natural companion pieces to his essays on education were the essays on the nature and prospects of marriage. Contrary to the general impression that he was a breezily optimistic enthusiast for open marriage, companionate marriage and what has come to be known as 'serial monogamy', he was in fact a very hesitant writer on such matters. He was also surprisingly sober in his approach to writing *Marriage and Morals*. He thought of books such as *The Conquest of Happiness* as unequivocal pot-boilers, but thought of *Marriage and Morals* as an almost uniquely satisfying chance to write something which was both serious and well thought out and financially successful. His hesitations sprang from sociological rather than moral uncertainties; he could see that changes in the economy were bringing about great changes in marriage arrangements, but thought that their direction was as yet unpredictable. Moreover, though he was confident about what needed to be taken into account in assessing the emotional gains and losses from change, he emphasized the impossibility of making sensible assessments in advance of the experiment.[35] It was the more ironic that *Marriage and Morals* became the most notorious of his works, and cost him his appointment at the City University of New York in 1940 when an anxious Catholic mother, convinced that a course in formal logic from the notorious lecher would entirely subvert her daughter's morals, found a judge silly enough to take her seriously and overturn the appointment.[36] In 1928 when he wrote it, Russell was mostly concerned to keep Beacon Hill afloat, though he very much enjoyed the research he did for it. It is rightly thought by many readers to be one of the deftest blendings of sociology, history, psychology and moral uplift which even Russell set before the public. Those who enjoy it find it deeply engaging; those who do not, find it maddening.

As usual, Russell was more confident about his enemies than his friends. Nor was he any more willing than usual to make the best case he could for his opponents' point of view. Throughout *Marriage and Morals* he writes as if the Christian – or, more exactly, the whole Judaeo-Christian tradition – had been entirely and pointlessly hostile to rational thinking about the purpose of marriage and about any form of sexual activity other than that between incompetent husbands and reluctant wives. Behind the invective, however, lay a serious point. Reading Westermarck and Malionowski, Russell concluded that behind the varied marital institutions of different societies there always lay material underpinnings of some kind. Once societies had discovered – what the Trobriand Islanders seemingly did not know – that sexual intercourse produces babies, and once they had developed beyond the most rudimentary forms of the division of labour, they instituted patriarchal systems of social organization in which the father bore economic responsibility for 'his' children. This made it necessary for fathers to have some control over their children and over the sexual behaviour of their wives, lest they find themselves saddled with responsibility for the offspring of others. Interestingly enough, this is very much the same explanation that is offered by later sociobiologists, just as it was by Hume in the eighteenth century.[37]

Russell does not say that he is largely following in Hume's footsteps, but he very probably knew it. For he follows him in explaining the notorious 'double standard' which demands much higher standards of chastity from women than from men in terms of the economic needs of the first societies which took any interest in property and its succession. Similarly, he follows him in explaining the morality he sees in the twentieth century in just the same terms as Hume explained the morality of the eighteenth; part is genuinely utilitarian, part reflects arrangements which once had a utilitarian point and now do not, part reflects the panic and anxiety inflicted on us by the defenders of the faith.[38] Unlike Hume, Russell writes as a reformer; the task of the rational moralist is to start from the facts and sentiments of the twentieth century and work out a rational system of sexual ethics, and then to consider how to get round the obstacles to its introduction. Hume was content to describe in a none too hostile spirit how things came to be as they were; moreover, he had a much higher regard for habit than did Russell, and thought mankind was almost certainly better off carrying on as it was used to, rather than launching out into uncertain seas. What good the philosopher did was done by discouraging fanaticism rather than by encouraging wholesale reconstruction.

The first step towards a rational ethics was the wider diffusion of knowledge.[39] *Marriage and Morals* largely reproduces the same arguments as his educational essays, chiefly that knowledge is the one great remedy against fear. He has some murderous asides about the stupidity of magistrates and police in prosecuting respectable booksellers for selling useful scholarly works such as those of Havelock Ellis, while doing nothing to catch or prosecute the clandestine sellers of real pornography. Russell argues a three-pronged case. Children who do not learn the facts of life soberly and in an atmosphere of respect for sexuality will learn them in an atmosphere of guilt and smut; they may become obsessed with sex, frightened of sex, convinced that it is dirty or disgusting. None of this offers much help in forming happy intimate relationships in later life. Secondly, parents who lie to their children about sex do great damage; they create distrust and in the eyes of the children cease to be friends whom they can rely on for help and information. If they are successful in stemming childish curiosity they probably damage the child's education – Russell thought that one reason why girls do less well at scientific subjects at school is precisely because they carry a great burden of this sort of sexual protectiveness. If curiosity is not simply stamped out, it will be turned into prurience. Finally, we need to know quite a lot about sex if we are to be half-way adequate lovers. Readers who have grown up on a diet of popular discussion of the clitoral orgasm and the existence or otherwise of the 'G-spot' will find it hard to recapture the sense of relief with which liberated young women in the 1920s discovered that there were straightforward physical and mechanical reasons why they did not enjoy sex, and that there was much that could be done about it. Russell no doubt overstated the case when he said that almost no married women and very few of their husbands got any pleasure at all out of married sex – he was in a gloomy frame of mind about his own marriage at this point. None the less, he is surely right that 'silence and decency' aren't much help in securing sexual harmony.[40]

Russell's defence of sex education went further than that, however, just as his insistence on the need to understand the social and economic bases of marriage was more than the defence of one branch of sociology at large. He thought that a proper understanding of sex would make it more *manageable*; one can see the romantic and the rationalist sides of his character struggling for the upper hand as he balances the fact that sexuality well understood is the source of great happiness with the fact that, ill understood, it is a powerful force for misery. In essence what he wishes his readers to understand is that romantic love is a terrible basis for long-term relationships, though wonderful in itself. Romantic love tends to flare up and die down unpredictably; it is no recipe for constancy because most of us will fall in love with a good many people in addition to our spouses. If we spend all our time stamping on such romantic inclinations, we shall suffer a double loss – ill-temper and sourness because it is so disagreeable to stamp on one's impulses, and the loss of the love that we might have had. Those who think that love and marriage must always hang together are, therefore, in for a terrible time – they will be miserable where divorce is difficult and much married where it is easy.[41] Even where it is easy, miseries will frequently spring from misconceptions – where people mistake a passing infatuation for real passion and end in recrimination and unhappiness. Knowledge is no guarantee against disaster, for this is an area in which there are no guarantees at all. However, knowledge may move social opinion in a direction which encourages people to avoid disasters rather than to plunge into them.

This straightforward view dominates his discussion of marriage as such. His views on marriage flow directly from his account of what the social and economic purpose of marriage is: marriage is essentially an arrangement for the procreation and care of children, and the rights of the parents take second place to the rights of the children. If there are no children to a marriage, the relationship of husband and wife is absolutely their own business and nobody else's. This does not mean that it is all the same how they treat each other, and that they cannot be condemned *at all* if they are promiscuous and 'easy come, easy go' about their sexual behaviour. Russell had very high standards for what one might call the proper use of sexual desire to strengthen and deepen a lasting and intimate relationship, though I do not suppose that he or anyone else would have claimed that he lived up to them more than intermittently.[42] All the same, there is a sense in which the childless marriage exists only to please the partners to it, and if it fails to do so, they are at perfect liberty to break it up.[43] Writing against the background of a system where divorce was difficult even for utterly incompatible childless couples, Russell never saw the need to discuss in detail what ought to be done about marriages which one partner wished to end but the other did not; nor did he have anything to say about the financial arrangements which ought to be made on break-up. 'Palimony' would have come as a terrible shock. A marriage which has resulted in children is an entirely different matter; here the interests of the children are paramount. If it seems on reflection that it is essential for the children's welfare that the parents should stay together, then they must grit their teeth and try to behave better.

Russell insisted on the duties which parents owed one another as parents rather than lovers; this was an insistence which he himself thought of as the proper balance to his insistence on the duties of lovers towards each other. Any assessment of the value of Russell's views on love and marriage depends very largely on one's view of the possibility of squaring the twentieth century's 'search for liberty and love' – to invoke the subtitle of Dora's autobiography – with the demands of stability and social coherence. Russell thought that if people understood that they had to combine the durable commitment which would enable them to survive the long slog of child-rearing with the flexibility, tolerance and self-control which would enable them to turn a benevolently blind eye to their spouse's emotional adventures and not get unduly distracted by their own, then they would indeed do it. It is plainly not impossible that people should combine these somewhat disparate commitments, since many people do it without much strain. What is less clear is that most people could live up to it in quite the way Russell sometimes seems to demand. For he alternates between so praising the life of passion that it becomes hard to see how someone who subscribes to this ecstatic vision will be able to sustain the long haul of 2 a.m. feeds, and so insisting on the demands of the mundane that it is hard to see how anyone who subscribes to this matter-of-factness would have the energy to fall in love. Against this sceptical view one might reply that this is an optical illusion created by Russell's rhetoric. To be sure, he sometimes suggests that passionate love is worth the sacrifice of all else and sometimes that mundane tasks are so important that they demand the sacrifice of all else; but what lies behind the exaggeration is much simpler. It amounts only to saying that people need to develop a sense of the importance of the long run; husbands or wives who fly into jealous rages at each other's affairs threaten what they themselves most want in the long run. We must not become so tidy-minded that we are invulnerable to others, but we must know how to reject temporary ecstasy for the sake of long-term happiness.[44] It is, perhaps, more nearly banal than outrageous; what saves it from banality is the view that none of these things can be just a matter of habit. The liberal, the puritan and the philosopher unite in their conviction that living up to these goals demands a continuous and wide-awake process of reflection and self-examination.

It is in this essentially rather orderly and decorous way that Russell defends the idea of 'companionate marriage' which had been proposed by the American judge Ben Lindsey a few years earlier.[45] (The proposal had cost Lindsey his job, just as it later cost Russell his.) We have seen that Russell was severe on the subject of wasting time on sex which ought to go on academic work. Like many English visitors, he found the spectacle of American teenage sex pretty off-putting. It involved too much bad drink – this was Prohibition America where it was *de rigueur* to produce gallons of illicit alcohol at parties; and the existence of the automobile meant that the young spent much of their spare time in heavy petting with people they would not have liked when sober. This was little fun in itself, and was liable to result in unwanted pregnancies which gave all the relatives a splendid opportunity to vent their sadistic spleen on the young.[46] One may detect here the odd hint of resentment at the meaner spirits among his first wife's relatives, but the serious point is that students would be happier and learn more if they could live together openly. Then as now, married students got better results than unmarried ones, and Russell's ideal – unsurprisingly – was the student who was simultaneously happier and better educated.[47] In all these discussions, Russell was extremely sensible in his recognition of the clumsiness and ineffectiveness of the law. So he concluded that the law should recognize easier divorce – in his day, one could not divorce a partner who went insane, for instance, and adultery was almost the only ground recognized by English courts; but public opinion should be opposed to parents who deserted their posts while their children still needed them. Companionate marriage was entirely experimental and revocable; the real thing was serious and should be taken seriously.[48]

Russell's broadly utilitarian approach is less remarkable today than it was in 1929. He was right to say that he was on the same side as the wise conservative, since he was concerned to make institutions adapt to such unstoppable changes as the rise of reliable contraception and the increased financial independence of women. In many ways, things have gone in the directions he feared rather than those he hoped. The high divorce rates of the 1980s owe a lot to the unrealistically romantic expectations of the young, though he may have underestimated the extent to which middle-aged men run away, not so much because they have fallen for the newest dumb blonde in the typing pool as because they find family responsibility too much to bear and flee in something like panic.[49] Russell was, and most fathers now are not, insulated from the burdens of child-rearing by the presence of maids and nannies. Equally he was not, and many of them are, making his way up the managerial or professional ladder and subject to the burdens of progress. The fear that the decay of old superstitions would lead to various kinds of self-destructive behaviour seems to have been justified, although, contrary to the fears of critics of the 'permissive society', it looks as if more of the trouble is caused by desperate attempts to find stability within marriage than by generalized racketing about.

What, however, is most characteristic and most engaging about the whole book is Russell's rather wistful defence of the thought that love is the most important thing in the world. Not that it is the *only* important thing, nor that its demands are absolute; frequently we must sacrifice it to something else. None the less, intimacy with someone whose intellectual, emotional and sexual tastes you share is infinitely valuable. Though Russell was an individualist of a very marked kind, he always wanted to break down the barriers between individuals. Loneliness he always placed at the heart of the human condition; the universe was a large, cold place, wholly indifferent to the affairs of suffering humanity, and from this glacial indifference only passionate love offered a consolation and an escape. Russell's godfather, J. S. Mill, reluctantly decided that the rapturous beauties of Shelley had to be placed lower than the calmer, more reflective and more moral poetry of Wordsworth; Russell stood by Shelley to the end. Even when it is not wholly convincing as either social theory or political prescription, it is an engaging stance in a man approaching sixty and beginning to feel old.

SIX

PEACE, POWER AND DEMOCRACY

THE 1930s and the early 1940s were unhappy years for Russell. His marriage to Dora broke down irretrievably in 1932, after Dora had had a second child by Griffin Barry, and Russell had become increasingly close to Patricia (more usually known as 'Peter') Spence – she had come to them as a governess during the Oxford summer vacation of 1930, and became his third wife in January 1936. His third marriage produced a second son and some moments of happiness, but was not on the whole a success, even before its final collapse in 1949. Russell and his wife worked together amicably enough on *The Amberley Papers*, a two-volume collection of the letters and other documents of his parents set in historical and personal context, and Peter had earlier contributed a good deal to the research for and writing of *Freedom and Organization*, one of the best things ever to appear over his name. Something must have been amiss even then, however, to produce an erratum slip which told the reader to insert the word 'valuable' in the preface which thanked her for 'many suggestions'.[1]

Things were against them from the beginning. The process of separation from Dora involved long-drawn unpleasantnesses with the lawyers over money and access to the children.[2] The age gap between Russell and his new wife was larger than even his vitality could readily bridge; he was in his sixties, she in her twenties, he set in his ways, she growing up. It was one thing to be a beautiful undergraduate who had captured the heart of a great philosopher, quite another to be a stepmother, mother and household manager against the background of the financial and emotional insecurity which beset them for the next ten years.

He, meanwhile, found life deeply unsatisfactory. The political scene was utterly gloomy, as the world started on the long descent from the Japanese invasion of Manchuria in 1931 through the Italian adventure in Abyssinia in 1935 and the Spanish Civil War of 1936–9 into the abyss of the Second World War. Though he was not directly affected by the Depression and the mass unemployment of the 1930s – and wrote almost nothing directly about it – his books sold less well and American tours were out. The worst feature of life in his own eyes was his relative failure to do anything academically worth while. It was obviously far too late for him to relapse into a conventionally academic role, but it proved impossible to go back to Cambridge, and surprisingly difficult even to stitch together a series of financially satisfactory visiting professorships. Worse yet, those that were to be had were in America; he loathed American universities, which were departmental, hierarchical, uncollegiate places, dominated by the kind of professionalism which might be acceptable in a law firm but hardly in the groves of academe. Even then, there were difficulties. What should have been an open and shut election to a chair in the Institute of Advanced Studies at Princeton was vetoed by the Director, Abraham Flexner; Flexner was yet another of the East Coast Quaker establishment whom Russell had alienated by his treatment of his first wife and by his mockery of life at Bryn Mawr; Harvard, too, was cool to the idea that he should join the philosophy department. However, a series of lectures in Oxford in 1937 was popular and well attended, and in the spring of 1938 he landed an invitation to Chicago for the new academic year.

He left England in September 1938 and was not to return until 1944. The year in Chicago went well enough, but the hoped-for extension to his professorship did not materialize, and he was glad to accept an invitation to spend the next three years at the University of California at Los Angeles. He disliked the University in general and President Sproul in particular; when offered a chair at the City University of New York in the spring of 1940, he at once resigned from Los Angeles and accepted the New York offer. Then the trouble started. Bishop Manning of New York circulated the press with a denunciation of the appointment; Catholic journals elsewhere joined in, and a Mrs Kay brought an action in the New York courts to have the appointment overturned. Her lawyer denounced Russell as, *inter alia*, 'lecherous, libidinous, lustful, venerous, erotomaniac, aphrodisiac, irreverent and narrow-minded'; comic though it all was, it none the less cost him his job. Russell was not a party to the action, which had been brought against the Board of Education of the City of New York who had proposed to hire him. There was no way he could defend himself, or refute the allegations made against him. The court found in Mrs Kay's favour; in spite of the urging of academics throughout America, who feared what would happen elsewhere if the Mrs Kays of this world were to triumph in relatively enlightened New York, the Board would not appeal against the court's decision, and that was that. He faced the prospect of unemployment in a strange country, with two college-age children to support, as well as his new son, Conrad. War had broken out by now, and there was precious little chance of getting back to England – the authorities were unlikely to be enthusiastic about using what little spare room they had on transatlantic shipping to repatriate a notorious pacifist.

He was rescued by Albert Barnes, founder and head of the Barnes Foundation of Philadelphia, who hired him to give a series of lectures spread over five years on 'the history and social bearing of philosophical theories from the ancient Greeks to the present day'. This appointment also ended in the courts, but not before Russell had lectured for Barnes for two years and had given something like half of *A History of Western Philosophy*. Part of the trouble, which led to another court case, was that Barnes took against Patricia Russell; and Russell himself gave Barnes some cause for complaint by continuing to give popular lectures and to write popular articles when Barnes had thought he had bought the exclusive rights in Russell's services. Barnes reacted by sacking Russell in December 1942. Russell sued for breach of contract and won – $20,000.[3] Not long after that victory, he was able to return home. Almost since the beginning of the war, he had been a convinced supporter of the British struggle against Hitler and Nazi Germany and had longed to go home. John was in the navy, and Kate happy to return, and he had calmed his own terrors of what might happen in the event of the German bombing of Britain. Meanwhile, Trinity College, Cambridge, had learned that he was, so to speak, 'stuck' and had created a fellowship for him to come back to. In 1944 he returned to Britain, and began an astonishing period of respectability and public esteem, during which he was awarded the Order of Merit and the Nobel Prize and was chosen to give the first – and in many people's view the best – Reith Lectures. That, however, is the setting for much of the next chapter.[4]

Russell's alienation from academic philosophy in the 1930s owed something to the rise of logical positivism on the one hand, and to Wittgenstein's gradually emerging post-*Tractatus* philosophy on the other. He was much more sympathetic to the first than to the second; indeed, he was one of the begetters of the first and a target of the second's criticisms. Wittgenstein's reluctant and defensive filtering of his new ideas to a few chosen disciples meant that Russell knew nothing much about them – and when he learned of Wittgenstein's new direction he was hostile. The idea that philosophy was no more than a technique for dissolving linguistic cramps seemed to him to trivialize the discipline, a view he expressed in numerous post-war observations on so-called 'linguistic analysis'. The logical positivists by contrast regarded him as an ancestral hero, as Carnap, for instance, observed many years later when he wrote him an immensely affectionate and admiring letter on his ninetieth birthday; but, of course, they were much younger than he and busily pressing on in directions he did not find wholly congenial. *An Inquiry into Meaning and Truth* – the text of the William James Lectures he delivered at Harvard in the autumn of 1940 – was more nearly an essay in their mode of analysis than anything else he wrote; but even then it was plain that he had little interest in analysis for its own sake, and was more interested in traditional epistemology and metaphysics than the Young Turks allowed themselves to be. The most substantial works of the mid-1930s were historical, *Freedom and Organization* and *The Amberley Papers*. Three other books which framed the decade are also more than pot-boilers, and well worth the reader's attention fifty years on; *The Scientific Outlook*, published in 1931, sums up his philosophy and sociology of science and his fears of what a wholly scientific culture might mean for human freedom; *Which Way to Peace?*, published in 1936, made out the most far-reaching case for 'defeatism' or pacifism that he ever made; and *Power*, published in 1938, was always regarded by Russell himself as his most thoughtful and carefully worked-out contribution to political sociology. He put together several collections of essays culled from his lectures and magazine writing, but he was quite sure what he took most seriously.

The Amberley Papers do not concern us here, though they remain a very useful source for historians of the 1860s. *Freedom and Organization* on the other hand epitomizes what one might call the sober liberal in Russell, as opposed to the preacher of utopia and railer against the sins of the world. It is a combination of the history of ideas and the history of institutions with a moral for twentieth-century liberals. The moral is that we live in a world in which freedom is threatened both by traditional authoritarianism and by the impact of science. Historically, science had been the enemy of authority and conservatism, but it now offered those who wanted them techniques of social control which would eliminate freedom much more effectively than any tyrant had been able to do in the past. Yet the organizational techniques which threatened freedom were also needed for its preservation; the scientific control of work, of the forces of nature, even of our genetic endowment, could liberate mankind from the old tyranny of toil and disease, and nothing else could do it. There could be no *simple* solution to the tension between organization and individual liberty. This was the Russell of the post-war Reith Lectures on 'Authority and the Individual' who owed allegiance to John Stuart Mill rather than to Lady Ottoline Morrell.

The Scientific Outlook and *Which Way to Peace?* are much more characteristic of the 'all or nothing' Russell. *The Scientific Outlook* predicts the arrival of something very like Huxley's *Brave New World. Which Way to Peace?* defended defeatism. It argued that military resistance to Nazi aggression would be misguided and war a much greater evil than a German occupation.[5] Russell thoroughly regretted having written *Which Way to Peace?*; he hardly believed it even when he wrote it, and in 1940 was so eager to tell everyone that he had changed his mind that he asked the editor of the *New Statesman* to announce it in the magazine. In his *Autobiography* he wrote that his defence of passive resistance 'had become unconsciously insincere. I had been able to view with equanimity the possibility of the supremacy of the Kaiser's Germany; I thought that, although this would be an evil, it would not be so great an evil as a world war and its aftermath. But Hitler's Germany was a different matter.' Some commentators have suggested that Russell was half conscious of the fact that his revulsion against war was emotional rather than consequentialist and utilitarian, and that his feeling that he was writing only half sincerely stemmed from that. That may have been part of the reason. It is more likely that Russell was ashamed of the lightness with which he had all along treated the Nazi threat to European civilization. He had preached appeasement throughout the 1930s, assuring his readers that if the grievances of the Germans were met, the Nazis would have nothing to fight for and would be ridiculed out of office. The *Autobiography* certainly says that the atrocities of the Nazis had shaken his faith in passive resistance – it would work 'only when the holders of power were not ruthless beyond a point and clearly the Nazis went beyond this point'. But even when he wrote the book, his faith had already been shaken by private experience. At Beacon Hill, he had discovered that 'such instances as the hatpin in the soup could not be left to the slow operation of a good environment, since the need for action was immediate and imperative'. And his marriage to Dora had taught him the limits of his own capacity for 'forgiveness and what may be called Christian love'.[6]

Power was written in a very different mood again. It was his most serious essay in what would now be called political sociology. He hoped it would make a great stir, but, although it received several careful and courteous reviews, it did not. Its failure to astonish is not something for which Russell can be blamed, however. He held two views, both sensible and largely correct, the first that power was the crucial term in analysing politics, the second that there was almost nothing to be said *in general* about the ways in which particular kinds of power, for example military, religious, and economic, would be converted into other kinds or employed against them. Together, these views explain why neither Russell nor anybody else could have the impact on social thinking that he and Frege had had on formal logic, say. Deftness in the detailed assessment of the balance of power in particular social and political contexts is a great political virtue; but it does not have the same intellectual impact as the reconstruction of a whole abstract discipline.

The Scientific Outlook focuses on issues in the philosophy of science, on the relations between science and technology and on the nature of a 'scientific society'. Russell's philosophy of science is hard to pin down because he covers so much ground so quickly; but one interesting aspect of it is the way he begins with a straightforward empiricism which promptly leads on to extreme idealism. The empiricist Russell declares science to be a matter of observation and inference. We see some connection between events and try to discover what natural law it instantiates; we drop a penny and a cannon-ball from the Leaning Tower, see that they hit the ground together, and extrapolate to Galileo's laws of motion. Scientific virtue requires us to resist the temptation to say 'it stands to reason' that heavy objects fall faster than light ones; we must experiment and observe and so build up our understanding of the universe empirically. However, the paradoxical effect of careful observation and experiment is to unsettle our naïve conviction that we see the world exactly as it is; indeed, it unsettles the belief that we see it at all. Physiology tells us that what we call 'seeing' is the reaction of the nervous system to a stimulus which might be produced in all sorts of ways. 'People say they see the sun; but that only means that something has travelled through the intervening ninety-three million miles and produced an effect upon the retina, the optic nerve and the brain. This effect, which happens where we are, is certainly not identical with the sun as understood by astronomers ... The sun is an inference from what we see, and is not the actual patch of brightness of which we are immediately aware.'[7] This is the scepticism of Bishop Berkeley, with no prospect that God will guarantee the universe some sort of objectivity; where Berkeley held that God perceived the same ideas that we do, and so made the universe orderly and predictable, Russell suggested that the more we learn the more likely it seems that we know nothing.

Although Russell begins by suggesting that science starts with settled observations and extrapolates to less settled laws, his preferred view of science soon turns out to be what is now called 'fallibilism'. Scientists do not begin with observations and generalize from them; they begin by guessing a law of nature and then 'trim it with the shears of reason'. The point of experiment is to test our guesses rather than prop up weak generalizations. Russell does not go far in developing these insights – which are more generally associated with the work of Karl Popper, therefore – because his eye is on the sociology of science rather than its philosophy. His major concern is with the frame of mind which motivates scientific thinking in the first place. After contrasting scientific and religious forms of authority, he explains science as the product of 'power thinking', the desire to exert control by setting out determinate goals and finding effective means to achieve them. He did not mean that all science was 'practical'; he was as quick as anyone to insist that technological advances had commonly been accidental by-products of dispassionate research, and that the most spectacular advances had usually depended on advances in very different areas. Indeed, 'a race of men without a disinterested love of knowledge would never have achieved our present scientific technique'. Faraday and Clerk Maxwell discovered the phenomena of electromagnetism and evolved the mathematical theory of wave transmission while engaged in a wholly dispassionate investigation of media of transmission. Without them, however, there would have been no Marconi, and no radio. Nobody invented the internal combustion engine as a way of powering an aircraft, but if the Benz dogcart had not been invented, the Wright brothers would have had no power plant.[8] Russell had something close to a religious veneration for the dispassionate search for knowledge and thought of science at its best as a moral discipline in the monastic sense; he ends *The Scientific Outlook* by urging his readers to remember this aspect of science. The greater part of *The Scientific Outlook*, however, concentrates on the social pressures which lead to scientific progress and on the social consequences of this progress.

Russell fought, as so often, on two exposed flanks. In part he was writing a rationalist, anti-Christian tract. *The Scientific Outlook* is unremittingly hostile to old-fashioned Christian doubts about science and secularism. Galileo's persecution by the Inquisition is therefore dwelt on a good deal. However, Russell succumbs to the temptation to turn the heroes of science into pasteboard figures. Galileo's enthusiasm for occult and mystical theories of the universe and for the mythical figure of Hermes Trismegistus is not mentioned, nor is Newton's enthusiasm for numerology. This has an unfortunate effect; in reducing intellectual history to set-piece battles between heroes and villains it reduces its intellectual interest along with its complexity. Almost worse, it hides the extent to which Russell's heroes were like the real Russell rather than the public intellectual front he imposed on them and himself alike. Locke, for instance, who is rightly regarded as the begetter of British empiricism, did not think that the laws of nature were really nothing but regularities in our experiences; ultimately, they were like geometry, confirmed by experience but prior to it and as it were, built into the fabric of the universe. Mankind might have to be content with registering regularities, but God the author of all things understood his universe as a mathematical and logical construction. Galileo had thought the same; far from leaving his theories to the mercy of every observation an ignorant critic cared to make, he insisted that only some observations could be relevant, and that apparently discrepant observations showed errors in our instruments or defects in our skill, rather than defects in his theories.[9] Russell himself had pursued his studies in geometry and logic with such passion only because he thought they held the clue to the structure of the universe. On being persuaded by Wittgenstein that the logic was purely a matter of convention, he lost much of his interest in those subjects. It is strange that Russell never felt a greater affinity for the real characters of his heroes; for they, like him, were divided souls, convinced that the universe *had* to display a rational structure which would reveal itself in clear-cut general laws, but ready to hazard their ideas about what that structure was on the outcome of a single decisive experiment. Real empiricists were bolder, more passionate and more heroic than he let on.

Russell's account of Darwin makes the point by negation; Darwin was, as Russell knew very well – though he did not admit it – the most implausible of scientific geniuses. He was a late developer, an idle under-graduate content to read for a pass degree, always tempted to become a country clergyman. Unlike almost every other scientist of comparable genius, he set himself to work by accumulation and waited until he was irresistibly pushed by the facts into his world-shaking theory of evolution. Even in his case, there is a good deal of doubt whether he did float so guilelessly on the tide of the evidence; what is quite clear is how atypical he was if he did. Yet Russell's simple contrast between empiricists and authoritarian bigots makes it very surprising that all great scientists were not like Darwin.[10]

These criticisms are to some extent beside the point. Russell's aim was not to write good history but to *écraser l'infame*, and in that light the Church was bound to appear as the villain of the piece, walking in darkness and hostile to the forces of the light. Compared with the Russell of thirty years before, the Russell of *The Scientific Outlook* is simply brutal in his insistence that science and religion are irreconcilable foes. The dialectical point, however, is less to denounce the authoritarianism of the Church than to warn of the new dangers to intellectual freedom which science itself has come to threaten. This is the other flank on which he has to fight – and he fights, it must be said, a much more interesting battle on that flank. It is interesting because Russell is torn between admiration for the potentialities of modern technology and his gloomy foreboding that they will fall into the hands of those who would enslave their fellow creatures rather than liberate them. Russell's guesses as to the future direction of technology are – as those in all books of any age are – a quaint mixture of the prescient and the misdirected. The great omission is the rise of computer-based technology. He gestures towards the growth of robotics and the general lightening of toil, but fails to note the way growth in that area hangs on advanced information-processing techniques and these in turn on replacements for old-fashioned radio valves and the like. This is no sort of criticism; in the nature of the case, one can hardly *predict* the invention of the transistor and the silicon chip.[11]

He was deft at conveying a general sense of the way in which advances in productivity might be almost limitless and yet their social consequences turn out dreadful. If it is all to the good that agricultural production can grow at a great pace, while the birth rate in advanced countries drops (so reducing the burden of toil demanded by mere subsistence), one plausible result of this might well be that the underdeveloped world, where population was rising rapidly and the threat of famine was ever present, would launch an international war in the name of redistribution. Still, it is less the side-effects of economic growth that most concerns him than the direct growth of techniques of social control. As something of a cinema addict, he foresaw the day when whoever controlled the mass media would be able to control all the ideas and beliefs of vast populations. Although he first resorted to civil disobedience as a way of grabbing media attention only in 1961, he foresaw the difficulties which radicals faced in getting their views in front of the public thirty years before. He was perhaps unjustifiably pessimistic about the susceptibility of the lay public to whatever was pushed at them on the cinema screen, but right to suppose that the covert values put across by Hollywood movies would in general be favourable to big business rather than to radicalism. He combined this anxious view of the scope of indoctrination with some scepticism about psychology; he would cheerfully draw on either Freud or J. B. Watson to discredit his opponents, variously explaining their absurdities either as a misguided response to elementary stimuli or as a distorted expression of repressed urges; but he was dubious about their claims to explain the whole of human psychology. Commonsensically, he thought that what the Jesuits had achieved by old-fashioned means, modern societies would surely improve on.[12]

This is merely a prelude to the account of 'the scientific society' which occupies the last quarter of the book. There he lets his imagination run free, with results that are rhetorically effective even when the reader thinks he has gone altogether too far. He drew a picture of a society in which technique was highly developed but only the simplest and crudest utilitarian values were followed – the world which radicals such as Herbert Marcuse claimed they saw around them in the 1960s. This world would not be wholly like what he took to be the America of his own day, since it would fall into the hands of experts and administrators rather than businessmen. He took it for granted that what passed for American democracy in the 1920s and '30s was a sham, where businessmen pulled the strings which made the politicians dance; the future would have to be rather different because unrestricted capitalism was hopelessly inefficient and would lead to another world war. After that war, a planned economy combining American productivity and Russian authoritarianism would be instituted. Genuine democracy would be abolished; what would replace it would be a planned division between an administrative élite and all the rest. Russell assumed that the élite would draw up a blueprint and then build a new society to that plan; unlike Huxley's more elaborate gradations of alphas, betas and gammas, a simpler division between the leaders and the led suffices for Russell, though he throws in the thought that Blacks and other coloured people will be landed with the menial tasks in even his 'hi-tech' world.[13]

The new élite would be educated in ways which preserved their initiative in chosen areas and destroyed it everywhere else. It would be like Sparta or an English public school applied to the creation of a scientific élite rather than a military caste. Such a training would inculcate public spirit combined with contempt for the lower orders and would have to include tests of physical hardiness and initiative. Students would be encouraged to challenge their teachers on any issue in scientific or mathematical subjects but, if they ventured heresy on social issues, they would be ignored in pained silence. The world's great literature and poetry would be locked away from all but a very few. An interest in 'love themes will be discouraged on the ground that love, being anarchic, is silly, if not wicked'. Sexual pleasure would be available for everyone on a guilt-free basis, since it would make for contentment. It would, however, be entirely divorced from breeding – which would be eugenically organized – so no family loyalties or affections could spring up. Yet another way in which

Russell anticipates Huxley's *Brave New World* is in his suggestion that such a society would not wait until children were five or six to begin the process of education and indoctrination; subliminal conditioning would go on prenatally, and intensively from birth.[14]

The lives of ordinary people would be extremely comfortable; unemployment would not exist; jealousy would have been abolished along with romantic love; work would have become easy; there would be ample leisure and ample entertainment to fill it. Russell does not quite anticipate Huxley's thought that euthanasia would await everyone as soon as they began to feel that life was a burden, but he may well have inspired such a thought, for he certainly says that the idea of the sanctity of life would vanish in such a society and we would live or die as the utilitarian calculations of our rulers decided. He very obviously anticipated Huxley in arguing that the one thing that such a society would require and that we so far lack is a substitute for alcohol which will produce the same euphoria without a hangover.

Russell occasionally suggests reasons why such a society might not work: mainly that the élite might not sustain its enthusiasm for the job of making it work, sometimes that there might be palace revolutions among the élite and this would breed instability.[15] His belief in original sin ought perhaps to have made him somewhat more sceptical of the chances of stable oligarchical rule. His aim, however, is partly to voice his own ambivalence about such a society, partly to induce the reader to share it. In 1942, when he gave the lectures at the Rand School in New York that provoked Albert Barnes into firing him, he seriously suggested a Platonic dictatorship as the only hope for the post-war world. Nobody was to teach in any school anywhere in the world who had not been taught in an approved education institute, itself staffed by educationalists who had been trained in universities licensed by the World Government. Behind national universities there had to stand a world university staffed by peripatetic great teachers who would be wholly committed to the goals of world government and whose authority would be backed up by the political authorities.[16] The lectures were called 'Problems of Democracy'; but Russell almost gave the impression that democracy was so fragile that it had to be locked away entirely. In *The Scientific Outlook*, he wrote more sceptically of such proposals and stressed the disagreeable side of this benign totalitarianism. It is as if there were two Russells, one the nineteenth-century liberal or social democrat, the other a twentieth-century Plato, writing his own version of the *Republic* to console himself for the collapse of his liberal hopes. Like Plato, he starts from the belief that things will go right only if the right people have the power to make them go right, and follows the logic of this view. Unlike Plato, who believed that philosophers were in touch with the Good, the True and the Beautiful, he retained his essentially democratic view of human values; desires were born equal, and nobody is an expert on what suits other people. The result is that he writes almost more aggressively in favour of illiberal policies than Plato ever did, just because his heart is not in it. When this tension is added to the other tensions in the book, something very ambivalent results: his sympathy with the ordinary man's sufferings through war, fear, ill-health and oppression struggles with his doubts about handing him over to any sort of élite, while his dislike of all élites struggles with his belief that ordinary politics is a waste of time and rational administration is the answer to our problems. Above all, the old nightmare persists that peace and security may demand the sacrifice of intellectual freedom and the untrammelled life of the mind. The reader is swept backwards and forwards on Russell's uncertainties.[17]

The final rhetorical *coup* of *The Scientific Outlook* is the most effective of all. Having led the reader through the journey from war to oligarchy to tranquil totalitarianism, Russell confesses that it is all a waking nightmare – 'Nasty New World' so to speak. If mankind can hang on to the *non*-technological values of science and live by its contemplative, non-power-hungry values, we may yet avoid war and dictatorship. The temptation to accuse him of laying it on thick in his vision of the technocratic future is defused by this final admission; he was showing us the horrors of one world in order to make us happier in another. In the 1960s, writers such as Herbert Marcuse and Jürgen Habermas accused Anglo-American empiricism of complicity in the creation of a technocratic universe; like Russell, they argued that technocracy was philosophically shallow and confused the ability to manipulate people and things with a deep understanding of them. Like Russell, they thought that something very like dictatorship by manipulation was consistent with a politics based on giving people what they thought they wanted, a politics of bread and circuses. Like him, they thought that science, properly understood, contained in its practice values of a less crassly utilitarian kind than those which the 'affluent society' had elevated to its supreme principles. Where *The Scientific Outlook* is brisk, lucid, overstated and entertaining, *One-Dimensional Man* is lumbering, turgid and scholastic; none the less, it is not far-fetched to see most of what is worth while in the latter scattered among the abundant insights of the former. It would not be surprising if it were true, seeing how readily the student radicals of the 1960s took to the ninety-year-old Russell and the seventy-year-old Marcuse.

Engaging as *The Scientific Outlook* is, it is not surprising that we remember *Brave New World* even better. Even if Russell was right to think Huxley had stolen almost every idea for his novel from him, what Huxley did with them was brilliant and original. Russell's belief in the omnipotence of the movies was left far behind by Huxley's invention of the 'feelies'; Russell's dry account of the place of sex in dystopia was entirely trumped by Huxley's chants of 'orgy-porgy'. Russell was neither the first nor the last to announce the need for an intoxicant which produced neither hangovers nor brawling in the street, but it took Huxley to call it 'soma'. Russell was writing a mixture of sociology and propaganda, and did it very well; but he was himself in Huxley's debt for a spectacular vision of a happy hell.[18]

Freedom and Organization, which came out three years later, is a more substantial piece of work. Based on a good deal of research – much of it done by Peter Spence – it is a solid contribution to social, political and intellectual history. Its stance is left-liberal, as readers can see at once by noticing how indebted Russell is to J. L. and Barbara Hammond for his economic history, to E. D. Morel for his diplomatic history, and to Charles Beard for his view of the American revolution and its aftermath. It displays many more allegiances which are personal to Russell – unlike sentimental 'one nation' Tories, he does not contrast aristocratic benevolence with middle-class meanness towards the working poor, but this is less because it is bad history than because he chooses to cold-shoulder Holland House and the great Whigs; similarly, he grudgingly admits a certain cunning in Bismarck, but will hear no good of anyone responsible for the imperialist adventures of Britain, France, Russia, Austria, Germany or Japan. The overall effect of the book is sober, and its author the rationalist liberal Russell; none the less, there are plenty of bald-headed assaults on '*l'infame*' in its pages. The very layout of the book says much about Russell's allegiances, especially when one learns that he had hoped to write a companion volume on the rise of the romantic tradition and its social and political impact. The neatness of the time-span – 1815–1914, the Congress of Vienna to the assassination at Sarajevo – is fortuitous. Its theme is the rise and fall of liberalism, of individualism and individualist democracy, and the way that history was intertwined with the downfall of conservative, agrarian, feudal, monarchical and Christian Europe and the rise of industry, the growth of America, the 'march of mind', the challenge of socialism and the attempts first of the middle and then of the working classes to take the reins of power from the hands of the socially privileged. There is no one moral which Russell seeks to draw, though the underlying political conviction which shapes the book is much like that which shaped *The Prospects of Industrial Civilization*. Old-fashioned individualistic capitalism was a threat to world peace; first, big business rose to power in every modernizing country; then those countries fought each other for economic domination of the world. The familiar anxiety reappears: can we replace anarchy with organization and retain enough intellectual and social freedom to make life worth living? 'It is not by pacifist sentiment but by world-wide economic organization that mankind is to be saved from collective suicide', he wrote in conclusion, but nothing suggested such organization was to be had at anything less than a very high price.[19]

The other theme that dominates *Freedom and Organization* is the importance of ideas, and the importance of the idiosyncratic individuals who come up with those ideas. There are, no doubt, 'tides' in social affairs which men can hardly resist or turn back; 'industrialism' is one such. Much of our intellectual life is only to be explained as a response to such tides; but within such broad limits there is a great indeterminacy as to how we shall respond, and what we shall make of events around us. Liberalism was partly a response to industrialism, partly a defence of the bourgeoisie and the way it benefited from the new world – but only partly, for in many ways it cast a critical eye upon both the bourgeoisie and the world the bourgeoisie was creating. At a less exalted level, quirks and accidents matter enormously. Who can doubt that the Russian revolution would have turned out very differently if Lenin had not returned from Switzerland? Did not Edward VII's fondness for France and his dislike of his cousin the Kaiser have an impact on the alliances which paved the way for the First World War? Wilhelm II's withered arm was as accidental as could be, but it made him more touchy, more determined to show his manliness, and therefore more determined to have a fleet to match the British fleet. The Kaiser himself wrote, 'When, as a little boy, I was allowed to visit Plymouth and Portsmouth, hand in hand with kind aunts and friendly admirals, I admired the proud English ships in those two superb harbours. Then there awoke in me the wish to build ships of my own like these some day, and when I was grown up to possess as fine a navy as the English.' Though he kept his toys in harbour throughout the war, it was his wish to have them which drove Britain to contract the sort of continental alliance British foreign ministers had avoided like the plague.[20]

The drama Russell depicts might, if we took the analogy lightly, be thought of as a Hegelian struggle in which contending principles of social order battle with each other, the winner taking on some of the colouring from the ideals it has vanquished, and in turn giving way to a new principle which it similarly colours. Unlike Hegel, Russell saw nothing in the process to suggest that behind History stood God or Reason. By the early 1930s he had come to think that the nineteenth century had been an untypically happy interlude in human history, and that the twentieth century would do well to escape disaster, let alone make further progress. *Freedom and Organization* opens with the downfall of Napoleon; momentarily, the principle of legitimacy is triumphant. The Congress of Vienna established that sovereigns were appointed by and answerable to God alone; hierarchy and piety were the order of the day, and the Emperors of Austria and Russia their chief protectors, with such aid as could be had from the King of Prussia, the restored Louis XVIII, and assorted electors, margraves and prince-bishops. The presiding genius, however, was none of these but Prince Metternich, whose entire career was devoted to impeding liberalism and nationalism, either of which might destroy the far-flung Austrian Empire by itself, their conjunction being certainly fatal. He was aided by Alexander I who had had liberal inclinations when first he came to the throne but who had found, as tsars generally did, that *vox dei* spoke in favour of absolute hereditary monarchy where *vox populi* did not. Until 1830, he was 'the gendarme of Europe'. Naturally, he and Metternich did not succeed in stopping change; but they did succeed in making it slower and bloodier.[21]

Metternich was a narrow-minded reactionary; but he had a genius for obstructive manoeuvring. Europe was tired of war. The British disliked what they saw of European despotism, but thought it none of their business. None the less, immobilism could not last for ever. The French threw out their legitimist king and installed Louis-Philippe as what one might call a middle-class monarch; the Belgians seceded from Holland; revolts against Austrian rule spread. In the next generation, absolutism and tradition were cleverly preserved by Bismarck's cunning; by 1848 Metternich's policy of inflexible immobility was played out. Nationalism was something he could not control – Austrian nationalism was too likely to turn into pan-Germanism and threaten the integrity of Austria on that front; but nothing else could stop Italian, Bohemian and Hungarian nationalism from flaring into revolt. Nationalism was something of a problem for liberals and socialists whose loyalties were to humanity or to the working class rather than to a particular state; neither liberalism nor socialism in the nineteenth century made much of a show of understanding it or controlling it. None the less, the 1848 revolutions, if they were primarily nationalist explosions everywhere outside France, were also liberal and sometimes socialist outbreaks, too. Russell insists that they were also what later sociologists call revolutions of 'modernization'; it was not exactly that Metternich was inconsistent with steam power and an industrial workforce, but he was certainly inconsistent with the outward-looking and reformist frame of mind the new technology induced. If Russell was no Hegel, thinking that 'the cunning of reason' used individuals and tossed them aside when they had served their purpose, he sometimes seemed to suggest that Metternich had not only failed to stem the tide of nationalism but had been bowled over in 'the march of mind' as well: '... the long peace generated new energy, and new energy made immobility intolerable. In this new mood, the world saw Metternich as he was: pompous, vain, vapid, incapable of stating his own principles interestingly, and closed to all new ideas from the moment of Napoleon's disappearance ... Before he was hissed off the stage, his style had long been antiquated.'[22]

Russell's account of 'the march of the mind' is a *tour de force*; it is in some ways better, because calmer, than much of his *History of Western Philosophy*, though it displays the same talent for blending social history and intellectual exposition. 'The march of mind' is an imprecise label, but refers sweepingly to the movement which looked to the dissemination of knowledge throughout society as the great step towards reform and prosperity. Its most characteristic institution was Lord Brougham's Society for the Promotion of Useful Knowledge (rechristened 'the steam intellect society' by the sceptical novelist Thomas Love Peacock). Russell broadens his canvas to take in the transition from Whiggism to liberalism, and the movement which pressed liberalism in socialist directions. He was wholly at ease across the whole range, not only because he was in any case immensely well read, but because Holland House had been one of the resorts of his grandfather's youth, and J. S. Mill, his 'godfather in a secular sense', had summed up a whole liberal tradition in his career.

Russell took it for granted that, after Waterloo, English life was grim. It has since been hotly disputed whether the process of industrialization rendered the working class temporarily worse off; Russell, following the Hammonds, had no doubt that during the thirty years following Waterloo the condition of the working class was horrible. Labour was abundant, productivity was increasing, agricultural enclosures were throwing more and more farmworkers on to the market, so unemployment was rife, wages were low, and the hated Combination Acts prevented workers from unionizing themselves. It is often forgotten – though not by Russell – that the Tolpuddle Martyrs were agricultural labourers and that agricultural distress was an even greater evil than the squalor of the industrial towns. The Corn Laws kept food prices high, and the disorganized state of the workers and the political monopoly of the landowners ensured that the landowners continued to enjoy the benefits of high prices without undue challenge. Incipient conflict between the manufacturing middle classes and the landowning aristocracy was occasionally visible, but equally typical was the case of a magnate like Lord Londonderry who neatly bridged that gap with huge estates and profitable coal-mines.[23] The role of the dispossessed in Russell's story is that of a reproachful chorus, as it were pressing their noses against the windows of Holland House, whose anxious inmates discussed their plight in general and ineffectual terms.

The surprising thing about Russell's tour of English social theory in the first half of the nineteenth century is how much he approves of Robert Owen. Bentham had not unreasonably dismissed Owen as a 'man of one idea', obsessed by the implausible view that we could give anyone 'any character from the worst to the best' by an appropriate education. Russell ignores all that. He praises Owen's sweetness of character and sides with Owen's conviction that what was wrong with his attempts to create utopian communities at New Lanark and New Harmony in Indiana was that they were too modest; seeing that Owen once negotiated with the Emperor of Mexico for two million acres of Texas on which to experiment with two million utopians, one wonders what a less modest experiment might have looked like. Russell was captivated by Owen's niceness, enjoyed his attacks on Christianity, and lightheartedly sided with his belief in the social value of dancing.[24]

Russell's view of nineteenth-century social theory was complicated. He liked Cobden's pacifism but disliked the economic theory behind it; he liked Owen much more, but utterly disbelieved the labour theory of value which justified Owen's belief that 'labour exchanges' in which goods were traded for labour tickets could replace money and the marketplace. Against this background, Marx stands out for intellectual penetration and political seriousness. Russell thought no less well of him in 1935 than he had in 1896; his emphasis on material forces, his disregard of values, his consequent toughness as a historical analyst – all these Russell praises again. But Marx is once again indicted on a variety of counts. The theory of surplus value will not do, since it rests on the labour theory of value which will not do; failure to distinguish between owners and managers had made it harder for socialists to attract just the managerial stratum they most need to attract if socialism is to work; moreover, this is but one aspect of a stress on class war which encourages the working class to be hostile to all forms of intellectual work and all forms of authority, and which therefore bodes ill for socialism.[25] Everything worth having in Marx's theory of exploitation could be translated into Henry George's attacks on monopoly. It was not – as it was in George – just a matter of landownership; capitalists monopolized the means of production which the workers were obliged to work with, and naturally drove an exploitative bargain for access to them. 'All power to exploit others depends on the possession of some complete or partial, permanent or temporary monopoly, but this monopoly may be of the most diverse kinds.' Land is one, credit another, cartelization in industry another. 'The real enemy is the monopolist', but class warfare is unlikely to be the best way to defeat him.[26]

Apart from technical issues in economics, Marx's real failure was political; he turns politics into something akin to a war of religion rather than politics as usually practised. Marx's emphasis on the dialectic bred a fanatical conviction akin to that which drove the medieval crusades; under most conditions, most workers would not join such a crusade. Countries where there were real gains to be made, but where there was a substantial Marxist socialist party, found the forces of reform hopelessly split between the liberals, who had good sense on their side but insufficient energy and intransigence to attract the bolder spirits, and revolutionaries who had plenty of passion and energy but too few supporters to get anywhere at the ballot box and too little talent for conciliation to be able to attract middle-class sympathy.[27] The wildness of Russell's rhetoric in the 1960s and the limited success of the British Liberal Party after 1922 disguises from many readers the ease with which he slipped back into traditional Lib–Lab ideas – and the good sense of those ideas in a British context.

It is almost with relief that Russell abandons the complexities of European socialism for the brave new world of early-nineteenth-century America. Russell was a devoted reader of Charles Beard's account of the economic background to the American Constitution, and was well insulated against any temptation to idolize George Washington – who did very nicely out of the country he had invented, ending his life as the richest man in the country. None the less, Russell is enthusiastic about Thomas Jefferson, whom he sees as an engaging representative of a doomed political outlook. Jefferson was a republican of the ancient Roman stamp, though he believed, as the ancient world had not, in a realm of inviolable individual rights as set out in the American Declaration of Independence of which he was the author. His allegiances were agrarian;

like Machiavelli and Rousseau, he wanted a republic of virtuous, public-spirited freeholders. He distrusted urban financiers and manufacturers – who, unfortunately, were precisely the people who lined up behind the new constitution. It was Jefferson who had the ten amendments which form the Bill of Rights attached to the constitution, and so turned what would otherwise have been a simple carve-up of power between central and local governments into something altogether more noble. However, the first congress elected under the new rules showed which way the wind was blowing: it passed a bill to redeem the more or less worthless securities issued during the War of Independence at face value – after members of congress and their agents had gone round the country buying up securities at their previous depreciated level. 'There was an orgy of corruption, in which shrewd business men, most of whom had taken no part in the war, profited at the expense of old soldiers and other simple folk. There was much indignation, but it was powerless to influence the course of events.'[28]

This kind of corruption was favoured by Alexander Hamilton, the greatest conservative force among the original framers. He would have preferred a monarchical constitution if one could have been agreed, or a president and senate chosen for life rather than the elected officers he grudgingly accepted. If these could not be had, the preponderance of the upper classes could none the less be secured if money was allowed to buy influence; this would provide the necessary balance between the conservative few and the poor (and therefore presumed to be radical) many. Russell's summary account of the history of American politics depicts a long-drawn-out struggle in which Jeffersonian democracy failed to establish a firm grip on the economic forces unleashed by Hamilton. Nineteenth-century American history suited Russell's quick and acid analysis to perfection. Without underestimating the effect of more-or-less autonomous ideological forces and racial antagonisms, he spells out the way economic pressures led to the opening of the west and thus to the conflicts which brought about the Civil War. If the Civil War is put in its economic context, it is not in order to 'debunk' it. Though Russell acknowledges that self-interest as well as abstract justice sustained the north in its struggle with the slave states, he acknowledges that Lincoln was a great man and that he moved slowly and painfully towards his eventual abolitionist position out of a wholly admirable concern to carry a united country with him and not out of any timidity or moral uncertainty. It is not, however, the Civil War which occupies centre stage in the story; it is the rise of the capitalist barons. When Russell advocated an American world hegemony, he did so in the knowledge that it was going to benefit Standard Oil and

J. P. Morgan. The rise of the capitalist robber barons such as John D. Rockefeller and Commodore Vanderbilt is for Russell the culmination of American economic history. As one might expect from the *Principles of Social Reconstruction*, ambivalence is again the order of the day; wicked though the tough and ruthless characters who built industrial and financial empires out of nothing were, he could not help being swept along by their vitality and audacity.[29]

Cheerful cynicism is, however, not the dominant note. At the end of *Freedom and Organization* lay 1914 and war. The final section of the book is an account of the rise of German nationalism and its inevitable issue in world war. Russell could not but admire the skill with which Bismarck had created a united Germany out of heterogeneous kingdoms, dukedoms, palatinates and bishoprics, and had made the result into a great power. The sharpness of Bismarck's intellect and his mastery of *Realpolitik* fascinated Russell almost as much as the end result appalled him. Russell followed historical orthodoxy in thinking that Bismarck himself would not have steered German politics in a direction which made a war with Britain inevitable, but that by making his master an emperor and encouraging militarism in all ranks of society he had conjured up forces a lesser man could not control. Conversely, he had so effectively contained liberal pressures and had so decisively outflanked and obstructed German socialism, that the forces which might have made for peace and held in check the forces of imperialism and adventurism were simply too weak. It was a mixture of social forces and personal quirks which gave the final disaster its form. Social forces which no one man could resist or do very much to shape made Britain and Germany competitors; physical and psychological insecurities peculiar to Kaiser Wilhelm in particular led him to resent his aunt – Queen Victoria – and his cousin – Edward VII – and to encourage his ministers in policies which he intended to spite his relatives and which inevitably led to war.[30]

There is a shift of emphasis between Russell's contemporaneous analysis of the origins of the First World War and his judgement twenty years later. *The Entente Policy* represented the foreign policy of Lord Lansdowne and Sir Edward Grey as obviously stupid and disastrous, and argued that it would have been easy to avoid hostilities by a sensible division of the imperialist spoils. *Freedom and Organization* is not exactly fatalistic, nor does it represent statesmen as mere clay in the hands of fate. It is, however, more dispassionate and less progagandist, and therefore more ready to recognize that politicians were susceptible to public opinion, the pressures of special interests, the dictates of their party superiors and so on; foreign policy was more largely the effect of domestic pressures than the calculated actions of any one man. In any case, the policies of Grey and Lansdowne 'were really dictated by the permanent officials of the Foreign Office, about whom, since there has been no revolution in England, we know less than we do about Holstein'.[31] Reorganization was more important than replacing wicked and stupid men with good and clever ones. That indeed is the general message of *Freedom and Organization*; the book's title is the tag on which his moderate radicalism of the 1940s and '50s was hung. The liberal virtues of freedom, toleration and individualism no longer shelter easily under *laissez-faire* and a capitalist economy; what we need is democratic socialism at home and some form of effective international authority abroad. That is the central core of Russell's politics; it was to that view that he returned and from that view that he launched out into more extravagant positions.[32]

One such extravagant foray came in 1936 with *Which Way to Peace?*, the book he repudiated when war broke out. Although Russell changed his mind about many things, and usually said so when he did, this was the only occasion on which he publicly declared that he had been straightforwardly wrong, and said nothing to excuse or justify his original view. This was very different from his later changes of heart about how to avert nuclear war.[33] The book starts with the simple question whether peace in Europe could be preserved by British rearmament and, if necessary, war with Germany. His answer was that rearmament would infallibly lead to war and war would infallibly lead to the total destruction of European civilization. Since nothing could be worse than that, it followed that a German invasion was not to be resisted and defeat was not to be avoided.

Which Way to Peace? states the case for a policy of 'passive resistance' in its most extreme form. None the less, its basis is the basis of all his views on war, and Russell claimed that even it was not strictly a 'pacifist' work.[34] This is a misleading, though not wholly unwarranted, claim. That it is misleading is plain enough. In his *Autobiography*, he describes his earlier conversion to a 'pro-Boer' view of the Boer War as a conversion to pacifism. It seems odd therefore to demur at calling his extreme defeatism a form of pacifism. Yet what he meant is clear enough. He was not a principled adherent of absolute non-violence. Alys Pearsall-Smith's family were Quakers, as were many of the members of the NCF; they were, as he was not, individually committed to the view that nothing justified the deliberate taking of human life. Although one might think that a policy of non-resistance to Nazism was almost definitive of pacifism, Russell was quite right to point out that his grounds for advocating non-resistance were not those of Quakers. *Which Way to Peace?* does not claim that *nothing* can justify war, nor that no wars have ever been justified; there are worse things than violence and there are many goals which we are justified in attaining by violence. Some wars are good wars. The American War of Independence was a good war, and so was Caesar's conquest of Gaul. It is the disproportion between the evils of German conquest and the evils of wholesale destruction which makes modern war morally unthinkable. The argument is, as ever, the application of Russell's brand of utilitarianism, where 'civilization' rather than 'happiness' is the supreme goal, and 'civilization' embraces the search for knowledge, the cultivation of passionate relationships, the development of art, music and literature. To these, everything else is instrumental. Russell was as ready as Machiavelli to employ violent means to preserve civilization if they would work. In 1945 he encouraged American policy-makers to think of using their nuclear weapons to bomb the Soviet Union into a greater respect for the values of civilization.[35]

Which Way to Peace? was in line with much of Russell's popular journalism at that time, and not out of line with much contemporary thinking. It was widely read and very well thought of by the kind of people who joined the Peace Pledge Union (of which Russell himself became a sponsor). Conversely, it was deplored by Gilbert Murray, who stood by Russell's former view that a willingness to support League of Nations sanctions against international aggression must entail a readiness to support the League in making war on an aggressor state – the view which Russell returned to after 1939. It was deplored, too, by everyone who thought that the fascist uprising in Spain, and the intervention by Germany and Italy in the Spanish Civil War, demanded a forcible reply. Replying to Gilbert Murray on this point, Russell insisted that even if it were a question of war against Hitler, 'I feel that, if we set to work to stop them we shall become exactly like them & the world will have gained nothing. Also, if we beat them, we shall produce in time someone as much worse than Hitler as he is worse than the Kaiser. In all this I see no hope for mankind.'

The basis of Russell's argument was his conviction that any future war would involve the total destruction of Europe. This was a view he had held since the early 1920s and had from time to time reiterated in alarmist essays defending the thought that for Europe to submit to an American despotism was better than 'self-extermination'. Appealing to the Swedish military analyst Major Bratt, Russell held that the invention of long-distance bombing aircraft had made war unthinkable by making it too destructive to wage. This view infected orthodox circles. Stanley Baldwin resisted demands for a crash programme to build new fighter aircraft for the RAF with the gloomy reply that 'the bomber will always get through'. The general belief was that bombing raids would render all major cities instantly uninhabitable and that rioting, the collapse of government and complete civil disorder would be the immediate result. 'Picture, if you can, what the result will be: London for several days will be one vast raving Bedlam, the hospitals will be stormed, traffic will cease, the homeless will shriek for help, the city will be a pandemonium. What of the Government at Westminster? It will be swept away by an avalanche of terror.' It turned out that there was no real evidence behind this widespread belief. Reports of the panic caused by bombing in Spain turned out to have grossly exaggerated both the casualties and the disorder involved. British experience of bombing was of small-scale punitive raids on dissident tribesmen in Afghanistan or the Sudan; naturally enough, unarmed villagers scattered in all directions when attacked from the air. Nobody knew the likely impact on cities like Berlin or London, but it was not absurd to think that their greater complexity and density of population would make them even more vulnerable than tribal villages. In the event, it turned out that that was far from the truth.[36]

What this assumed was that defence by fighter aircraft and anti-aircraft guns would be unable to intercept incoming bombers; but nobody stopped to speculate that, even if bombers got through, their losses in aircrew and machines before they got home might make the mass-bombing of civilian targets ruinous for the attackers. Nor did commentators anticipate that bombing would be as inaccurate as it proved in practice. Both the morality and the effectiveness of the British bombing of civilian Germany during the Second World War have been called into doubt; the slaughter of civilians was gratuitous and the German economy not much damaged – morale was stiffened rather than destroyed, and German output was at its highest in 1944.[37] None of this could have been guessed in 1936; Russell was in the mainstream thinking that all-out attack on civilian targets would smash the physical and organizational basis of all civilized life. Where he differed from the mainstream was in concluding that radical unilateral disarmament was the only answer; he never seems to have reckoned with the 'deterrent' argument: that if Britain and Germany could *threaten* each other with total destruction, both would have been terrified into keeping the peace. He only contemplates the idea in the context of a possible policy of isolationism, but even then he dismisses it. 'There are those who say: Let us have such big armaments that every one will respect us, and let us then steer clear of foreign entanglements; then our own territory will be safe, and we can keep out of other people's quarrels.'[38] He seems to have taken it for granted that rearmament programmes inevitably lead to war as they had before 1914, and that the advantage to the attacking side was so overwhelming that deterrence could not work; the side which struck second would be unable to strike at all. Deterrence would lead to one side or another making the perfectly rational decision to launch a first strike.

The ultimate cure could be nothing less than a world government with a monopoly of offensive weapons – Russell demanded a world airforce based on multinational rather than national units, in much the same 'philosopher-king' spirit as he demanded a world university to enforce an educational monopoly for internationalist thinking. His intention, however, was not to discuss world government in any detail; his only concern was to point out how far the League of Nations was from being it. In the absence of a central directorate and independent military force, the League was a talking shop which was bound to be too slow to challenge aggression. In any event, its supporters were generally pacifists and he could see that it was 'a difficult thing to use pacifist sentiment as the driving force in a war'. Nor could orthodox international alliances do any better. Public opinion lurched from a desire to 'hang the Kaiser' in 1918 to the feeling that Versailles had been too hard on the Germans and that Hitler ought to be conciliated rather than stamped on. Keeping public support for an alliance with teeth was an impossible prospect. In any case, if the goal was to have *overwhelming* superiority in men and material to Germany and Japan, it was impossible to achieve; as fast as the alliance armed itself, so would its probable opponents. Russell's incidental speculations on what might happen in the European arena are quite prescient – he guessed that Hitler would successfully try to detach Stalin from the West, and his suggestion, that the best the Europeans could do was hang on until America came to their rescue, was not far from the mark either.[39]

What dominated everything, however, was the belief that another war in Europe would be the end of civilized life. A government which began by fighting *for* democracy would have to take such a firm grip on its population to fight the war successfully that it would end up as a military dictatorship. Meanwhile the population would be driven back into the Dark Ages. Mobs would try to lynch politicians, airmen and anyone else they could blame for their miseries; libraries, laboratories and other sources of knowledge would be destroyed. Peace on any terms would be better than that. That entails individual and national non-resistance. What he envisaged was a unilateral declaration that under no conditions would Britain fight and the subsequent dismantling of the means of so doing. Since Britain still possessed an empire which excited the greed of other nations and needed a good deal of policing, this entailed its abolition, too. The African colonies were to become League protectorates, India was to become self-governing, and the West Indies were to be sold to the United States 'for a good sum'.[40]

A disarmed Britain would not fall prey to Germany or any other militaristic state; British disarmament would make their militarism look silly. Certainly non-resistance would be hard to pursue; we all like fighting for what we think right, and we all like the thought of making other people act as we think best. None the less, we can educate ourselves out of this urge; we can come to see that persuasion may do more good than force. All we should lose would be the satisfactions of pride: in 1936 there was still a substantial source of pride in all those red areas of the map, but Russell insisted that we could readily 'substitute a civilized standard of values for the lust of domination'.[41] All this, however, was advice to governments. What of the individual? For him the message was bleaker. His duty was to do nothing to make war likely. It was not clear to Russell that there was in fact much an individual could do to prevent it breaking out, but one can see why Russell and the Peace Pledge Union were temporary allies. Individuals could at least promise not to provoke conflict. As for stopping it once it had started, Russell recalled the dangers to which conscientious objectors had been exposed in 1916, and declared that it was likely that in the next war objectors would be shot: 'We may also assume that unless the war resisters are very numerous they will not again escape the death penalty.'[42] What is very strange is that Russell never discussed in any detail how it was possible to survive an invasion by passive resistance. The French had found themselves baffled in their occupation of the Ruhr by the strikes and non-cooperation of the German inhabitants. Twenty-five years after *Which Way to Peace?*, Russell and the Committee of 100 tried to change a government's mind on nuclear weapons by civil disobedience; and throughout the 1930s and '40s, resistance to British rule in India was led by a man whose followers specialized in passive resistance. Even under Hitler's occupation, non-cooperation sometimes worked. Russell, however, merely suggested in *Which Way to Peace?* that if we were to treat the invaders nicely, they would feel too embarrassed to go on – which was plainly silly – and in his *Autobiography* swung to the opposite extreme of claiming that passive resistance could not work at all against the Nazis. The second is obviously nearer the truth than the first, but it is not the whole truth.

Which Way to Peace? was less a thought-out defence of pacifism than the expression of a mood. It was too obsessed with strategic logic, and too little tempered by common sense, to persuade anyone but the already convinced. Russell's ideas about war reflected a lifelong urge to quantify Armageddon; both before and after *Which Way to Peace?*, he displayed the same obsession with assigning large numbers to indefinite facts. At the beginning of the First World War, his friend Bob Trevelyan had been shocked when Russell insisted on working his way through the strategy and tactics of the Battle of the Marne – like many pacifists, Trevelyan wished not to think about the mechanics of war at all. Russell wanted to be able to say that a new war would kill one, two or three hundred million people, and wreck Europe for one, two or three centuries.

This desire looks like the product of a rational, calculating intelligence, but it was not. It displayed the logic of the paranoiac, not that of the detached observer. Russell more than half realized that the fact that the Second World War had not yet broken out showed that there was something wrong with his scenario for total war. If nations which struck first were infallibly successful, it was odd that Britain and France were not in ruins already – one could hardly suppose that Hitler would have scrupled to take advantage of the chance of overwhelming victory. When Russell explained why this pre-emptive strike had not occurred, he destroyed the basis of his defeatism. The crucial obstacle to a pre-emptive strike by air was much the same as the crucial obstacle to organizing a sneak invasion with a large modern army: it was an enormous logistical job to assemble the aircraft and weaponry for a serious campaign, and one which was impossible to perform in secret. He probably never fully realized quite how complex a task it was, but he at any rate had some conception that it would take an enormous tonnage of bombs to lay waste much of London, and therefore an enormous number of aircraft which could not be assembled unobserved. What he and others failed to see was how many more raids would be needed than the one overwhelming strike he pictured; visions of a swift knock-out blow were destroyed by the reality of bombers which were usually several miles off target. The only serious attempt to deliver a devastating blow prepared in secret was the Japanese attack on Pearl Harbor. That was enormously assisted by American obtuseness and wishful thinking, but it was not, and was never expected to be, decisive, even by its perpetrators.[43] It was not possible to strike a single knock-out blow; the country attacked would be terribly damaged but would certainly be able to retaliate in kind. The logic of that, however, is peace rather than war. *Which Way to Peace?* is thus logically flawed, however interesting as the precursor of arguments which were better founded after the invention of nuclear and thermonuclear weapons.

The realization that he had made a moral misjudgement turned Russell against the book. He had begun by assuming that Nazism was just another nationalist movement; his newspaper articles suggested that mockery and an insistence on the liberal verities were enough to defeat it.[44] It is not clear quite why he was so blind; he knew German scientists and scholars who had been driven into exile, and there was nothing secretive about the regime's ill-treatment of its political opponents or its anti-semitism. Perhaps he could not believe that anyone as mad and evil as Hitler could attract so much support. He was tempted to believe that Hitler was only pursuing traditional goals, even though Russell himself had pointed out he was not; if so, it was natural to assume that a German invasion would have been no worse than submitting to the Kaiser's government would have been in 1914. Even in 1936, he can only have half believed it. Almost as soon as the book was published he knew it was nonsense; by 1940 it was clear to him that any amount of destruction was preferable to Nazi domination of Europe.[45]

Power, on the other hand, is well worth reading still. Its incidental insights into such matters as the psychology of revolutionary leaders was shrewd at the time and has become even more apt in the world of Pol Pot and Idi Amin. The one complaint one might level at it is that, like many other books on its topic, it begins by claiming that it will give us a comprehensive theory of its subject matter, but ends by providing an essentially anecdotal and fragmentary account of the forms and nature of power. If one is sceptical of the prospect of a global theory in the first place, the disappointment may well not be very intense. Russell certainly starts by announcing that power is the fundamental concept in political analysis, just as energy is in physics; the analogy suggests Newtonian ambitions – but Russell instantly admits that the analogy does not hold up. We know, as the mugger knows, that brute force can be converted into wealth, and we know, as the hirer of mercenaries knows, that wealth can be converted into brute force; but we have no equations to display the way the process works. 'Like energy, power has many forms, such as wealth, armaments, civil authority, influence on opinion. No one of these can be regarded as subordinate to any other, and there is no one form from which the others are derivative.'[46] All we can do is set out as clearly and cogently as we know how the variety of ways in which individuals or groups manage to make their wills effective. At the very least, this will cure the Marxist illusion that the economic form of power is more fundamental than the rest. This general aim is seconded by another more local aim: 'to make the present and probable near future more intelligible than it can be to those whose imaginations are dominated by the eighteenth and nineteenth centuries'.[47] In the light of that, it is not surprising that a relatively abstract account of the various kinds of power should give way to soon to a discussion of the problems of democracy, centring on the difficulty of giving democratic governments sufficient power to defend themselves while not giving them such a monopoly of power that they can murder democracy itself. The background is dominated by the new totalitarian states and the prospect of the next war, the foreground by the familiar argument that liberal values cannot be sustained by *laissez-faire* capitalism. The relative peace of the nineteenth century in which rationalist liberalism flourished was an interlude, not a guide to the future. The ancient world, the Italian Renaissance, the horrors of the Thirty Years War all have more to teach us than the exceptional century of liberal tranquillity. Russell resembles Machiavelli trying to teach the warring Florentine republic of the sixteenth century how to learn from the triumphs and failures of their Roman predecessors; Lenin is compared to Cromwell, Mussolini to Napoleon and the *condottieri* of the Renaissance. In the face of revolutionaries and demagogues such as Stalin, Hitler and Mussolini, Russell has to follow Machiavelli in drawing the distinction on which *The Prince* and *The Discourses* rest, the distinction between 'new' power and power based on old habits of obedience. Machiavelli's dissection of Cesare Borgia's rise to power is matched by Russell's dissection of the appeals of fascism and communism.[48]

Russell defines power as 'the production of intended effects'; it is a quantitative notion, in the sense that, comparing two men with identical aims but very different degrees of success in attaining them, we should incline to say that one had more power than the other. None the less, it is only loosely quantifiable; there can be no exact comparisons when men with very different goals employ very different means. Distinctions have to be drawn to a large extent *ad hoc*; we may, for instance, contrast the impact of more mechanical assistance with less. The medieval soldier fighting face to face had a different view of those he killed from the modern aviator dealing death from 20,000 feet. Like many writers of the 1930s, Russell was more than a little obsessed with the figure of the aviator. It seemed to him – and to them – that a man who saw his fellows as little more than scurrying ants could hardly help but become more bleakly merciless than the conquerors of earlier ages.[49] Mechanism was only one face of power; reflection on it led to an equally important distinction, that between power over men and power over nature. Political and social power is primarily power over persons; even the use of power over nature requires power over people to make it effective. An unwilling army which leaves its weapons in the barracks is not much use, as the Tsar discovered to his cost in 1917. Trotsky understood that rifles need willing fingers.

Three large subjects most interested Russell. The first was the role of opinion in creating and undermining power; the second, the peculiarities of large modern organizations; the third, the ethical and other constraints on power. Although he devotes separate chapters to such topics as 'The Biology of Organizations' or 'Power and Forms of Government', his real concerns run through every argument. He was eager not to overstate or understate the role of opinion: ideas are not merely epiphenomenal, but it is certainly not true that poets and philosophers are the legislators of mankind. A totalitarian state with a monopoly of the means of propaganda can fight off competing ideas, but will not survive defeat in war.[50] A monarchy with God on its side, such as imperial China, might endure indefinitely because of its hold on men's minds; none the less, it could not survive the arrival of the superior weapons of the West – trying to survive meant modernization, modernization weakened the belief in the divinity of the state, and the game was up. All societies give their citizens plenty of reasons for revolt, for all societies contain a great deal of injustice, poverty and brutality; all the same it takes some spectacular defeat to bring most of them down. Tsarist Russia was brutal, inefficient, poverty-stricken and seething with discontent, but it took the negative fact of the regime's defeat in war to make revolution possible, and it took Lenin's ability to convince enough of his followers that revolution was practicable and desirable to make it actual. Although revolutionary regimes – presciently he took fascism and communism to be examples of the same phenomenon – depend on agitation and propaganda, these will work only for a time. They may make a revolution; they cannot sustain it indefinitely. Stalin murdered the recalcitrant and harangued the rest, but all his urging could not overcome the Russian desire for peace and quiet which led most of his wretched subjects to evade both trouble and their duties by whatever means they could. 'The ultimate limit to the power of creeds is set by boredom, weariness, and love of ease.'[51] This scepticism is something to set against his habitual tendency to intellectualize politics and overestimate the importance of intellectual conversion.

Russell had a strong sense of what it was that was distinctively 'modern' about the modern world. Like Durkheim, he claimed that society was 'denser' than previous societies, that is that people were more closely integrated and for more purposes; interdependence on a large scale was dictated by the modern economy, modern technology and modern communications. Governments, too, were more implicated in social life. Though it was only totalitarian regimes which took things to an extreme, all governments now undertook responsibilities which had formerly been left to self-help. Like Durkheim, Russell believed that men spent so much time in functionally organized groups, such as firms, schools, armies, government departments and the rest, that their sense of their own capacities was very tightly bound up with their estimation of the powers of the organizations they belonged to. This density makes modern states more stable than their predecessors; their internal lines of communication and the control they can exercise over their subjects gives them greater internal power than their predecessors. This inspires Russell to reflect on the possibility of world, rather than merely national, government. Great-power rivalry is an uncertain way of keeping the peace, and transferring powers to a wider authority is the only way to improve on it. Since modern states are so well organized, there is room to hope that the victor in a future war or the most powerful of the neutral states may be able to impose world government.[52]

Unlike Durkheim, Russell saw no strong connection between modernity and liberal democracy. Modern governments had to be technically efficient and to have a solid base in public opinion, but this did not imply democracy. He could see that a government which secured the sincere support of party cadres and the military would be able to impose itself on the rest of the population more or less indefinitely. The American system of democracy had advantages over autocracy in securing good leadership and the willing cooperation of the populace; but what matters to many societies is speed of response and military weight, and for these democracy is no help.[53] He took it for granted that in any future global flare-up America would emerge on top, but that was not due to democracy, rather to American technology and her inexhaustible supply of raw materials. The late-nineteenth-century confidence about the spread of liberal democracy was simply out of date. In the twentieth century it was the cool oligarchs, typified by the airmen and their commanders, who were in tune with the spirit of the age. None the less, the democratic ideal would not vanish, if only because American survival was assured and her brand of democracy with her.[54]

When Russell asks how power can be 'tamed', all the familiar hopes and fears come to the surface. The power of the nation state is the great problem; it is essentially geared to making war, but in the twentieth century the war of all against all must mean universal death. If we do not learn to live together we shall assuredly die together instead. How we were to learn this lesson is another matter entirely. Russell's suggestions would not have surprised Viscount Amberley, though his language might have done. Philosophers, says Russell, write about power much as they do about sex; some – and here he thinks of Nietzsche and Fichte – are brazen in their power worship and long only to yield to natural leaders; others – most liberals among them – pretend that they never feel tempted to push other people around or give them orders or even press unwelcome advice upon them. None of this will do; most of us are more or less happy to wield power if we can, and unless we recognize this we shan't talk sense about it.

The sense Russell talks is very much of a piece with the arguments of *Principles of Social Reconstruction*, and it looks forward to the doctrine of *Human Society in Ethics and Politics* and his emphasis on the fact that 'a world in which the aims of different individuals or groups are compossible is likely to be happier than one in which they are conflicting'.[55] Human beings have a multitude of desires, some of them such that everyone can satisfy them at once, others such that one person's satisfaction excludes everyone else's. We cannot all be richer or more powerful than anyone else; that is the most obvious drawback to the ethics of the superman. The pursuit of such goods leads to mutual destruction. The remedy is hard to practise but less hard to discern; a wide and optimistic education so that a happy childhood leaves no grudges festering in the adult mind, a search for useful work, and the restoration of democracy to the world of work, avoiding both the oligarchical organization of capitalism and the bureaucratic tyranny that socialism had turned out in Soviet practice.[56] Liberal democratic politics are not perfect, but – in this anticipating Popper's defence of democracy – Russell thought liberal democracy embodied a version of the true scientific spirit, institutionalizing the means of detecting errors and making new experiments in social and political organization.[57] As he said for the next twenty years, democracy works best when its adherents have the sceptical optimism of the scientist: 'The temper required to make a success of democracy is, in the practical life, exactly what the scientific temper is in the intellectual life.' That sceptical optimism is what he preaches here. After another half-century of war, tyranny, revolution and military *coups*, it remains hard to see what better case could be made for a lively and unaggressive liberalism. Russell always thought *Power* an underrated little book. He was quite right. If it did not establish him as the Newton of political science, it showed that he was capable of writing better sense in ten pages than most sociologists in ten volumes.

SEVEN

THE NEW VOLTAIRE?

THE years after his return to Britain in 1944 were unusual in many
ways. Until his opposition to British nuclear weapons set him at odds
with orthodox political opinion, Russell was, as he remarked with some
astonishment, both famous and 'respectable'. 'I began to feel slightly
uneasy, fearing that this might be the onset of blind orthodoxy. I have
always held that no one can be respectable without being wicked, but so
blunted was my moral sense that I could not see in what way I had
sinned.'[1] The truth was that the world had caught up with him; his views
on sex and marriage were no longer thought outrageous – opinion divided
on whether the fact that he eventually married no fewer than four times
showed he was unsound or merely that he had lived a long time; a wife
every twenty years was hardly an extravagant allowance. His dislike of
the Soviet Union – intense enough to lead him to say to Gilbert Murray
during 1941 that Stalin's government was even worse than Hitler's – had
been unfashionable during the war but was now seen to be entirely
rational; and his anxiously liberal brand of socialism was wholly in tune
with the public opinion which sustained Britain's post-war Labour governments. The creation of the Third Programme opened an outlet which
might have been invented with him in mind; debates with the orthodox,
lectures on the impact of science on philosophy, light-hearted remi-
niscences of his years at Cambridge[2] and gloomy prognoses for the atomic
future were all grist to his mill and brought him before a wide public.

His *History of Western Philosophy* 'took off'; its faintly scurrilous attacks
on authoritarians and time-servers attracted the liberal-minded; its sly jabs
at the godly attracted the sceptical; and it was crammed full of genuine
philosophical insight, too. So popular did it become that for the first time
in his life Russell was able to relax about his financial situation. For the
foreseeable future, the *History* would keep the wolf from the door. Even
if it had not provided him with a pension, he was sufficiently in demand
to make a very satisfactory living. Two tours of America in 1950 and 1951

and a spectacular tour of Australia in 1950 added jam to the post-war bread and marge and extended the audience for his popular essays; a glance at the printing history of almost any of them illustrates the twin effects of his post-war popularity and the paperback revolution.

His academic respectability was confirmed with the bestowal of the Order of Merit by King George VI in 1949 – 'funny-looking chap' the king is said to have murmured to an ADC, but as G. E. Moore reported after collecting his own OM, 'the king had never heard of Wittgenstein' and probably had his doubts about the soundness of philosophers who supported conscientious objection during one war and nuclear blackmail after the next. He received the Nobel Prize, which he was awarded in 1950, with mixed feelings; he could hardly wish not to be honoured, but wished it had been for philosophy rather than literature. (Seeing that there is no prize for philosophy, the Nobel committee could hardly have done much better than they did; but one sympathizes with his desire to be honoured as the author of *Principia Mathematica* rather than *Marriage and Morals*.)

Domestic life until 1952 was no smoother than before. Peter Spence found him increasingly unbearable and left for good in 1949; on his side, he regretted being parted from his second son a good deal more than he minded being parted from his third wife. All this was put in the shade by his first son's nervous breakdown and the collapse of John's marriage and domestic arrangements generally. For a time, it looked as if Russell was going to be landed with three grandchildren and an incapable son to look after. But Dora Russell was eager to shoulder these burdens, and Russell's own marital misadventures were finally put behind him at the end of 1952 when he married Edith Finch, an old friend of his and of Lucy Donnelly from Bryn Mawr. She became friend, counsellor, political ally and nurse; what might have been a lonely old age became as sunny in its private aspects as its public aspects were stormy.

The decade between Russell's return to Britain and the beginnings of his anti-nuclear campaigning – marked by the radio broadcast on 'Man's Peril' at Christmas 1954[3] – was the high point of his career as gad-fly, educator, counsellor to the perplexed, and intellectual entertainer. It was in that decade that the public got used to the thought that he was an intellectual ornament in something of the style of Voltaire – anti-clerical but morally serious, cynical but public-spirited, a stern rationalist, but perhaps more of a romantic than he liked to let on. He had been fulfilling a good many of these roles for thirty years; yet he had never been wholly at ease doing it. He had always regarded his popular writings as a poor second-best to his serious philosophical work. More importantly, he had also regarded his interventions in politics and public life as very much less valuable than his work in pure philosophy. Now, however, he seemed not unhappy to have ceased to be a professional philosopher, almost as if he had come to like the human race better than before and to think better of his own work as educator and propagandist because of that.

However, Russell would have been the first to insist that the comparison with Voltaire was in crucial ways misguided. In an essay published in 1958 on 'Voltaire's Influence on Me', he pointed out that Voltaire had been much more of a moral sceptic that he was. In *L'Huron* Voltaire sets a Red Indian, a Jesuit and a Jansenist to argue with each other about their creeds; as usual in eighteenth-century morality plays of this sort, the poor Red Indian is shown to be utterly unable to see why Europeans should persecute one another over the mysteries of the faith, or why they should be willing to suffer at one another's hands for those same mysterious doctrines. Russell observes that he had not always sympathized with Voltaire's attitude; a willingness to suffer for one's faith had hitherto seemed to him noble, even if the faith itself was absurd. After years of living under the threat of nuclear warfare, he was more sympathetic to the thought that creed wars must at all costs be averted.[4] When he changed his mind, it was out of a humanitarian concern for the survival of the human race, not out of contempt for doctrinal disputes that he adopted this 'Voltairean' position.

Russell, moreover, was more often in the thick of political controversy and less often in the thick of religious controversy than Voltaire; Voltaire's noble campaign to secure posthumous justice for Jean Calas – judicially murdered by the *parlement* of Toulouse in 1762 – has blinded later ages to the extent to which this public-spirited campaign was out of character. For most of his life, Voltaire was a man on the make, financially and in most other respects. Voltaire was sent to the Bastille once, and then only because of a private quarrel, but in eighteenth-century France Russell would have stayed in the Bastille or would have fled the country. He could never have spent his life seeking the literary fame that Voltaire sought, and he would have been far too incautious to survive in the Catholic despotism which operated in eighteenth-century France. His political allegiances were also quite other than Voltaire's – Voltaire preached enlightened despotism at the court of Frederick the Great, and the success of his plays and histories depended on the favour of the court of Louis XV; Russell on the contrary always preached liberal democracy and had earned his living by writing for popular journals and giving lectures whose success was entirely a matter of his hold over a lay audience. The tone of voice, the ability to drive opponents wild by making them look silly – these they certainly had in common. All the same, analogies with writers of a wholly different stamp are always dangerous – and wide though Russell's range was, it is as hard to imagine him writing classical tragedy in measured alexandrines as to imagine Voltaire knocking off 1500 words on 'Who May Use Lipstick?'.[5] In fact 'Who May Use Lipstick?' was a light-hearted defence of the proposition that schoolteachers should be permitted by their employers to use cosmetics if they felt like it. It ended with a high-spirited defence of the proposition that jolly, high-spirited people should educate children. Its high spirits did not mean that it was not seriously intended. Russell's popular and polemical writings were meant to educate a democratic public, to encourage rationalists and liberals in the age of fascist and communist intolerance, to put pressure from the non-doctrinaire Left on the Conservative governments of 1920s and '30s Britain. We should therefore pause, before turning to Russell's last campaigns to save his fellows from the nuclear holocaust or the horrors of imperialist wars, to look directly at the question of his successes and failures as a social conscience and political educator.

The intellectual who has the intense political passions of Russell is in a difficult position in countries such as Britain and America, more difficult than his counterpart in France and more difficult than his forebears in eighteenth- and nineteenth-century England. To be of any use, he needs to be simultaneously a responsible and an irresponsible figure. He needs to insist on the difference between the duty of the intellectual to think ideas through to their conclusion and the duty of the politician to remember the needs of party cohesion and public acceptability, which is why he must be irresponsible; he must at the same time understand that the price of influence is a willingness to remember that he is thinking about the everyday lives of his fellow citizens and not the far future of a race of supermen, robots, party activists, or crusaders for the faith, which is why he must be responsible. A crucial step in achieving this is to establish an appropriate relationship with his audience. Nor is this something which lies entirely in his own hands. The ability of the audience to listen, to criticize and respond makes an enormous difference to the quality of the exchange an intellectual and his audience can have. Jean-Paul Sartre, Maurice Merleau-Ponty or Albert Camus had an audience of more or less alienated intellectuals and more or less committed left-wing activists to write for, and much of the literary life of post-war France was in their hands. One of Russell's difficulties for much of his life was that cultural and political life in Britain was so vastly different. In a way, the potential prize was greater, because Britain did not have such a 'ghetto-ized' oppositional intelligentsia, and Russell could hope to influence a broad band of public opinion. On the other hand, Britain had always been more sceptical of intellectuals in politics, and in the twentieth century was short of obvious channels through which engaged intellectuals could 'permeate' public opinion.

Nineteenth-century liberal writers had had an obvious forum in the great quarterly reviews such as the Whig *Edinburgh Review* or the utilitarian and radical *Westminster Review* and its successor, the *London and Westminster Review*. Most of Mill's philosophical and political essays appeared in such reviews. Walter Bagehot made an art form out of the much quicker and snappier commentaries he contributed to the *Economist*, but even he turned to the quarterlies for his masterpiece, *The English Constitution*. By the time Russell wrote, that kind of superior journalism was almost dead; what was left of it after the First World War soon vanished, leaving behind only the thinner weeklies like the *New Statesman* (itself having incorporated the Liberal *Nation*). Acerbic asides in the *New Statesman* diary are no substitute for considered essays addressed to readers of whom the author is sufficiently respectful to take them entirely seriously. When the peace debates of the 1930s spawned a host of leftish magazines, their effect was largely confined to the converted, and their content was decidedly thin. *Which Way to Peace?* and Aldous Huxley's pacifist essays would hardly have been taken less seriously by their readers if their readers had had anything like the nutritive diet the nineteenth-century quarterlies had provided. For all that, the great pleasure of reading Russell's popular essays is that they almost always engage their audience in a brisk, light-hearted but intelligent exchange; the anxiety they sometimes induce is the corresponding doubt whether they take that audience entirely seriously. Whatever else liberal politics can be, it cannot be the politics of condescension.

The conjunction of the thinner medium and the more diffuse audience did a good deal of damage to many more writers than Russell. Intellectuals with political aspirations found themselves short of a natural platform, and academic journals and scholarly books are no substitute for access in a considered way to politicians and senior administrators. This would not, of course, have been enough by itself to make it more difficult for someone like Russell to exercise a benign political influence. A further problem was that the First World War seems to have marked a turning point in the relationship between the press and the public too, as though newspapers had decided that what their readers wanted was entertainment, with only as much information as could readily be digested between gossip and sport. Russell could never have wanted to become an editor or a leader writer in any case; but this was less important than the fact that, if someone like himself was to address a wide audience, he either had to seize their attention by being 'outrageous' or had to write on entertaining topics, as he did for the Hearst press. None of this is to belittle the impact of Russell's own character. For much of his life he plainly felt a contempt for uneducated people which is entirely at odds with the sentimental profession of solidarity with humanity's sufferings which opens his *Autobiography*. The assertion that Darwin was worth thirty million ordinary men is not easy to reconcile with the claim that 'Echoes of cries of pain reverberate in my heart. Children in famine, victims tortured by oppressors, helpless old people a hated burden to their sons, and the whole world of loneliness, poverty and pain make a mockery of what human life should be. I long to alleviate the evil, but I cannot, and I too suffer.' Max Eastman recalled an alarming moment when Russell observed, after a very successful public debate in the 1920s, 'Anyone who takes these debates of ours seriously must be an idiot.' Eastman recoiled, and so might most of us.[6] Russell was more vulnerable than most to the temptation to treat his readers like fools. That, however, is the point; a more sober public media might have controlled his tendency to say the first irritated thing that came into his head rather than encouraging it.

Nor did everything hang on Russell's character and the character of the mass media either. The changed political scene, and the difference between British politics and continental politics, also made a great deal of difference. British politics was orderly, party-based politics. After 1914, Russell could never have returned to his Liberal allegiances; the only focus for his efforts had to be the Labour Party. However, to make much impact on the Labour Party, it was necessary to embroil oneself in the party organization, as distinguished academics like R. H. Tawney and somewhat less distinguished figures such as H. J. Laski did. Russell decided that the experiment of the NCF proved once and for all that he was not an organization man. He may well have been wrong about this, although the acrimonious history of CND and the Bertrand Russell Peace Foundation inspires a fairly jaundiced view of his effect on organizations.[7] What he was right to believe was that anyone who wanted to have an impact on what happened to education (to take an obvious example) under a Labour government would have had to resign himself, first, to working away on policy subcommittees, secondly, to risking having his work thrown away either because Conference did not like it or because the most likely candidate for Minister of Education did not like it, and thirdly, to waiting a very long time for a Labour government to get elected. It is easy to see that shouting loudly from the touchline might seem more interesting than spending one's life in the scrum. Moreover, the former offered an income, the second did not.

Russell's intellectual peers, such as Keynes, the Webbs, Gilbert Murray and Leonard Woolf, were not natural 'party men', and nor was he. Their natural audience would have been senior administrators and senior members of government; these were, in fact, the men whom Keynes and the Webbs did affect. One consequence of the First World War was the creation of what writers often term 'big government'. Departments set up to run the war effort did not vanish when the war was over but found an infinity of new tasks to perform. The bigger government grows, the more amorphous it tends to become, and the more amorphous the governing élite becomes, too. Once again, anyone intending to have an impact on the operations of government would have to specialize, as Keynes and the Webbs did, to target a particular group of administrators, members of the cabinet or shadow cabinet, or influential back-benchers – he would have to become a public-spirited lobbyist. In the last thirty years, we have become used to such people and the organizations they have created playing a valuable role in waking us up to the needs of sections of the community which have been neglected; organizations such as the Child Poverty Action Group and Shelter have done enormously useful work of this sort. It does, however, demand full-time attention and a fairly narrow focus. This was just what Russell did not wish to give and what he did not wish to confine himself to.

It is not surprising then that Russell induces in many readers something of the ambivalence he felt in himself. He offered utopian schemes for wholesale social reconstruction, but seemed unwilling to do anything about getting them implemented. He was chronically unwilling to spell out the details of their practical implementation in a way that might convert the unpersuaded. He lurches – it is an unkind word, but it surely fits the abruptness of his shifts – between utopianism and reformism, as if he first thinks his status as a detached intellectual allows him the first, and then decides that the fact that people might take him seriously imposes the second. Because he set so much store by emotional attachments and moral allegiances, he set too little by the humdrum question of how good intentions were to be translated into a better world, so that his reformist suggestions are neither very persuasive nor very thoroughly worked through. For a man who wrote an essay on 'The Harm that Good

Men Do' – admittedly using 'good man' in a decidedly tongue-in-cheek fashion – he was remarkably casual about the effects of his own brand of goodness.[8]

It cannot be said, then, that he had the impact on the political climate he sometimes hoped for; nor can it be said that he was really entitled to it, since he never occupied a sufficiently stable and articulated position to warrant it, and never set himself to the patient hard work which might have achieved it. Yet if he had done everything he could have done, and had had a sufficiently different temperament to give him more chance of success, the odds were still against him in the social and political climate of twentieth-century Britain. Given the temperament he in fact had, he was probably right to erupt in crusades rather than slog away in committees; and, given his unique philosophical talents, he was in any case better employed dominating twentieth-century analytical philosophy than trying to rescue the Lib–Lab alliance of the 1890s. However, there is one respect in which his impact on a wide audience was as benign as one could wish. What I want to suggest in the rest of this chapter is that, even if he was not the perfect 'intellectual in politics', he deserves the gratitude of several generations for his career as gad-fly. If he was politically inept and absurdly optimistic about the possibility of changing the entire political climate by mere argument, the way in which his popular essays and radio talks enlivened the intellectual life of his day gave pleasure in itself and was benign in its effects. If he did not reorganize the educational system, introduce industrial democracy, abolish armies and destroy the authority of the Church, he woke up the middle-aged and encouraged the rebellious young. This was a cause to which he was avowedly committed; almost any collection of his essays – 'Sceptical', 'Unpopular', 'In Praise of Idleness' or whatever – are models of how to do it.

The Conquest of Happiness was not a book which Russell thought much of. It was firmly in the pot-boiler category, designed to make a few pounds for Beacon Hill. None the less, it is in many ways an excellent example of Russell's ability to make just the right point in an engaging and memorable way. This is true, even though his chronicle of the varieties of unhappiness is certainly overblown and overcoloured. Consider his description of a social evening in America: 'It is held that drink and petting are the gateways to happiness, so people get drunk quickly and try not to notice how much their partners disgust them. After a sufficient amount of drink, men begin to weep and to lament how unworthy they are, morally, of the devotion of their mothers. All that alcohol does for them is liberate the sense of sin, which reason suppresses in saner moments.'[9] There are plenty of parties which end up like that, but there are very many more which do not. However, there is a tongue-in-cheek quality about the whole thing which suggests that we are not to take it entirely literally as an account of the inevitable outcome of every party, so much as an account of the logical stopping-place of the misguided belief that booze and sex will cure real misery. The same is true of his denunciation of the pleasures of power; Napoleon was a small poor schoolboy who was mocked by his aristocratic classmates. The urge to get back at them made him Emperor, and seeing the *émigrés* crawling back home made him happy; but it all got out of hand because it 'led to the wish to obtain a similar satisfaction at the expense of the Tsar, and this led to St Helena'. Are we supposed to take this as the last word about the history of Napoleonic Europe? Evidently not; the point is the moral: 'Power kept within its proper bounds may add greatly to happiness, but as the sole end of life it leads to disaster, inwardly if not outwardly.'[10] If we wonder why, Russell explains: no one can be omnipotent, there are always obstacles which cannot be overcome, and the knowledge that this is so must lead the man in whom omnipotence is a fixed ambition to deny the existence of the obstacles or to eliminate people who might provide evidence of them. Russell wrote all this twenty-five years before the last days of Stalin were revealed to a horrified world; but what should we think of the man who could, and did, murder any of his close associates on a whim, but who was reduced to living in three identical bed-sitting rooms in the Kremlin, tormented by fears of assassination and betrayal? Was Russell not right, and did his caricatures not serve precisely the purpose they were designed for?

Similarly, when offering recipes to fend off the worst forms of unhappiness, Russell may not be entirely persuasive. Anyone who knows anything of his life is inclined to respond by asking why the recipes worked so ill with him. The answer is that they did not work so ill with him. Nobody who did not actively and thoroughly enjoy thinking and writing could have written even his pot-boilers; his defence of 'zest' as one of the great ingredients of a happy life is all of a piece with the way he defends it. As always, there are acute asides which hardly lose relevance after half a century: 'In women, less nowadays than formerly, but still to a very large extent, zest has been greatly diminished by a mistaken conception of respectability. It was thought undesirable that women should take an obvious interest in men, or that they should display too much vivacity in public. In learning not to be interested in men, they learned very frequently to be interested in nothing, or at any rate in nothing except a certain kind of correct behaviour.'[11] Even today, when feminists have alerted us to the dangers of 'sexist' institutions and attitudes, it is a rare feminist who bases her feminism on the simple principle that the freedom to do as you choose and enjoy yourself doing it is a valuable freedom which men take for granted and women ought to be able to take for granted too.[12] One might think the defence of zest too truistic to be worth bothering with – until half an hour's conversation with the depressed promoters of good causes inspires the thought that they seem to get very little out of the life of virtue. At that point, zest can seem much underrated after all and its defence a necessary complement to sober public spirit.

The moral philosopher who pauses to read these popular essays will also find something interesting; in particular, what he or she will find is that Russell's arguments are at once less utilitarian and less dependent on appeals to high-flying ultimate values than one would expect from what one might call his official moral philosophy. The doctrine Russell preaches is very much closer to eighteenth-century moralists such as Bishop Butler or David Hume, who emphasized that ethics was not entirely about sacrificing ourselves for the good of others, and that one powerful argument for cultivating a benevolent disposition in ourselves was that benevolence led to happiness, while misanthropy and envy generally did not. The argument is very simple, very old and absolutely persuasive; it was also, and very oddly, an argument which had somehow gone underground thoughout the high tide of utilitarianism on the one hand and Kantianism on the other. The envious person's goals are at odds with everyone else's; he wishes them to do badly, while they naturally wish to do well. Every success other people achieve is gall and wormwood for him, but there is nothing he can do about it, since they are not likely to fail in their undertakings simply in order to gratify his meanness. Benevolence on the contrary finds happiness in the happiness of others, finds opportunities to do good for ourselves in doing good for others. The benevolent person counts himself or herself lucky when others are too. Russell, of course, incorporated this into his enthusiasm for 'compossible' desires; what we ought to cultivate in ourselves is desires whose satisfaction is consistent with the satisfaction of our other desires and the desires of other people. The world will not always allow us to do it; too many people and too little food, for instance, pose moral dilemmas which no amount of cultivating compossible desires will cure. None the less, it is often possible and, where it is, it is what any sensible person would do.

It is advice which, given baldly, may seem too obvious to bother with, or impossible to heed at just those moments when one most needs it. This, however, is hardly a complaint which is to be levelled against Russell rather than any other writer who chooses to offer advice on how to lead the good life; neither Aristotle nor the New Testament have proved particularly efficacious against ill-temper and self-deception. Any book of this kind can do no more than induce its readers to set off in an appropriate direction, recognizing that they will occasionally slip up and that nothing will inoculate them against the human condition or original sin. What is very much in Russell's favour is that his advice, trite or not as the reader may think it, is set against a particular background and is directed at a particular sort of reader. That is, Russell takes it for granted that certain kinds of unhappiness are much more likely to occur in the twentieth century than in previous centuries, and that certain kinds are not – the art of cultivating a stoical indifference to pain was a much more valuable route to happiness or resource against misery in the days before modern medicine and modern anaesthetics; conversely, the ability to stand up to public opinion, not be distracted by notions of success and failure which do not suit us, and not give in to the excesses of competition is much more necessary today than it was for someone living in an isolated village where economic life went on as it had done for half a millennium. Equally, Russell's readers are not the children of the upper classes who might have been brought up on Cicero's *De Officiis* in the middle of the seventeenth century. They are essentially twentieth-century readers, anxious, probably, and willing to consider how they might try to improve their lives. They are the sort of people who are readily mocked – Roy Campbell's *Georgiad* memorably denounced

> All who of 'Happiness' have learned the ropes
> From Bertrand Russell or from Marie Stopes[13]

but his criticisms might well have left Russell cold. We do not live in a century when it is possible merely to will ourselves back into a framework where we know by mere feel or by tradition what to do, and where happiness of a sort comes easily. Freud, of course, insisted that there was no recipe for happiness and that his therapeutic art confined itself to replacing neurotic misery with 'ordinary unhappiness'. Russell did not believe that there was a recipe either; *The Conquest of Happiness* was not much like the self-improvement manuals of a later day which insisted that absolutely everything could be absolutely wonderful absolutely all the time. Russell, like Freud, was insistent that life is at best a risky business, that every source of happiness is also a source of loss: friends die, lovers grow cold, favourite theorems display a flaw, beloved landscapes are built over. If we dwell on such things, Byronic unhappiness will fill our days (and, one might unkindly add, tempt us to write essays such as 'The Free Man's Worship'); if on the other hand, we do not, we may, if lucky, find ourselves happy before we have noticed it.

The same complaints and the same defences might be levelled against and erected on behalf of almost every piece of popular social and political writing he produced. Consider his Reith Lectures on *Authority and the Individual*. Reduced to the barest bones, they do little more than tell their hearers that they live in a world in which it is more urgent than before to achieve a proper balance betwen the demands of order and security on the one hand and the demands of freedom and individuality on the other. It is more urgent because modern tyranny is nastier than any previous form of tyranny was, and because modern chaos is likely to be a nuclear chaos which will simply terminate human history. However, part of their cleverness is just that they start from such an obvious, indeed banal, position. Anyone who failed to feel after the Second World War that individual initiative had to be satisfied in a peaceful fashion and social order preserved in a non-tyrannical fashion would have been very eccentric indeed.

Russell's rhetorical trick, if that is not too impolite a term, is to get the discussion off the plane of banalities by generalizing it and particularizing it simultaneously. That is, he sets it in a much more general setting than most of his hearers would have done by calling in historical examples, anthropological examples, the supposed findings of modern psychology and the like; it is not just the discontents of post-war Britain that he addresses, but the human condition. Do we feel somehow let down by the fact that the war has ended, even though we fought in order to end it? If we do, it is not surprising; the Crow Indian, safe on his reserve, says bring back the old dangerous existence, 'there was glory in it'.[14] Freya Stark reports that South Arabia was full of brigands and murderers – and of astonishingly cheerful inhabitants. 'When war comes the bank clerk may escape and become a commando, and then at last he feels that he is living as nature intended him to live.' The need for excitement, adventure and fear is built into us; once it served an indispensable evolutionary purpose. Now it cannot be satisfied in the old way, since its satisfaction will lead to us all blowing ourselves to bits. It must be satisfied somehow, or we shall blow ourselves to bits out of sheer boredom.

The message is fundamentally the message of *The Principles of Social Reconstruction*, as indeed emerges plainly enough when he says, 'The general principle which, if I am right, should govern the respective spheres of authority and intitiative, may be stated broadly in terms of the different kinds of impulses that make up human nature ... Broadly speaking, the regularizing of possessive impulses and their control by the law belong to the *essential* functions of government, while the creative impulses, though governments may encourage them, should derive their main influence from individual or group autonomy.'[15] The discussion is cut down for a radio audience, and chastened a little by the passage of time: we are not looking towards utopia so much as trying to make life safe but not uninteresting. This calmer tone is characteristic of the whole set of lectures. Unlike the earlier Russell, the Russell of *Authority and the Individual* is less inclined to divide mankind into murderous leaders and their virtuous opponents. He is more inclined to look to the general human vulnerability towards paranoia, rage and the desire for revenge in order to explain the lunacies of the politics of the recent past, almost as if he thinks that we could produce an equation of the form: *frustration plus scapegoats equals fascism*, though he plainly does not mean that to be taken entirely seriously.

What he does mean to be taken seriously is the need for an appropriate combination of institutional restraints on populist excesses and the inculcation of an ethic which will make people self-controlled and tolerant and therefore less vulnerable to demagoguery. What he is particularly deft at is showing just how difficult it is to bring this about. Democracy, for instance, is supposed to be a political system in which the ruled control the rulers; we the public put our leaders in power, and the decisions of government are executed by people who are known as 'civil' or 'public servants'. It does not work out like that. 'The ordinary voter, so far from finding himself the source of all the power of army, navy, police and civil service, *feels* himself their humble subject, whose duty is, as the Chinese used to say, to "tremble and obey".'[16] The non-utopian Russell of the Reith Lectures does not claim that there is any easily available way of remedying this; there is no prospect of bringing back the Athenian assembly and parading our generals and admirals in front of the assembled citizens for judgement. The equality and social justice which are the revolutionary ideals of our own age cannot be achieved at all without the resources of a complicated, technologically advanced society. It is no good thinking that we can give every individual a direct say in government in such conditions as these. Like a good many academic writers some twenty years later, Russell suggests that one way round the problem of what came to be thought of as the alienation of the ordinary citizen from the democratic process was the democratization of whatever aspects of life were amenable to it, and in particular the workplace.[17] Sadly, the one example of success he points to – the John Lewis Partnership – is still extremely unusual in the world of large commercial undertakings, even though the cooperative movement generally has continued to make steady if unspectacular progress.

The great virtue of the Reith Lectures is a rather un-Russellian virtue, namely their steadiness and sobriety; though he was very ready to say that money is not everything and that when human beings have satisfied their needs for food and shelter they then look round for something *useless* but interesting to do, he was entirely unwilling to suggest that the welfare state is a bad idea or that it must inevitably weaken initiative. To say that there is more to life than security is absolutely not to deny the value of security. Forty years on, his emphasis on the need for the state to see to conservation appears particularly prescient, even though the example he looks back to is the creation of dust-bowls in America – but he looks forward to future troubles with oil supplies presciently enough, too.[18] In general, the argument cannot be faulted; if one sets out from a liberal democratic perspective, asks how authority is to be carved up and how individuals are not to be excessively regimented, the answer must be that power should be devolved as far as possible and that, when in doubt, we should devolve it rather than centralize it. This means that the state must protect each of us against violence, must administer justice, must coordinate economic activity lest we render the globe uninhabitable, but otherwise ought to encourage us in self-help. These rules for liberal democracy might have been drawn up by his godfather. Where Russell's own anxieties obtrude, and then only briefly, is in the momentary defence of world government. If the logic of liberalism is to concede to centralized organizations those powers which cannot safely be left in individual hands, the logic of liberalism implies the creation of a supranational authority to eliminate war.

To go on at any length to show that this sobriety marks the Russell of *The Impact of Science on Society*[19] would be wearisome; while he was not exactly repetitious, he certainly stuck to the same general message, the illustrations and asides alone varying a good deal. To argue that the verve and high spirits of all of it are entertaining and enlivening would be equally tedious and pointless; Russell's own essays carry more conviction than any argument on their behalf could do, and no one writing *about* Russell would be well advised to quote him at length – the contrast between his prose and one's own would be too depressing. Two last points and two last illustrations will suffice.

The first is that one of his underrated merits was to make what one might call middle-of-the-road politics something other than merely half-hearted compromise. He knew that one of the attractions of fascism and communism for the younger generation of the 1930s was that they gave a great sense of activity; the fascist and the communist might be filled with a terrible intensity, but perhaps that was more agreeable than lacking conviction. Russell could dismiss them in such a way as to stop that attitude dead in its tracks. 'The view that the only practically possible choice is between Communism and Fascism seems to me definitely untrue in America, England and France, and probably also in Germany and Italy. England had a period of Fascism under Cromwell, France under Napoleon, but in neither case was this a bar to subsequent democracy. Politically immature nations are not the best guides as to the political future.'[20] It is hard not to hope that the Webbs re-read that last remark in due course. Marx's prognostications are rebuked in eight crisp paragraphs, ending with the objection that regimes begun in hatred will go in hatred and become hideous dictatorships; as for fascism, it is less a doctrine than a bundle of resentments, and as such beneath contempt. There is no question of somehow pursuing a middle way between Left and Right; liberal socialism is the only doctrine a rational person could accept and the sort of existence a liberal socialist society could guarantee most of the population is an ideal very worth working for.

If one of his merits was to make his brand of democratic socialism energetic and appealing enough to be attractive to the young, the other was to make it clear that, whether or not the unexamined life was not worth living – as Socrates had rather aggressively insisted – the examined life was very well worth living. 'Social dynamics is a very difficult science ...' he observed; and most of his readers must at times have felt that he could with advantage have recalled the fact more frequently.[21] But even his lightweight essays are a splendid encouragement not to be got down by the difficulties and to persevere with the inquest into how we can contrive to be both human and happy.

In the twentieth century, philosophy has become increasingly a professional discipline and increasingly inaccessible to a lay public. Like most disciplines that fall into the hands of academics, there is a great temptation to create obscurities and difficulties which only very clever young people can tackle; it is in this way that they prove their fitness to join the profession. Russell understood this process very well. In 'How I Write', he observed: 'I am allowed to use plain English because everybody knows that I could use mathematical logic if I chose. Take the statement: "Some people marry their deceased wives' sisters." I can express this in language which only becomes intelligible after years of study, and this gives me freedom. I suggest to young professors that their first work should be written in a jargon only to be understood by the erudite few. With that behind them, they can ever after say what they have to say in a language "understanded of the people".'[22] Sadly, reality has overtaken the joke, save that professors get into the habit of using the jargon and rarely stop to address the public in plain prose thereafter. Russell, of course, is somewhat to blame for this. It was the success of his conception of philosophy as essentially a form of critical analysis that set it on the path to the technically difficult subject it has become. However, there was also the Russell who thought that philosophy ought to give one insights which it was worth passing on to the rest of mankind in language the rest of mankind could grasp. He may have made a lot of money doing it; he also did a lot of good.

EIGHT

WAR AND PEACE IN THE NUCLEAR AGE

FROM 1945 until his death in 1970, Russell thought, wrote and campaigned endlessly in the hope of bringing sanity and order to world politics and persuading his fellow creatures to turn away from the impending nuclear catastrophe. His career as polemicist, agitator and amateur world statesman fell into three phases. The first was his reaction in the early post-war years to the invention and use of nuclear weapons and his call for a world government which would have a monopoly of such weapons. From the outset he thought Britain should remain a non-nuclear power; and the second stage of his public career came when he took his advocacy of nuclear disarmament for Britain on to the streets with the creation of the Campaign for Nuclear Disarmament in 1958. The last was his increasingly fierce criticism of American foreign policy from 1960 onwards, culminating in his part in the campaign against America's intervention in Vietnam.

The quarter of a century between the end of the war and his death in 1970 saw some striking reversals. Immediately after the war, while America still had a monopoly of nuclear weapons, Russell was ready to see world government instituted by the threat or even by the actuality of a nuclear war. By the time he died, he had long been convinced that the Soviet Union was no threat to world peace and the United States a real menace. It is an intriguing question: what had changed in the interim – Russell, America, or the balance of world power? British readers whose memory stretches back to the 1960s will have a clear picture of Russell addressing large crowds in Trafalgar Square, organizing 'sit-down' campaigns and other forms of civil disobedience, getting himself arrested and spending another week in Brixton prison, forty-three years after his first visit. Why was he so committed to British unilateral disarmament that he supported 'direct action', such as invading airfields and submarine bases and 'sit-down' campaigns in central London, when he did not advocate American unilateralism, and was as ambiguous a 'pacifist' in the 1950s as he had been in the 1930s or during the First World War?

In his final decade of active campaigning, Russell was a very public presence; he operated successively through the Pugwash conferences, CND, the Committee of 100, the Bertrand Russell Peace Foundation and its offspring, the War Crimes Tribunal. As a very old man, he worked through a variety of other people, above all his secretary Ralph Schoenman, the young American who largely controlled what the public saw and heard of Russell between 1961 and 1967. Distinguishing Russell's views from those of his helpers and the various groups he worked with becomes more difficult as he becomes more and more the spokesman of a movement. Cynics said at the time that Russell was the captive of his followers and that his role was to sign what Schoenman made up; even before that, they had said that Russell was unduly under the influence of his fourth wife – who was certainly radical in her politics – if not, on the face of it, more so than her notably strong-willed and independent husband.

In the absence of an unvarnished account of Russell's last years by those who worked with him, common sense and caution have to go a long way. Russell maintained to the end that his position had been consistent from 1945, and that although he had followed the practice of governments and businesses in employing spokesmen to state his position, what came out under his name was exactly what he wanted to say.[1] This chapter will broadly confirm that. His views on international affairs were not so very different from what they had been before. The curiously bloodless bloodthirstiness of some of his proposals and the hostility he displayed towards America were not aberrations of extreme old age or thrust upon him by wild young men. His extremist proposals for a world government with a monopoly of destructive power were of a piece with views he had expressed in 1915, and his hostility to America was much like the contempt he displayed in 1918 when he was jailed for it.[2] In the 1920s, as well as in the 1940s and '50s, he had described America as an illiberal, hysterically anti-communist, lynch-mob-governed, racist slum which ought none the less to take up the reins of world government. His readiness to distinguish so sharply between the benefits of world peace and the squalor of American society and politics was in its own way admirable. We expect a historian to remain appalled at Roman brutality even while admiring the benefits the *pax Romana* brought to the (compulsorily) civilized world; and Russell displayed just this distance when he demanded that the unlovable United States should assume the mantle of world leadership. Even when he lost his temper and said things he regretted afterwards – as when he declared that Harold Macmillan was more wicked than Hitler – he still made sense.

What we may more seriously complain of is not the wild ideas foisted on him by his helpers, but that at some times he flatly contradicted himself, and at others was disconcertingly evasive. Whatever the merits of his advocacy of an aggressive American foreign policy in 1945–9, for example, he ought not to have denied having put it forward – especially when he went on almost at once to withdraw the denial too. Nor should he have simultaneously declared that the Russians' overriding duty was to move with extreme caution and that they had every right to put missiles into Cuba if they chose to.

Russell was seventy-three when the war ended, eighty-eight in 1960, and ninety-five at the height of the campaign against the American presence in Vietnam. After 1954 he produced no sustained philosophical work. Although he had been an energetic traveller immediately after the war, he made few foreign trips after the mid-1950s, and after 1956 was increasingly unwilling to leave his home in North Wales; in his late eighties he was increasingly frail and suffered digestive disorders which prevented him going out very much. He was inevitably cut off from much that went on in the outside world. How seriously should we take his last writings on politics: his attacks on America over the war in Vietnam, his denunciation of the Warren Tribunal's inquiry into the assassination of President Kennedy, and so on? One obstacle to taking them seriously is that he did not compose all of them; after 1958 he received endless requests for messages of encouragement, to disarmament meetings, then to anti-Vietnam war meetings. By the mid-1960s messages went out in large numbers, were distributed as news releases, and were inevitably constructed on 'boiler plate' principles – the same paragraphs were endlessly re-used in different contexts. Russell justified this by observing, 'It is a curious thing that the public utterances of almost all Government officials and important business executives are known to be composed by secretaries or colleagues, and yet this is held unobjectionable. Why should it be considered heinous in an ordinary layman?' This would be fair enough if the only question was whether Russell the campaigner was *responsible* for the campaigns waged in his name. However, nobody expects government press releases to reveal the real thinking of politicians; but we are concerned with what Russell thought, and the fact that these statements offer little evidence of that is a difficulty. Indeed, they can bear rather little intellectual scrutiny. Read in the mass, the products of what one might call 'the Schoenman years' are alarming; the proportion of abuse to argument is very high; disputed facts are confidently asserted without any suggestion that they are open to reasonable doubt – Russell rightly insisted that he always cited 'sources' but seemed unable to see that it was the reliability of those sources which his critics questioned. Throughout the campaign against the Vietnam war, every horror is explained by conspiracy and malice. America is declared to be a near-fascist state in the hands of mad generals; the Vietnam war is doubly genocidal, setting Negro soldiers and Asians to kill each other; the atrocities which indubitably did mark the war are put down to policy rather than panic. Kennedy was killed by the FBI, or the CIA, or at any rate by their friends.[3] And so on.

Russell got angrier as he got older. With not long to live, he felt that he must make what difference he could, and he became readier to sacrifice both coherence and accuracy to impact. In reply to a critic in *Tribune* who had complained of the 'unsociological' quality of Russell's writings on nuclear warfare, he wrote, 'I used to deal with wide sociological questions, for example in *Principles of Social Reconstruction, Roads to Freedom* and *Power*, but the Bikini test of 1 March, 1954 persuaded me that there was no time for long-term solutions and that some more immediate and specific movement was necessary for the preservation of mankind ... if you saw a man dropping lighted matches on heaps of TNT, you would feel it necessary to stop him without waiting for vast schemes of social reform. And that is the present situation as I see it.' So we cannot be sure when he meant to be taken seriously, or when he was simply happy that his name would help the opponents of American folly and wickedness; letters to friends are notably more cautious and measured than his public blasts against American imperialism. Since he thought the superpowers might blow everything sky-high by mischance or blind stupidity, it was not only old age that made him angry and impatient. As he remarked more than once, there is little point studying logic if nobody survives to understand the results. In that perspective, veracity came a poor second to impact. When the Bertrand Russell Peace Foundation was founded in 1963, its chief asset was his name, and he was ready to lend it to his helpers without overmuch scrutiny of the terms.[4] The reader does not need to be adept in political theory to realize that Russell did not pen everything which went out over his signature – a knowledge of English grammar suffices.

It is not their hostility to America or their extravagance which makes Russell's last writings inauthentic. There is nothing inexplicable in Russell's antipathy to American foreign policy after 1957; it became sharper after the Cuban missile crisis of 1962, but that is not surprising. Nor is the wildness which was always likely to break out in anything he wrote.

What is at odds with his earlier views is quite different. When he assails American policy in Vietnam he is sentimental about the Vietcong, who, he claims, are a 'non-communist, neutralist, popular front' trying to keep the South Vietnam government to the terms of the Geneva accords of 1954. He asks us to applaud their bravery and to admire their fastidious concern not to injure the civilian population, or to injure only those who have collaborated with the American enemy. This legalism was a characteristic New Left trope, as was the rhetoric of such passages as this: 'The people of Vietnam are heroic, and their struggle is epic; a stirring and permanent reminder of the incredible spirit of which men are capable when they are dedicated to a noble ideal. Let us salute the people of Vietnam.'[5] All his life, Russell had been a resolute opponent of the doctrine of 'the superior virtue of the oppressed'. Then he had written of the delusion that subject peoples were peculiarly admirable, 'One by one these various nations rose to independence, and were found to be just like everybody else; but the experience of those already liberated did nothing to destroy the illusion as regards those who were still struggling.'[6] He had thought it enough to point to the horrors of war and oppression; he had never thought the victims of oppression were made better by their sufferings, and would have thought their moral merits irrelevant. The belief that the Vietcong were morally special was a piece of New Left sentimentality which one can imagine Schoenman swallowing, but not Russell. Again, Russell attacked American imperialism in flatly Marxist terms that he would formerly have mocked.[7] He had always thought America was an imperialist power which used its military strength to make life easier for big business, but he also thought nations were driven by autonomous ideological forces, too. Powerful states simply wanted to make the world conform to their image, and Marxists looked for economic explanations where none were to be had. Schoenman wrote of Russell's wonderful openness to his young collaborators;[8] judging by his final repudiation of Schoenman, the truth is rather that Russell thought little of Schoenman's intelligence, but was happy to employ his energy and unwilling to waste time on quarrels with his own side.[9] The causes of American intervention mattered less than stopping it.

Twenty years earlier, Russell was one of the first laymen to come to terms with the existence of nuclear weapons. He was one of the few who were wholly at home with the physics of nuclear warfare, and he was an opponent of British nuclear weapons before the British government had seriously thought of producing them. The numerous articles and broadcasts he made in the 1950s advocate world government, appeal for verifiable disarmament, and suggest ways of reducing military tension by diplomatic means; but they also display an unostentatious familiarity with the new technology which would have been astonishing in anyone but the author of *The ABC of Atoms. Has Man a Future?* contains perhaps the clearest couple of paragraphs on the nature of nuclear fusion and fission and on the difference between atomic and hydrogen bombs that anyone ever wrote.[10] One of his first interventions in the nuclear debate came in a speech to the House of Lords on 28 November 1945, in which he appealed for a world government strong enough to contain the new menace. His familiarity with the physics of the bomb did nothing to make him happier about its existence. For one thing, many scientists involved with the bomb had worked on it only because they feared that German scientists must be close to creating a nuclear weapon. Like them, Russell was horrified at its use against Japan – by August 1945 Japan was close to defeat and was known to pose no nuclear threat. A demonstration of the bomb's destructive capabilities would, they thought, have been enough to bring about a Japanese surrender. Its use against undefended cities conjured up visions of future wars in which whole cities were reduced to radio-active ash and their inhabitants annihilated with them or stricken with lingering radiation-induced diseases. Russell's fears were even more vivid than his hearers'. When most laymen had hardly any idea of the nature of the new weapon, Russell could look ahead and see the dangers of more powerful weapons yet, for he understood the implications of the fact that atomic bombs momentarily created temperatures sufficient to launch nuclear fusion, and warned the House of Lords that 'some mechanism analogous to the present atomic bomb could be used to set off a much more violent explosion which would be obtained if one could synthesize heavier elements out of hydrogen'. That was the recipe for thermonuclear weapons.[11]

Russell was not alone in his fears. Where he was almost isolated was in his insistence that America must use her monopoly of nuclear weapons to create a world government armed with the power to destroy any country which tried to create nuclear weapons of its own. In 1945 the only possible target of this pressure was Stalin's Russia. For the next few years he was ritually denounced by the Soviet press as a mad warmonger, a fact which caused him some amusement in view of the way American newspapers treated him as a raving Red – but he was also treated with some suspicion by his friends on the English Left. Russell proposed that America should lead a confederation which monopolized nuclear weapons and the right to manufacture them, individual nations abandoning that right and reducing their non-nuclear armaments.[12] Once founded, it would have no trouble surviving, for it would possess overwhelming nuclear superiority over any nation tempted to go its own way. Russell accepted that Russia might well refuse to join on any terms; what was to be done about an intransigent Soviet Union? Russell's answers varied in brevity and clarity, but the essence was that the USA should seek a *casus belli* which would allow it to launch a war to end war. 'A *casus belli* should not be difficult to find. Either Russia's voluntary adherence or its defeat in war would render the Confederation invincible, since any war that did occur would be quickly ended by a few atomic bombs.' This was not quite to embrace pre-emptive nuclear war, but it came close. Later he sometimes expressed regret at having advocated such a policy, but by no means always, and even at the height of his campaign for British unilateral disarmament he was willing to defend his old views as appropriate for their time.[13]

Russell was not a pacifist, because he was a consequentialist. Even the horrors of nuclear war could in principle be outweighed by a good enough outcome. War was almost invariably bad in fact because it set civilization back, aroused the most obscene human passions and was inherently uncontrollable. Most wars were aimed at futile goals such as national glory or the conquest of useless territory. But absolute pacifism was not warranted. 'I have repeated *ad nauseam* that I am not a pacifist, that I believe that some wars, a very few, are justified, even necessary.' The Second World War was a good war; it would have been better had Hitler been stopped by other means, but Nazi domination would have been vastly worse than the war. Russell observed in October 1945, 'I should, for my part, prefer all the chaos and destruction of a war conducted by means of the atomic bomb to the universal domination of a government having the evil characteristics of the Nazis.'[14] Was a one-sided nuclear war with Russia a reasonable way of achieving a world without national nuclear armaments? Russell had no doubt that it was. Non-consequentialists might think it was not. There are many good ends we must not achieve by illicit means: the police must not get a murderer to confess by threatening to kill his wife and children, governments must not keep rents down by murdering the occasional landlord, and so on. By analogy, it would be illicit to bomb the Soviet Union into non-nuclear virtue. 'Just-war' doctrines which many people, non-Catholic as well as Catholic, find intuitively attractive would condemn it as the murder of innocent Soviet citizens for an uncertain future good. Russell never took such views seriously. Indeed, he was chronically incapable of believing that anyone could. Yet it is not hard to see their appeal. Even if it were true that a pre-emptive war against the Soviet Union would have made the world safer in 1986, most of us would think that it would have been iniquitous to murder large numbers of 1946 Russians to achieve it. *Our* survival is *our* business. There is a large moral gap between thinking that our forebears have left us a dangerous world to cope with and thinking that it would have been quite all right for them to massacre several million people to make life easier for us.

To all this Russell was deaf; nor were his opponents particularly acute in making the point. When critics complained of the inconsistency between his earlier advocacy of American aggressiveness towards Russia and his later defence of an extremely conciliatory policy, they missed the target. He replied, reasonably enough, that only idiots would advocate the same policies in changed conditions.[15] Once Russia had nuclear weapons it was impossible to bully the Soviets into disarmament. On his own terms, Russell was right; altered circumstances are decisive. His critics were prone to believe that they had scored a decisive blow by pointing out that by the early 1950s he no longer held the views he had held in 1945–8; they failed to point out that the earlier policy was intolerable in its own right. Few remarked on the curiously detached way in which Russell discussed a policy which by his own estimate would involve the deaths of up to half a billion people.[16]

Nor did they point out that Russell's advocacy of an aggressive American policy had varied in tone but never in content. The content always included the probability of a war. The tone varied according to whether Russell thought it would be a long war or a short one. It became less optimistic. Initially he thought the war would last a few weeks, reducing Moscow and Leningrad to rubble and bringing the Soviet Union to heel. A look at the map and at the capabilities of American bombers might have made him less sanguine; second thoughts about the bombing campaign against cities like Hamburg might have done the same. As time passed the scenario changed: bombers could not stop the Red Army before it reached the Channel. To win the war, America would have to bomb Europe to bits. Five hundred million dead was a plausible casualty figure and European civilization would be set back by five centuries (by what standards, he did not say); none the less, the war was worth fighting because it would establish world government and save European values.[17] It is an open question whether the claim makes sense, let alone whether it is morally acceptable. We often speculate in an idle way whether the Black Death was an utter disaster or whether it did some good, too; and we ask similar questions of man-made catastrophes such as the Thirty Years War; but Russell's arithmetic was not meant as idle speculation. He thought it the proper basis of foreign and military policy. One may doubt that it is. To claim that 'European values' will be preserved by killing half a billion people and setting civilization back half a millennium is somehow absurd. It is like a surgeon offering us an operation in which our vital organs are removed as a prophylactic and telling us it would be a fair price for survival – 'Survival as what?' we might well ask.

Russell's later reaction to all this was also odd. Though he had published his views prominently, he claimed that he had lost interest in them once he had changed his mind: as he later wrote, '... at the time I gave the advice I gave it so casually without any real hope that it would be followed, that I soon forgot I had given it'. Moreover, he seemed to think, even when he published his *Autobiography*, that he had held these views only during 1948 – which is quite false. More than once he denied that he had ever advocated the policy of leaning hard on the Soviet Union at all – then admitted when shown the evidence that it had looked like a good idea at the time and he had simply forgotten doing it.[18] Whether this was old age catching him out, it is hard to say; if it was a deliberate attempt to deceive, it was uncharacteristically cowardly, and inept too, when the printed record was all too easily accessible. It is hard to believe in a lapse of memory, however; he wrote several defences of his position, not just one, and they were spread over three years, not confined to one occasion. He did not write as if he was suggesting something 'off the cuff'.

Two things about those early post-war years stand out. The first is the ferocity of his hatred of the Soviet Union; he thought no policy too barbarous if Russia was its target. The basis of Russell's hostility to the Soviet Union was very much what it had been twenty-five years earlier when he had written *The Practice and Theory of Bolshevism*, the main change being that he concluded from the Yalta agreement that Stalin had the same territorial ambitions as the tsarist regime a century earlier, and that he was appalled by the behaviour of Soviet troops. This comes out particularly clearly in the article in *Cavalcade* in which he spelled out his policy of creative blackmail for the sake of world government. If world government proved unattainable, the second best was an alliance of western powers under the American nuclear umbrella – in essence, NATO.[19] Russell thought that it was only American nuclear superiority that stopped Stalin pressing on into western Europe and installing universal totalitarianism. Russell's views were not ill-founded. With hindsight, one can see that the Greek Civil War, Tito's escape from Russian hegemony, and the tightening of the Soviet grip on the rest of eastern Europe were episodes in the establishment of the post-war balance of power in Europe. Between 1945 and 1953 they looked like evidence of a settled Soviet ambition for universal political and military domination. For all that, Russell's anti-Russian stance had nothing in common with the hysterical anti-communism of McCarthyite America; it was an old-fashioned liberal hostility to Russian despotism that had led him to oppose the Triple Entente before the First World War and Stalin now.

The other notable feature of Russell's views was his disbelief in sharing nuclear secrets with the Soviet Union as a second best to world govern-ment. Others at the time thought that, by sharing nuclear secrets with the Soviets, the USA would calm their anxieties concerning American intentions and allow them to pursue a more relaxed foreign policy. In 1945, Russell was cautious, if not positively hostile. Giving Russia the recipe for an atomic weapon without a *quid pro quo* would not appease Soviet hostility and would amount to arming the enemy. 'I am not one of those who favour the unconditional and immediate revelation to Russia of the exact processes by which the bomb is manufactured,' he told the House of Lords, 'I think it is right that conditions should be attached to that revelation, but I make the proviso that the conditions must be solely those which will facilitate international cooperation; they must have no national object of any kind.' In 1946, he wrote in defence of the Baruch Plan, which envisaged 'internationalizing' nuclear know-how by creating an international atomic commission which could inspect and supervise the dismantling of atomic weapon piles anywhere in the world. Even then, however, Russell was less interested in the plan itself (which many writers have since criticized as a plan to secure American control of nuclear weapons development by another name) than in the thought that its rejection by the Soviet Union would be evidence of aggressive intent, and the *casus belli* visualized by his policy of creative blackmail.[20] He later claimed that he had advocated an aggressive policy towards the Soviet Union only after the Baruch Plan had been turned down; but his memory again played him false. He had advocated an aggressive policy from the beginning. In his own terms, he need not have apologized. It was at any rate entirely in line with ideas he had held since the 1920s when he had first advocated a *pax Americana*; and, like almost everyone else who had lived through the 1930s and the war, he was affected by the desire not to repeat the errors of the 1930s and appease an unappeasable dictator.

Russell's hostility to Russia made him no less critical of the United States. He made two very successful lecture tours to the USA in 1950 and 1951, interest in his ideas having been aroused by his Nobel Prize. A wild success with his immediate audiences was matched by hostility in the world outside the lecture theatres and university campuses where he spoke. Russell thought, as educated Englishmen are prone to, that Americans suffered from snobbery about money, unwarranted anxiety about sex, and uncontrollable hysteria about socialism and communism; they were gullible, self-righteous and astonishingly ignorant about almost all of America and absolutely all of the rest of the world. Unlike most educated Englishmen, who have no opportunity to ventilate such thoughts, or who keep tactfully quiet if they do, Russell secured his bread and butter – or, rather, secured some jam to put on his bread and butter – by publishing his opinions in any paper or magazine that would take them.[21]

Reactions varied from one issue to another. Liberal East Coast readers enjoyed the splutterings of southern and mid-western fundamentalists when Russell explained why he was not a Christian; but they became tight-lipped when Russell mocked American anti-communism. Russell's views were quite old-fashioned, though he expressed them in inimitably offensive prose. In foreign affairs, great powers should settle non-vital matters as coolly as possible; the distinction between vital and non-vital matters ought to be clear-cut and universally understood and ought to be drawn in a defensive frame of mind; the conduct of international relations ought to be in the hands of professionals who could draw on appropriate expertise. America broke all the rules. The State Department yielded to congressional hysteria and sacked its China experts when they were most needed, and so tied America to Chiang Kai-shek.[22] In the Korean War, the American-led UN forces could and should have held the thirty-eighth parallel and pursued a waiting policy. General MacArthur's pursuit of the North Korean army up to the Chinese border produced the predictable result – Chinese troops and a string of disasters. Russell stood by old-fashioned *Realpolitik*. It was not America's business to save the Russians and the Chinese from communism; the Russians and Chinese had no doubt been ill-advised to install communist governments, but it was up to them to save themselves. It was America's business to draw a clear line beyond which incursions would be resisted – and that was that.

If American foreign policy was inept, American society was becoming increasingly repulsive. Fear of communism threatened colleges and schools as staff were forced to swear loyalty oaths, syllabuses were rewritten to make all forms of socialism seem wicked, and the timidity of the courts meant that teachers whose constitutional rights were threatened stood little chance of resistance.[23] Russell bombarded newspapers and magazines with denunciations of this 'reign of terror'; as McCarthyism grew more virulent, so he grew angrier. The trial and execution of Julius and Ethel

Rosenberg in 1951 (who may well have been guilty of spying for the Soviet Union, but who did not get an unprejudiced trial and, in less hysterical times, would not have faced treason charges and the death penalty in the first place) made less impact at the time than later; but they confirmed his ill opinion of American justice.[24]

This made little difference to Russell's views on nuclear policy, though it poisoned his opinion of American governments. It was Russia's success in detonating its own atomic bomb in 1949 which changed Russell's views on nuclear policy. It would no longer do to pursue a bold policy, since mutual destruction was the likely outcome. He did not argue for a more pacific foreign policy straight away, and in fact never suggested American renunciation of nuclear weapons; the best American response to Russian nuclear development was further development of its own weapons. Moreover, he initially had no doubt that Britain had to stick with the American alliance, even though he did not wish Britain to become an independent nuclear power – or perhaps even because he did not wish Britain to become an independently armed nuclear power. For all the American silliness about socialism and the ignorance of most Americans about western Europe, America was a broadly liberal, democratic, individualist society of the same cultural stamp.[25] Nor did Russell look on British neutrality as a plausible foreign policy option until much later in the 1950s.

Russell's views changed piecemeal as he came to terms with the full implications of a war fought with hydrogen weapons, and as scientists became increasingly fearful of the effects of testing nuclear weapons in the atmosphere. He later said that although his general perspective on war had not changed – he was still a consequentialist and a rationalist, still not an absolute pacifist – something had altered.[26] The emotional colouring of his ideas had been heightened when he contemplated the full effects of thermonuclear (hydrogen, or fusion) weapons. The prospect of genetic damage reaching into the distant future appalled him, as did the thought that the holocaust might be triggered off by mechanical malfunction, human error or lunacy in high places. Hardly a month went by during the middle and later 1950s without some tale of a near-miss: radar operators were frequently said to have mistaken a flight of geese for incoming missiles, and the story of the rising moon being mistaken for a missile attack was endlessly retold. Russell's imagination was stimulated by all this in a way that even his contemplation of the horrors of bombing in *Which Way to Peace?* had not quite matched.[27] As a mathematician, he was depressed by reflecting that in the long run it was certain that a nuclear war would occur by accident or design; in any week or month, the odds were not very alarming; over the long run it was a racing certainty. He was also struck by a sort of metaphysical horror at the prospect of the total destruction of life on earth. A recent bestselling book suggests[28] that a peculiar horror which many of us feel in the face of nuclear war is the sense that destroying all life and wrecking the entire planet on which everything lives is simply mad. We cannot contemplate it without feeling that our hold on reality is slipping. Russell had always taken refuge in his passion for the sea and the mountains whenever human relationships became unbearable; their detachment consoled him for personal and political disorder. When satellites were invented, he raged against the prospect of embroiling the heavens in our squalid terrestrial squabbles. 'In reading of the plans of militarists, I try very hard to divest myself for the time being of the emotions of horror and disgust. But when I read of the plans to defile the heavens by the petty squabbles of the animated lumps that disgrace a certain planet, I cannot but feel that the men who make these plans are guilty of a certain impiety.'

All the same, he always argued that America was right to develop the hydrogen bomb. Russell was sceptical of the value of any nation promising to renounce nuclear weapons, unless the promise could be made to stick by an external sanction. If war broke out, powers with the necessary technology would at once build and use the hydrogen bomb. It was not very sensible of him to denounce the half-loaf of abstention and insist so strenuously on the whole loaf of world government and enforceable disarmament, even though there was something to his claim that only pressures comparable to those which drove nations into nuclear armaments were enough to drive them out again. By 1958 he was less insistent on the whole loaf of world government and was advocating verifiable nuclear disarmament, along with most people in the peace movement. His belief that only world government and overwhelming military power would achieve anything was overtaken by events; technical progress allowed nuclear tests to be detected without on-site inspection, and a ban on atmospheric testing was agreed in 1963. Russell rightly thought that the partial test-ban treaty was a very small advance, and his belief that only pressures as strong as those which drove nations into arming themselves could drive them to disarm had much to be said for it. The fear of accidental war, and repugnance at the thought of poisoning our children, have been powerful forces, but not powerful enough to secure disarmament as opposed to greater caution in armament.[29]

All this was consistent with his belief that nuclear deterrence was a perfectly rational and morally acceptable way to conduct foreign relations.

Russell defended America's decision to develop the hydrogen bomb primarily because Russia would certainly try to develop it anyway,[30] and a world in which the Soviet Union had the hydrogen bomb and America did not would be horribly unstable. The point of maximum danger in nuclear strategy is when each side possesses effective first-strike capacity, but inadequate second-strike capacity – that is, in plain language, when each side might gain a victory if it initiated a nuclear attack, but cannot be sure that enough of its weapons would survive an attack on itself to allow it to launch a devastating reprisal. Under these conditions, both sides have an incentive to strike first. What gave Russell nightmares was the thought that a first strike would be less than wholly effective, so ensuring that both sides perished. A Soviet – or an American – lead in the arms race would be dangerous because the lagging side might think that the only way to prevent its rival getting far enough ahead to attack with impunity would be to strike first and cripple its efforts. The full hideousness of such unstable situations lies in the fact that since each side can make the same calculations, both sides know the temptations under which its rival operates and therefore have even more reason to strike first.[31] Until the beginnings of 'de-Stalinization' moreover, Russell continued to think that the Soviet Union was bent on world conquest, from which only the threat of nuclear catastrophe would deter her. Russell's view was wholly plausible, therefore. Mutual deterrence was intrinsically repulsive, but would work so long as both sides were cautious and avoided provocative or ill-thought-out action, and were conscious that a false move meant the end of the world.

This simple view underlay most of Russell's contributions to the nuclear debate of the 1950s. He denounced American and Soviet brinkmanship, appealed for the cessation of weapons testing and encouraged the British to renounce nuclear weapons and support a nuclear-free Europe. There was much to be said for this. It is self-evident that brinkmanship puts up the risk of accidental conflagration; testing weapons in the atmosphere was gratuitous environmental poisoning once the superpowers possessed the means to survive and retaliate for a first strike against themselves; British disarmament made sense as part of a campaign to avoid the 'balkanization' of weapons. Just as the great powers had been pulled into the First World War by the hostilities of the small Balkan countries, Russell feared that America and Russia might be pulled into a nuclear war by the Arab–Israeli conflict, or by the hostilities of India and Pakistan or a local flare-up in Europe; limiting possession of nuclear weapons to the superpowers would reduce such dangers, and since Britain was then the only other nation with nuclear capability, there was a chance that renunciation by Britain might be the start of a non-nuclear club.

Between 1954 and 1964 Russell wrote, broadcast, debated and organized endlessly, both among top scientists through the 'Pugwash' conferences and in the hope of reaching a mass audience through the Campaign for Nuclear Disarmament, the Committee of 100, and finally through the Bertrand Russell Peace Foundation. The essays and lectures of those years (his 'books' are no more than essays pulled together) are not intellectually elaborate; at their best they are cool, careful and persuasive. At their worst they are shrill and angry in tone, and hasty in argument. In this, they are very like the hastier and angrier productions of 1914 and 1915. The Russell of 1914 who accused the bishops of supporting the war because they hoped for large dividends on their armaments shares was very like Russell in 1961 accusing Macmillan of being 'much more wicked than Hitler'. In neither case ought we to take him too literally, nor ignore the small grain of truth embedded in the wild exaggeration. It is true that immersion in money-making dulls our moral sensibilities, and bishops need to remember that as much as anyone; and there are awkward questions to be asked about the ethics of a defence policy based on threatening to incinerate millions of innocent women and children. A government which launched atomic war would kill more innocent victims than Hitler ever killed, which is not a thought to be shrugged off lightly. Traditional just-war doctrines would condemn it as murder on a vast scale, and Russell was not alone in thinking that threatening to commit mass murder is morally dubious.[32] Whether he was the man to say it is another question; unlike theorists of the just war, he did not think that it was wicked to threaten what it would be wicked to do, and his own advocacy of an aggressive policy towards Russia in 1945–9 made him an unconvincing defender of the sanctity of innocent life. But in 1914 he had been an unconvincing superintendent of the moral standards of bishops.

The other similarity between 1914 and 1960 was the violent changes of mood he experienced when he contemplated the vagaries of human nature, and the extreme prognoses he offered for the future. As in 1914, he asked himself whether mankind was hopelessly addicted to violence and self-destruction. Save when feeling particularly depressed, he still answered, No. The world might become paradise or hell according to human choice, and it was up to individuals to decide.[33] It was noticeable that he hardly considered the possibility that things might go on in much the same way, a good deal sub-paradisaical, but a good deal super-infernal, with mankind very much disliking the fact of existence under the nuclear umbrella but learning how to minimize its risks and anxieties and reduce the dangers of catastrophe. One source of heightened gloom was his conviction that states with thermonuclear weapons facing other states in a fixed condition of mutual distrust would want ever more powerful weapons as an end in itself. He sometimes wrote of the invention of the hydrogen bomb as if it had been fuelled by a pure urge for destruction, rather than by the political considerations he had urged at the time. 'The A-bomb when it was new had caused a shudder of horror, and had even stimulated suggestions for international control of atomic energy. But people soon got used to it and came to realize that the harm which it could do was not enough to satisfy mutual ferocity.' The atomic bomb was already adequate to destroy urban populations and wipe our whole cities; but rural populations and peasant societies were not vulnerable to it. So the urge for wholesale annihilation had to be appeased by the H-bomb which would poison with fall-out those whom it did not instantly destroy by heat and blast.[34] Russell's tendency to libel human psychology in this way went oddly with his habit of depicting most of mankind as the long-suffering victims of wicked governments, mad generals and wild ideologues. It co-existed even more awkwardly with an ability to explain in entirely persuasive terms why nuclear scientists had begun by favouring the development of the atomic bomb (a rational fear that Hitler would get it first and would use it without hesitation) and why so many had now turned against it (an equally rational fear that human error would lead to universal self-destruction). The most eminent of the scientists Russell cited was Einstein, the most controversial Robert Oppenheimer, who had led the Manhattan Project to success and had been denounced as a security risk when he turned against the development of the H-bomb. Since his left-wing inclinations had been known since the 1930s, his disgrace was evidently a put-up job.

Russell's account of this in *Has Man a Future?* is an admirably calm review of the various letters, manifestos and meetings that led up to the creation of the Pugwash Conference in 1957 – and the only point at which his calm slips is when he contrasts the rationality of the scientists who managed (though only just) to set aside their political attachments and think of the welfare of the whole human race with the idiocies of Pugwash's critics in the US Congress.[35] Russell's irritation was more than justified. The Pugwash movement was one of the rare occasions when scientists from behind the Iron Curtain were readily able to discuss arms and disarmament with colleagues from the West; but the Senate Internal Security Committee investigating Pugwash in 1960 took that as evidence only that the American scientists present had been hoodwinked or, perhaps, were plotting treason. Twenty-five years on, it is hard to remember that the death of Joseph McCarthy in 1957 had by no means eliminated the obscene phenomenon of McCarthyism from American politics. When Richard Nixon and John F. Kennedy fought for the presidency in 1960, Kennedy's chief charge against Nixon was that he was vice-president in an administration which was (improbably) soft on communism and had allowed the Russians to take the lead in the production of intercontinental ballistic missiles – they hadn't, in fact, even if they had got into space first with the launch of *Sputnik* on 4 October 1957. Similarly, John Foster Dulles, the chief architect of foreign policy under Eisenhower, more than once declared that he was confident of America's ability to win a nuclear war; what he doubted was the nation's ability to win the Cold War. In such an atmosphere, Russell had some grounds for believing that American politics were dominated by madmen.

So by the late 1950s, Russell's position was that the primary duty of a great power such as the United States was to do everything possible to keep down the temperature of international politics. For the first time, he held a genuinely 'Voltairean' position, urging everyone to forgo the pleasures of ideological conflict and moral denunciation for the sake of peace. No moral ideal was worth the destruction of civilization. Russell's American critics concluded that he had become an enthusiast for the Soviet Union and had gone soft on communism in his old age. This was quite untrue. He had once more become an unrespectable radical, but he was as hostile to the Soviet Union as ever, and deeply sceptical about communists in the British peace movement. Even when enraged by American obduracy over the terms of a nuclear test-ban treaty, he still insisted that the Soviet Union was primarily to blame for the failure of attempts to ban atmospheric tests – paranoia was built into every Soviet institution and every Russian ruler, and Russian objections to on-site inspection showed as much. He held much the same anti-patriotic views which had so enraged everyone in 1914–15; his stupider critics thought he was pro-German then, and they thought he was pro-Russian now. That was wrong. What he believed was that since the West was not encumbered by the follies of the Soviet system, it could afford to be accommodating in a way the Soviet Union could not – just as the First World War could have been avoided by British concessions which Imperial Germany could not have been expected to make. This was not to side with Russia, merely to recognize Soviet inability to behave sensibly. It raised a question he never quite answered: did not this policy *encourage* Russia to behave badly, in the knowledge that this would induce the West to behave more and more cautiously?[36]

Domestically, Russell knew that the British peace movement contained fellow-travellers. His attitude to them was purely calculating; if their presence threatened the effectiveness of the peace movement or the Campaign for Nuclear Disarmament, then they must be got rid of. The communist Lady Tyrrell wrote inquiring whether it was true that he did not want communists in CND and got a very sharp little note to say she should choose between working for peace and working for Russia; and when he discovered that the World Peace Council was using his name as a respectable cover, he was quick to stop it.[37] Even when CND was at its largest and most welcoming, Russell did not object to its strikingly undemocratic constitution – its executive council was self-appointed and irremovable by the organization's supporters – a feature which appears to have been intended to reduce the risk of a communist takeover. Russell's reactions to changes in the Soviet Union during the 1950s were like most liberals': he welcomed the thaw which set in after the death of Stalin and hoped for rapid liberalization. For a while he thought it was happening, with Soviet scientists joining the Pugwash conferences and Khrushchev himself encouraging the publication of previously illicit works such as the novels of Solzhenitsyn. Still he did not overlook the continued bloody-mindedness of Soviet foreign policy; he was appalled by the invasion of Hungary in 1956 (and one of his last political gestures was to write a savage denunciation of the invasion of Czechoslovakia in 1968); he thought that the belief in the inevitable triumph of communism, which Khrushchev affirmed in the exchange of letters between Russell, Khrushchev and Dulles published in the *New Statesman* in the autumn of 1957, was quite mad; and his own advocacy of a nuclear-free zone in central Europe was coupled with an insistence that Hungary, Poland, Czechoslovakia and the other 'satellite' states must be free to choose their own form of government.[38]

The argumentative record from 1954, when he made his famous broadcast on 'Man's Peril', to the end of 1960 when he resigned the presidency of CND and embarked on a campaign of direct action and civil disobedience with the Committee of 100, is all of a piece.[39] The only ultimate solution was world government backed by a monopoly of force, implementing a system of legal agreements like those which keep the peace domestically. This ultimate solution would be a long-term prospect and its achievement a very long-drawn-out business. Still, it is the only wholly acceptable solution and we should not rest content with anything less. In the meantime, any government which does not bend all its efforts to securing a reduction of tension is guilty of reckless unconcern for the lives and happiness of mankind. As technology advances, the risks become greater and so does the wickedness of government inaction. The best thing the British government could do under these circumstances was to renounce nuclear weapons and adopt a neutralist foreign policy. This view, advanced from about 1956 onwards, was a real change of heart after Russell's earlier enthusiasm for NATO or an equivalent; Russell did not pause at the position of those unilateralists who hoped to leave nuclear weapons in the hands of the USA and the USSR only, but still envisaged a non-nuclear and conventional role for the other NATO powers. Russell's defence of NATO belonged to the years when he was also advocating a forward policy of pressure on Russia. Now that he was only concerned not to stir up tension, he believed a non-nuclear Britain would do more good as an influential neutral power than as a not very influential non-nuclear member of NATO. He also envisaged neutrality as an element in the creation of a nuclear-free Europe such as was envisaged in the Rapacki Plan, the Polish proposal for dismantling the Warsaw Pact and NATO. Searching for a vehicle for these views, Russell helped to create the Campaign for Nuclear Disarmament.

Russell's reflective thoughts on nuclear disarmament belong to what has usefully been labelled the 'pacificist' strain in defence thinking; that is, to the strand of thought which accepts that war may be justified from time to time, but which holds that these occasions are infrequent, and that the best policy for governments to pursue is a cautious and unaggressive one. Once nuclear weapons exist, caution becomes more imperative than ever. This thought readily leads to the view that for any nation other than the superpowers to possess nuclear weapons adds needlessly to the danger of accidental war, without doing anything for the security of their possessor. There are further considerations which press in the direction of unilateralism for a country the size of Britain which is not already locked into a situation like that of the USA and the Soviet Union where a sudden move by either side is perilous, and which does not have the excuse of a country such as Israel which faces enemies who regard themselves as in a state of permanent if not always active war. British dependence on American weapons put Britain at the mercy of American foreign policy; for anyone with Russell's grim view of Eisenhower and Dulles, that was unbearable. Far from being safe under the American nuclear umbrella, Britain had become an 'unsinkable aircraft carrier' and therefore a prime target for a Soviet strike. To get out of that situation, nothing would do but unilateral disarmament and neutrality. Russell may also have felt that the permanent confrontation between Russia and the West on the German frontier and in Berlin was so dangerous that it had to be dismantled at all costs. Russell was by no means the only distinguished intellect heading in the same direction; George Kennan, the chief architect of the American policy of containment immediately after the war, had by 1957 turned about and contemplated the dismantling of the two frozen alliances. He may well have had more impact than anyone on Russell's thinking and on the formation of CND.

Was Russell right to argue for unilateralism? It is impossible to say with certainty. It is obviously possible that one effect of British nuclear disarmament would be to make Britain more vulnerable to blackmail by powers with nuclear weapons, notably the Soviet Union, and it is largely on this argument that all British governments have rested their rejection of unilateral nuclear disarmament since 1958. Again, opponents of unilateralism often argue that it would be right to get rid of nuclear weapons but wrong to do so without exacting some reciprocal concessions from other countries, notably the Soviet Union. This was the thought which led Aneurin Bevan to change his mind about Britain's nuclear status; he wanted not to 'go naked into the negotiating chamber'.

To rebut such arguments is not the work of a moment, nor even of a shelf of books on nuclear strategy. A solid argument for Russell's neutralism was that a Britain which had renounced its imperial pretensions and was intent on avoiding external entanglements would not excite the suspicion of the Soviet Union and would not be vulnerable to blackmail. Russell himself was badly placed to argue this, since he would have had to change his mind about the aggressive intentions of the Soviet Union even more drastically than he did. He would also have had to take a stand on how Britain could square neutrality with a more 'European' economic and foreign policy. Unilateralist politics always wavered between an isolationist desire to cut Britain off from global conflicts and a moralizing ambition to lead the rest of western Europe into non-nuclear virtue. Russell was no more decisive than his followers. The best case for Russell is the simplest. The details of unilateralism would doubtless be as complicated as the details of any other defence policy, but the campaign for unilateral disarmament had a simple message – what one might paraphrase as 'we want out'. By insisting that the only policy prudence and morality dictated was unilateral withdrawal from the nuclear arms race and nuclear-armed alliances, Russell was at least briefly bound to be arguing the right case – if withdrawal was practicable, it was desirable; and if it was not, a pressure group firmly committed to it would restrain governments from adventurism and force them to scrutinize every step of the nuclear path. It was a view which led many sceptics – I was one – into the ranks of CND, and it may well have animated Russell for some of the time. In so far as the world is now marginally less alarming than in 1958, he deserves some share of the credit. He did not have the impact on public opinion that he did without assistance; in the first instance it was the Campaign for Nuclear Disarmament which provided it.

Russell's career in CND was quite brief and often stormy. CND itself emerged in a haphazard way from several different strands of anti-nuclear thinking. One was the Direct Action Committee under Michael Randle's leadership; this was a pacifist and anarchist movement which Russell did not intellectually agree with, but to which he contributed a few pounds a year, even after he had become President of CND. It was committed to demonstrative protest and civil disobedience. Another strand was Christian pacifist, or Christian 'pacificist'. Canon Collins was the chairman of Christian Action; he had not been able to persuade Christian Action to back a campaign against British nuclear weapons, but he brought a distinctively Christian contribution to CND. A third element was the National Council for the Abolition of Nuclear Weapons Tests, which had begun life as a Hampstead committee with which Russell had had several exchanges of letters over the previous years. CND was brought into being by a combination of events of which the testing of the British H-bomb in 1957 was probably the most important. The *Autobiography* cites George Kennan's Reith Lectures as an important stimulus, but a Labour Party conference which came very close to renouncing NATO and nuclear weapons, and J. B. Priestley's *New Statesman* article of 2 November 1957 advocating immediate unilateral disarmament, had done much to stir up opinion. Kingsley Martin's recollections of the creation of CND suggest that it was founded to appease the *New Statesman* readers who wrote in to demand that something should be done to follow up Priestley's article. Although he was not a prime mover in its creation, Russell's *New Statesman* correspondence with John Foster Dulles and Nikita Khrushchev in the autumn of 1957 had brought him together with Kingsley Martin, J. B. Priestley and others. Over Christmas 1957 they brought CND into existence, with Russell as President and Collins as Chairman; its public existence was confirmed by a rally in Central Hall, Westminster, in February 1958, and by the first of the Aldermaston marches at Easter. (This one started in London and advanced on the Atomic Weapons Research Establishment at Aldermaston; its successors took the opposite route.) The Aldermaston marches were an idea lifted from the Direct Action movement; they were hugely successful, and enjoyable, occasions.

Russell had a more realistic view of the movement's real influence over the next two years than did the cheerful mob of young people who walked down the Great West Road, slept in school halls over the Easter weekend, and rallied in Trafalgar Square to cheer Russell, Michael Foot, Canon Collins and J. B. Priestley. The campaign's impact on Labour and Conservative politicians was almost negligible; the committed remained committed, to whichever side they belonged. By the time the Labour Party conference in the autumn of 1960 was momentarily converted to unilateralism – or, more exactly, by the time the leadership of the Transport and General Workers' Union had decided to put its block vote behind unilateralism – Russell had despaired of CND. Labour was unlikely to return to power for many years, and the Conservatives were no more likely to espouse neutrality than they had been to vote against going to war in August 1914. In the summer of 1960 Russell and the Reverend Michael Scott laid plans for what became the Committee of 100. The idea was simple, though it is unclear whether it had been floated in discussion in Direct Action for some years already, or whether it was a genuine inspiration of Ralph Schoenman. One hundred people should sign a statement declaring their willingness to break the law in protest against the British government's possession of nuclear weapons.[40] The offences anyone would commit would be minor ones: obstruction, or trespass on military bases. The government would be embarrassed at having to jail or fine respectable people, and the hope was that each person lost to the original hundred by imprisonment would be replaced by another, so stretching the forces of law and order as well as embarrassing them. Russell's correspondence with the original signatories of the manifesto of the Committee of 100 is mildly amusing; he had to spend a good deal of effort reassuring some of his friends that they did not *have* to break the law and persuading others that, if they did, it would be possible to ensure that the time they spent under arrest would not interfere with their careers.

Russell wished to resign the presidency of CND in September 1960; he also wished to speak in favour of direct action at the Trafalgar Square demonstration on 24 September, but he was persuaded that to do so would be disastrous for the defenders of unilateralism at the forthcoming Labour Party conference. Russell's account of all this in his *Autobiography* glosses over a good deal of muddle and acrimony. The backers of the Committee of 100 contrived to make themselves look silly by sending the letter announcing their impending campaign to 'someone with a name similar to the intended recipient but with a different address, and, unhappily, entirely different views'. This was the conservative journalist and author John Connell (of the *Evening Standard*) who gave the game away to the paper. In spite of everything, a truce was patched up with Canon Collins until the Labour Party conference was over. Then Russell resigned, on bad terms with those he left, and creating a great deal of doubt and confusion among the ordinary members of CND – the majority of whom, however, supported him rather than Canon Collins, whose autocratic outlook on the organization of CND had always riled many of the rank and file. Dissident CND marchers were heard to chant, 'Fire the Canon and drop the Bomb,' as they marched. It has puzzled many people that Russell went down the path of civil disobedience; he was no Gandhian pacifist and *satyagraha* did not come naturally to him. The best explanation is the one he always gave in interviews and in reply to letters from disheartened members of CND who felt that he had deserted them. Appealing to the Corn Law League and the suffragettes as examples of successful 'fanatics' who had not stopped at defying the law, he argued that at a time when newspapers and the mass media were unable to take arguments seriously, dramatic gestures would grab maximum publicity.

Russell's position on civil disobedience was straightforward. He never thought we were obliged to obey governments which were acting stupidly or immorally. Disobedience as such did not pose moral problems; none the less, he had been cautious about issuing a general licence to follow the dictates of conscience, since some people's consciences were quite misguided. He argued along utilitarian lines; for the Committee of 100 it was not a question (as it later was for American soldiers in Vietnam) of a conscientious refusal to obey orders. The question was one of political tactics only. In the 1900s he had taken a squarely tactical view of the suffragettes; when they stirred up public opinion to appreciate their cause, they were justified; when they maddened the public they were foolish. The same was true in the 1960s. Ecstatic supporters such as Ralph Schoenman had wild visions of hundreds of thousands of protesters all joining in mass civil disobedience. Russell knew this was quite mad; there was no chance of assembling a people's army overnight with no organization – and his disciples soon discovered that they could not hire enough buses to transport a couple of hundred protesters to the airbases they hoped to picket, let alone master the logistics of moving an army.[41]

The respectable who complained that he was allowing himself to be used by the fanatical received a sharper brush-off. Past fanaticisms in a good cause had been justified by success; so would this be if it was successful. All he asked was good publicity and maximum embarrassment for the government. He had no enthusiasm for Gandhian campaigns of *passive* resistance such as motivated one wing of Direct Action; he would have accepted armed insurrection as a way of achieving disarmament if there had been any hope of such a thing succeeding. But he knew that the idea of a popular uprising against warfare – which featured in Schoenman's plans – was nonsense. The only question was whether demonstrations, sit-downs, and the activities of 'Spies for Peace' (who discovered where the government's wartime communications centres were located and published the information in defiance of the Official Secrets Act) would hasten the arrival of disarmament, neutrality, and an end to testing.

Although Russell himself secured as much publicity as anybody by being charged with incitement after a rally to mark Hiroshima Day in 1961, the campaign did not work. The government was not irredeemably stupid, and although the Committee of 100 gained support whenever the police were ill-tempered and heavy-handed in dragging protesters out of Trafalgar Square and elsewhere, the government's efficient use of the Official Secrets Act to send the most determined Spies for Peace to jail for eighteen months was a decided dampener – such sentences were too long to be a mere irritant to the victims, but not so long as to cause a public outcry.[42] Many of its members made themselves look foolish at the time of the Cuban missile crisis, too. Russell's own attention was being pulled away from British concerns. The signing of the partial test-ban treaty in 1963 persuaded him that governments had woken up to the perils of nuclear war, even if the Cuban missile crisis in October 1962 convinced him that in other respects they were still run by madmen. His attention was now turned outwards; and he embarked on his final career as what I. F. Stone has felicitously christened 'World Ombudsman'. In September 1963 he established the Bertrand Russell Peace Foundation and announced that he had resigned from the Committee of 100. The Foundation was largely run by Ralph Schoenman until he was swept up in the War Crimes Tribunal, and by a succession of other helpers of whom Christopher Farley was the most important. Until the accession of wealth which was generated in 1967 by the sale of Russell's papers to McMaster University and the publication of his *Autobiography*, it ran on a shoestring or, more accurately, an overdraft and whatever small sums Russell could raise for it. It spawned the Institute for Workers' Control, whose concerns were directly centred on industrial democracy, a juxtaposition which neatly reflected the concerns of the No-Conscription Fellowship half a century before; and it failed to spawn an Atlantic Foundation to study international relations.[43]

The main preoccupation of the Foundation and of Russell himself was the American involvement in Vietnam, but almost any piece of American misbehaviour, internal or external, came under attack. The assassination of President Kennedy in November 1963 and the subsequent commission of inquiry chaired by Chief Justice Earl Warren was one of many occasions when Russell and the Foundation joined in an internal fight, though the Foundation set up a 'British Who Killed Kennedy? Committee' to chase that hare. The Warren report was not thought by anyone to be wholly satisfactory; and its more energetic critics denounced it as a cover-up. Russell sided with the critics: the CIA had killed Kennedy because he had savaged them for their bungling of the Bay of Pigs invasion two years before.[44] A year later he joined in the great debate over increasing violence in the Black ghettoes. Twenty-five years before, he would have remembered de Tocqueville and thought the rioting a symptom of a revolution of rising expectations; now he claimed that the American government was genocidal, the police pretty much on a par with the camp guards at Auschwitz, and Black rioting a justified response to a campaign of extermination.[45] America received all this with rage and outrage; Russell was interfering where he had no knowledge and no business. Many English readers doubted whether Russell had read, much less written, what he now put his name to; it read like the rantings of the student Left, not like Russell's own immaculate prose. Russell's correspondence would have strengthened their doubts; writing to Jim Boggs, he argued in entirely persuasive terms that the idea of Black insurrection was a suicidal fantasy and that radical reformism was infinitely preferable to revolutionary zealotry. Even then, Russell's demands for the instantaneous restructuring of the American educational and economic systems to accommodate Black grievances were unpersuasive – *how* was any of this to be achieved in what he believed to be a racist state?

There was nothing novel about Russell making wild assertions about American wickedness – on his last visit to the United States in 1951 he had given the impression that he thought every tree in the southern states was hung about with the bodies of lynched Negroes and that any university teacher who defended racial equality would instantly be sacked. At the time the National Association for the Advancement of Coloured Peoples was steadily gaining ground in the courts, and three years later won the landmark decision in *Brown* vs *Board of Education of Topeka* which established that segregation was inherently unconstitutional. As always, Russell was not *entirely* wrong; the movement towards racial equality was marked by judicial evasiveness, rioting, police brutality, the murder of civil rights workers, the bombing of churches and the assassination of Black leaders – none of which Americans enjoyed being reminded of by an Englishman. But there was a change of intellectual style. Previously, Russell had held members of governments personally and individually responsible for the misdeeds perpetrated within their jurisdiction, the most striking instance of this being his indictment of Sir Edward Grey.[46] It was not particularly plausible to ascribe so much to the wickedness of individual politicians, but it was at least consistent with his markedly individualist approach to social and political analysis. Now he seemed to have acquired the habit prevalent among the 1960s radicals of blaming everything on 'the system'. He could now indict his opponents wholesale and retail, since the fact that President Johnson had not personally ordered the mass murder of Los Angeles Blacks was covered by the self-evident truth that 'the system' was racist and murderous and the President the system's servant.[47]

The sceptical Russell, who believed that men did both good and evil by accident and who frequently mastered the temptation to believe in conspiracy, seemed to have vanished entirely, leaving the Russell who saw conspiracy everywhere firmly in command. The sole cause of evil in the world was American imperialism. Whether it was internal American politics, the tangled politics of Greece, the Middle East or whatever else, the hand of the CIA and the dictates of American imperialism were surely there. At times he began to sound like the Ayatollah Khomeini denouncing the 'great Satan' – in itself a reason for wondering how much he wrote of all the articles he put his name to. After his death, Christopher Farley told a revealing story about Russell's attitude to every movement he allied himself with. Russell explained that he always felt an outsider; his companions would go on at length about the virtues of pacifism, or the glories of socialism, or the speed with which CND would convert the British people, and a small voice inside Russell's head would always say, 'I don't really believe all that.' Russell himself confirms this.[48]

We must approach Russell's increasing fear of America's impact on the world cautiously, then. The issue is more complicated still. Russell's hostility to American intervention in Vietnam had two very distinct aspects. The first was his belief that America had become increasingly aggressive and the Soviet Union more defensive and genuinely eager for a quiet existence and some movement towards disarmament; this view was sharpened by the Cuban missile crisis, which Russell saw as essentially caused by American aggression. The second was his belief in the right of Asiatic peoples to self-determination and a guarantee against intervention by colonial powers. The combination made Russell sound like a standard

1960s 'anti-imperialist', and at times led him to present the Vietcong as a band of saints whose patience had finally given out. It is, however, only that sentimentality which is particularly novel and disturbing; his hostility to British and American influence in Asia was genuine and of long standing.

Russell had loathed the British Empire since well before 1914. From the 1920s to the end of the war he had been a staunch defender of Indian independence; he had written angry articles on the Amritsar massacre, on the practice of what was euphemistically termed 'rigorous imprisonment', on the 1930s jailings of Gandhi and Nehru, and on the plethora of arbitrary decrees with which British rule was maintained. He had welcomed the speed with which independence was granted after the war. In all these years he had taken it for granted that one root of colonialism was economic – E. D. Morel, his friend and ally in the Union for Democratic Control, had, after all, made his reputation and earned Russell's admiration for the way he took on the Belgian crown and exposed the brutality of Leopold's exploitation of the Belgian Congo. But Russell was, if anything, more appalled by the tendency of colonial regimes to set up authoritarian police states in the colonies which brutalized national politics as well as the affairs of the colonies themselves.[49]

The only cure was independence; without independence the British would corrupt themselves by running a police state in India. He took it for granted that some Britons would oppose independence because they made money out of a dependent India, and many who had no economic interest would oppose independence because they took pleasure in the vicarious glamour of 'their' possessions. Nor did he apply such an analysis to India alone. After his long visit to China in 1921–2, he tried to persuade the British government to channel its share of the Boxer indemnity into Chinese education and away from narrowly selfish schemes; had Ramsay MacDonald's first government remained in power beyond 1924 Russell would have been a member of the Phillimore Committee which considered the disposal of the indemnity – as it was, the Tory government pushed him off the committee which then proceeded to behave as Russell feared it would.[50]

What Russell never put forward in the whole half-century was the doctrine he once mocked as the doctrine of 'the superior virtue of the oppressed'.[51] This he characterized as the obverse of the usual tendency to think well of ourselves and badly of others. The brutality of the oppressors was sufficient argument against their policies; there was no need to suppose that their victims were particularly attractive, individually or *en masse*, let alone that they had been ennobled by their sufferings. We forbid the police to torture captured burglars because torture is wicked, not because burglars are estimable people; nor do we need sentimental reasons for opposing colonialism. Throughout the 1950s Russell argued as he had for the past four decades: that America would try to preserve her economic advantages he took for granted; what mattered was that it should not threaten the peace. It was brinkmanship rather than imperialism which alarmed him, and it was the self-deception as much as the hypocrisy involved in American alliances with nasty right-wing regimes which received his sardonic analysis. Self-deception and dangerousness ran into each other; Chiang Kai-shek was both a tyrant and an obstacle to peace with communist China; American support for Leon Battista was disgusting rather than dangerous, but when it led to hostility to Castro's socialist revolution, it became dangerous because it invited Soviet competition for influence in the Caribbean. This had European implications. In the early 1950s Russell had had no objections to German rearmament; by 1961 he was ready to assuage Russian fears of a 'German finger on the nuclear button' at any price and terrified that the game of 'chicken' which Kennedy and Khrushchev were playing over the status of Berlin would erupt into nuclear war.[52]

In the 1950s, as we have seen, Russell thought the Soviet Union would become more liberal; then he realized that change would at best be exceedingly slow. He always agreed that Russia was a nastier place than the United States. Yet after he changed his mind about the possibility of pushing Russia into a more cooperative frame of mind, he became increasingly convinced that it was from America that the threat to peace now emanated. John Foster Dulles's policy of trying to roll back communism was more alarmingly echoed by senior military figures such as Admiral Radford, General Nathan Twining and Air Force General Curtis Le May ('bomber Le May' to both friend and foe) who would tell anyone who asked that, were it not for pussy-footing politicians, they could bomb the Soviet Union into good behaviour in the course of an afternoon.[53] Russell may have been more easily frightened than the facts warranted, but twenty-five years afterwards the men who gave him sleepless nights still seem pretty alarming.

The Cuban missile crisis, followed by the American build-up of forces in Vietnam, convinced him that American foreign policy was too dangerous to be tolerated. The build-up of the Cuban crisis was slow. Throughout 1961 the point of tension was Berlin, where the East German government faced an almost uncontrollable flood of refugees from its oppressiveness (and poverty), and finally took the drastic step of constructing the infamous wall. Another point of tension was Turkey, where the American government had installed Thor ballistic missiles, threatening Moscow from a new direction and at closer range than previous missiles had done – though there is some doubt whether this was any part of American policy, since Kennedy was annoyed to discover their presence there during the missile crisis, having believed that they had been pulled out for the sake of *détente*; and after the crisis was over he was happy to withdraw them as a face-saving gesture to Khrushchev. The Soviet government may have felt that something had to be done to counter these strategic gains; and putting medium-range missiles into Cuba may have looked a cheap way of making up ground. The missiles were on the 'wrong' side of the early-warning radar systems, which were largely geared to detecting long-range missiles coming over the North Pole; and, sited only ninety miles from the Florida coast, they were a clear warning to the American government not to do anything rash about Cuba. After the fiasco of the Bay of Pigs invasion in 1961, it was widely expected that the American government would try to avenge itself by full-scale invasion. The Soviet invasion of Afghanistan suggests that this is what the Soviet government would have done, and the Vietnam war suggests it must have been a serious option for Kennedy. In spite of these considerations, the Soviet move was foolish; militarily the missiles were useless since they had too short a range to hit civilian targets in the American north-east, or strategic sites in the mid-west. Their presence was symbolic and irritant.

To install irritants broke all the rules of diplomacy in the nuclear age. Whatever its motivation, it was bound to look like an attempt at unsettling the nuclear balance. It further broke all the rules by reducing both sides' time for manoeuvre during a crisis; the missiles were on indefensible sites, which meant that if they were to be used at all they had to be used as soon as any conflict broke out; but that in turn meant that the American airforce would have to destroy them sooner rather than later. The two things together meant that they were absurdly provocative, the more so when they added nothing to the firepower already possessed by the Soviet submarine missile fleet. No satisfying explanation of what went on inside the Kremlin has ever been given. Kennedy's reactions, on the other hand, have been described over and over again – usually in terms ordinarily reserved for hagiography.[54] In essence, he stuck to one demand: that any missiles already in Cuba should leave and that no new ones should be installed. He declared a blockade of Cuba and announced that the US navy would search Soviet vessels heading for Cuba. Technically, the blockade was a substantial violation of international law and its application to Russian vessels on the high seas could have been taken as an act of war; for two days the world held its breath. Happily nobody made a false move. Kennedy browbeat his admirals into allowing two Soviet vessels through the blockade in order to give Khrushchev plenty of time to reflect; Khrushchev backed away from direct confrontation after extracting an American promise not to invade Cuba, and agreed to withdraw the missiles. Face and lives had both been saved.[55] Though Kennedy has rightly been praised for the coolness with which he handled events, the subsequent history of the Vietnam conflict showed just how difficult it was for a president to keep control of the forces that had already brought him the Bay of Pigs, and that luck as well as good judgement were on his side for once. Nor does the successful resolution of this incident do much to redeem the inept record of American foreign policy before and after 1962.

Russell's view of events was firmly anti-American. He thought the crisis was largely the result of American bullying in Central America – a perfectly sensible long-term view; initially he believed that the missiles were a CIA invention, dreamed up to excuse another attempt to overthrow Castro. In this he was just wrong, though less wrong than the critics who said that it was inconceivable that the CIA would play such a trick on the world at large, let alone attempt to deceive the American government. Russell feared that Kennedy would box himself into a situation where neither he nor Khrushchev could avoid war except by a climb-down, for he saw that Kennedy would be under tremendous pressure to act tough after the previous year's humiliation. So it was always to Kennedy that he addressed demands for concessions and Kennedy whom he denounced as the likely begetter of World War Three. After the event, he praised Khrushchev, but only because 'I feel that support is due to the more pacific party. It is only for this reason that since, though not before, Khrushchev decided not to challenge the blockade, I have thought him more praiseworthy than his opponents.' He abused Kennedy as a warmonger, as the man who threatened to blow up the whole world for the sake of American high finance. One cannot but sympathize with Kennedy's retort that Russell's 'attention might well be directed to the burglars rather than to those who have caught the burglars'. Russell fired off telegrams to U Thant, Macmillan, Kennedy and Khrushchev, and eventually to Castro himself, urging moderation and suggesting the obvious compromise solution of an American pledge of non-invasion in return for the removal of the missiles. Astonishingly, both Khrushchev and Kennedy replied, and the world was treated to the spectacle of the two most powerful men in the world arguing with each other through the sitting room of a ninety-year-old philosopher. Although his aides made any number of exaggerated claims for his influence on events, Russell knew his role in the episode was almost accidental, and that it was the world at large that was being addressed, not he. None the less, he enjoyed the sensation of being at the heart of great events – and engaged in a repeat performance during the Sino-Indian conflict. It was at least flattering that the essential lines of the solution to the conflict were those he had suggested.[56]

The crisis convinced him that America was in the grip of bloodthirsty generals, CIA spies, armaments manufacturers and the peddlers of simple-minded myths. Russell's 'statement' on the crisis has rightly been derided as a hysterical and absurdly one-sided outburst: 'You are to die,' it announced, 'not in the course of nature, but within a few weeks, and not you alone, but your family, your friends, and all the inhabitants of Britain, together with many hundreds of millions of innocent people elsewhere. Why? Because rich Americans dislike the Government the Cubans prefer and have used part of their wealth to spread lies about it.' There is no reason to doubt Russell's claim that none of this represented any positive enthusiasm for the Soviet cause, and that his only aim was to point out that American bullying of Cuba was on a par with the Soviet domination of Hungary. None the less, continuous high-pitched denunciation aimed only at America hardly made him many friends or converts. It was in this frame of mind that he launched the Bertrand Russell Peace Foundation in September 1963, severed his ties with the anti-nuclear movement in the following spring, and embarked on his final campaign against the war in Vietnam.

Through the Peace Foundation itself he put forward proposals for settling the Middle East crisis, resolving the difficulties of India and Pakistan, and very much more besides. These proposals were carried round the world by Ralph Schoenman, who was uniformly unsuccessful and uniformly disliked, save by Edith Russell and, to a lesser extent, her husband. The campaign which dominated Russell's last years was the struggle against American involvement in Vietnam. Before he died, he had become merely one of innumerable opponents of what had turned into one of the more hideous wars of recent years. A very large minority of all Americans was hostile to the war. Young people felt that the government was at war with them as well as with the Vietcong, and Russell's voice was hardly needed or heeded in the general fury. It ought none the less to be counted in his favour that, whatever the merits and demerits of the way he fought against the war, he was one of the first people to understand what was going on and what it might lead to.[57] In 1963 large parts of the American press were still ready to accept the government line that there were no American troops in Vietnam, or that there were a few who acted as advisers, or that occasionally the advisers were attacked when the Vietcong attacked South Vietnamese troops and had to defend themselves. Russell argued from the start that there was large-scale intervention already, involving American pilots in missions flown by the South Vietnamese airforce, that this intervention was morally and militarily disastrous, that it was bound to increase in scale and to involve America in the cruelties and brutalities of the regime American weapons were propping up. In all of this he was absolutely right. Moreover, his acrimonious contests with American editors and pro- prietors – notably with *The New York Times* – were marked by the curious fact that Russell's chief source for his accusations of brutality and deception were the newspapers whose editors accused him of everything from senility to rabid communism; how they contrived to print on their news pages accounts of the war which they denied on their editorial pages is one of the small mysteries of journalism. That *The New York Times* later published the *Pentagon Papers* after an epic battle with the government and the courts only adds to the difficulty.[58]

Because Russell was increasingly frail and was protected against the outside world by his various secretaries and helpers, one can only sketch in a general way what he thought about the war. Chiefly he thought that the war was atrocious; in all his writings on the war he dwells almost obsessively on the physical brutalities and horrors of napalm bombing, torture by South Vietnamese troops and police, the self-immolation of Buddhist monks protesting against the Diem regime. Almost everything else was froth. Supporters of the Vietcong, who might have been expected to treat legality as an exploded 'bourgeois' notion, expended quantities of ink in arguing that America had violated the 1954 agreement which had been intended to unify North and South Vietnam under a democratically elected government. Russell went along with them, but it is doubtful that he cared about the rights and wrongs of the conflict as a matter of international law, any more than he did about the illegality of Kennedy's blockade of Cuba. To use one of his own images, he felt like a passer-by who sees a large adult beating a small boy with a stick; there's no point in asking how the fight started, the thing is to stop it.[59]

Russell was largely proved right about the atrocities committed during the war – often only after he was dead, when the *Pentagon Papers* revealed the extent to which the military had lied to the US government, and the government had lied to Congress and the American people. On the other hand, the passage of time makes the one-sidedness of his condemnation no more attractive; he was at best evasive on the question of Vietcong terrorism. His view that the oppressed look admirable only until they win would have been sickeningly verified by the Pol Pot regime in Cambodia, and it is hard to imagine which side he would have taken over the subsequent North Vietnamese invasion of Cambodia. One can at least observe that, forty years before, he had pointed out that socialists in power are no less likely than capitalists to be swept away by nationalist passions. That Hanoi and Peking should come to blows would not have surprised him. While the Vietnam war was raging, he was often right on the substance of American misdeeds where he was not right in detail; in 1963, for instance, he accused the American government of supplying lethal defoliants to South Vietnam and was rebuked by Dennis Bloodworth in the *Observer*, who claimed that what had been used was 'common weed-killer' – the truth being that the infamous Agent Orange *had* been used as a weedkiller in Nevada (where it had caused sickness in animals and human beings), but was lethal if used in the concentrations and quantities in which it was used in Vietnam.[60] Russell, as ever, gave his critics an excuse to write him off as a raving old man when he accused the American government of deliberate genocide, of encouraging torture, and of creating concentration camps under the guise of the 'strategic hamlets' into which the peasants in the countryside were herded to make it easier to protect them from the Vietcong. Even after all the post-mortems, leaked documents and partisan retrospectives, it does not appear that anyone in the Pentagon did want to use South Vietnam as an experimental arena for practising chemical warfare, and there was not much pressure for all-out bombing raids on civilian targets in the north – which were among Russell's accusations. None the less, Russell's view that the war was pointless, atrocious and heading for disaster was quite right. We may flinch at the tone of his appeal to Negro soldiers to desert and join the Vietcong because the war was a racist plot to get poor Blacks and Asians to kill one another; but Blacks and poor Whites were certainly prominent in the army and in the casualty lists, since they were less able to get deferments from the draft than the better-off and more articulate. The simplest case against the war was overwhelming, and Russell was at any rate intermittently sensible enough to stick to the simplest case. The Diem regime, and its successor under Marshals Ky and Thieu, was tyrannical, exploitative and brutal; the American government had made its usual mistake of thinking anti-communism a proof of moral worth and popular support. It was bound to find itself enmired in an unwinnable war. It could not create democracy in Vietnam, but it could undermine it in the United States.

If that was compelling, the rest was not. Russell's support of the Vietcong was at odds with everything in his career. The decayed condition of the South Vietnamese government and its armed forces meant that an American withdrawal was tantamount to a Vietcong victory; whether there would have been a takeover of the South by Hanoi had the Vietcong won in the very early 1960s is debatable, but there is no blinking the proposition that an American defeat meant a communist victory. It was perfectly possible to accept this without being enthusiastic about the Vietcong; the British Committee for Peace in Vietnam took the view that the Vietcong was likely to install a pretty dictatorial regime, but that it would be no worse than the Diem regime, and that the great thing was to end the civil war and get foreign troops out. Russell and his allies in the Campaign for Solidarity with Vietnam mocked this neutralist position, and gave their enthusiastic backing to the Vietcong, whom they depicted as a purely indigenous movement of national liberation, with scarcely a communist in their ranks.[61] This was either disingenuous or self-deceived, or both. It was also counter-productive; critics thought that if he could believe that, he could believe anything, and dismissed him as a senile idiot. Even more oddly, Russell attacked the Soviet Union for excessive timidity in supporting national liberation movements, and demanded Russian intervention on behalf of the Vietcong, and in support of Cuba, the Angolan independence movement, and the Palestine Liberation Organization into the bargain. Russia's chief duty was to send arms and advisers to every anti-American cause wherever it might be found, and in Vietnam to send in aircraft to shoot down the American bombers raiding North Vietnam.

This was a complete reversal of everything he had thought, even as recently as 1962. His view then was that the great powers must above all else try to keep down the temperature of international relations. He said during the missile crisis that defending Cuba to the death would be disastrous and praised Khrushchev's statesmanship in backing down gracefully. He had attacked nationalism as a threat to world peace for half a century and more; now national liberation was the cry of the moment, and world peace a secondary consideration – no wonder many people find it hard to believe that Russell was the author of such stuff. Nor is it easy to suppose that he believed Russia to be a natural ally of national independence. If he did think it, he certainly did not think it for long; in the summer of 1968, he wrote to President Kosygin pleading that the Soviet government should leave Czechoslovakia alone, and again in August to denounce the invasion.[62] What he made of the fact that Cuba and North Vietnam were almost the only countries outside the immediate Soviet orbit to support the invasion, there is no way of knowing. *The New York Times* regularly trotted out the complaint that he had become a communist dupe, dazzled by the flattering attentions of Soviet leaders. The small grain of truth in that is that he was readier than before to believe the worst of American generals, politicians, diplomats and journalists and spent no corresponding effort on denouncing Russian politicians, journalists, generals and diplomats. But soft on communism never was an apt description.[63]

The explanation of Russell's curious shifts in his last years lies perhaps in one thing above all else. Casting his mind back to 1914, he surely felt that the war in Vietnam was proof that western, civilized, rational, liberal, scientific man had reverted to something lower than the beasts. In 1916 angry Englishmen called for bombing raids on German cities in revenge for the Zeppelin attacks on Britain. They knew that they were suggesting something absolutely frightful. Dropping bombs on civilian targets, perhaps killing several dozen women and children, was the act of a barbarian; those who suggested that the British should do such a thing did so in the belief that German 'frightfulness' could be deterred only by similar frightfulness on the British side. Fifty years later, scruples seemed to have vanished. The Second World War had acclimatized mankind to high-tech murder, with the fire-bombing of Hamburg and Dresden every bit as obscene as the nuclear bombing of Hiroshima and Nagasaki. To employ the weapons the Americans first handed out to the South Viet-namese and then equipped their own troops with – fragmentation bombs, napalm, bullets with the properties of the outlawed dum-dum – was one more step on the road into the abyss. The gobbledegook in which the American government and military wrapped up the facts of mass murder must have grated all the more hideously on Russell's fastidious ear. At the age of ninety-three or ninety-five, what more could he do than cry out against the horror and lend his prestige and his name to those who seemed most energetic in combating it? Those inclined to sneer would do well to ask themselves how well they have lived up to the injunction not to follow a multitude in doing – or assenting to – evil.

NOTES

PREFACE

1. 'Is there an absolute good?', Russell Archives (BRA). This was a talk he gave to the Apostles on 4 March 1922; the same thought occurred to J. M. Keynes.
2. Two important examples are Russell's claimed 'conversion' to a pro-Boer pacifism and his discussion of his work for the NCF.
3. Ronald W. Clark, *The Life of Bertrand Russell* (Harmondsworth, 1974).
4. *Life*, pp. 334–5.
5. 'How I write', in *Portraits from Memory*, p. 207, discounting 'A Free Man's Worship'.
6. Katharine Tait, *My Father Bertrand Russell* (London, 1976).

CHAPTER ONE

1. 'Obituary', *Unpopular Essays*, pp. 221–3.
2. Russell's own *Problems of Philosophy*, in print since 1912, is as good an introduction as could be wished, both to philosophy in general and to his philosophy in particular. A. J. Ayer's *Russell* (London, 1972) and D. F. Pears' *Bertrand Russell and the British Tradition in Philosophy* (London, 1967) are excellent introductions to Russell's 'pure' philosophy. Benjamin Barber, 'Solipsistic Politics', in G. W. Roberts, ed., *Bertrand Russell Memorial Volume* (London, 1979) and Richard Wollheim, 'Russell and the Liberal Tradition', in G. Nakhnikian, ed., *Bertrand Russell's Philosophy* (London, 1974) are uniquely useful on his political philosophy.
3. The one notable exception was his speech on the danger of atomic weapons, 28 November 1945; see below, pp. 176–7. He made six speeches in all.
4. Below, pp. 61–2, and pp. 189–90.
5. *Marriage and Morals*, p. 57.
6. Michael St J. Packe, *The Life of John Stuart Mill* (London, 1954), pp. 501–2.
7. *The Later Letters of John Stuart Mill* (London, 1972), pp. 1681, 1692–3; *Life of Mill*, pp. 437, 500–502.
8. *Life of Mill*, p. 500.
9. *Which Way to Peace?*, p. 61; *Life of Mill*, p. 438.
10. *Principles of Social Reconstruction*, pp. 155ff.
11. *Amberley Papers*, *passim*.
12. *Amberley Papers*, vol. 11, p. 202; J. S. Mill, *The Subjection of Women*.
13. *Life of Mill*, p. 439.

14. *Autobiography*, p. 12.
15. ibid., p. 23.
16. ibid., p. 17.
17. ibid., p. 9; 'Prisons', *Papers*, 12, pp. 97–109.
18. *Autobiography*, p. 36.
19. ibid, p. 53.
20. *Autobiography*, p. 29.
21. *Autobiography*, pp. 80–81.
22. *Life*, pp. 35–7; *Papers*, 1, pp. 5–20.
23. *Papers*, 1, pp. 16–20.
24. J. S. Mill, *On Liberty* (Harmondsworth, 1974), p. 166.
25. Louis Greenspan, *The Incompatible Prophecies* (Oakville, 1978), pp. 9ff.
26. *On Liberty*, pp. 165–6.
27. *Life*, p. 556.
28. Even his lectures at the Rand School on 'The Problems of Democracy' are strikingly sketchy. BRA.
29. Below, Chapter 6, pp. 140–44.
30. Michael Freeden, *The New Liberalism* (Oxford, 1978); *Liberalism Divided* (Oxford, 1984).
31. *Roads to Freedom*, pp. 17–18.
32. J. W. Burrow, *Evolution and Society* (Cambridge, 1966).
33. H. Sidgwick, *The Moral Philosophies of Green, Martineau and Spencer* (London, 1883).
34. Review of L. T. Hobhouse, *Morals in Evolution, Independent Review*, 1907, pp. 204–10.

CHAPTER TWO

1. *Papers*, 12, sec. 7: 'Prisons', pp. 97–109.
2. *Papers*, 1, pp. 208–9; 'Seems, Madam. Nay, It is', op. cit., 106–11 (read to the Apostles in December 1897), explains why Russell rejects McTaggart's identification of the Good and the Real. 'Beliefs: Discarded and Retained', in *Portraits from Memory*, pp. 38–42, gives a knockabout account of Russell's emergence from Hegelianism into empiricism.
3. *Portraits from Memory*, p. 42, for instance. *Autobiography*, pp. 160–63, is characteristic. Murray's letter is dated 24 February 1902.
4. *My Philosophical Development*, p. 35. *Portraits from Memory*, pp. 13–18.
5. *Portraits from Memory*, pp. 11–12; *My Philosophical Development*, pp. 211–12.
6. *The Philosophy of Leibniz*.
7. *Portraits from Memory*, p. 39.
8. *My Philosophical Development*, p. 254.
9. Below, pp. 46–7.
10. *Portraits from Memory*, p. 41.
11. 'On Denoting', *Mind*, 1903.
12. *Portraits from Memory*, p. 20.
13. *Papers*, 12, p. 306.
14. *Autobiography*, pp. 53ff.
15. *Papers*, 1, pp. 61–2.

16. *German Social Democracy* (London, 1896); his *Autobiography*, p. 132, provides a dismissive account of its publication.

17. Georges Sorel, 'The Decomposition of Marxism', in I. L. Horowitz, *The Revolt Against Reason* (London, 1961), pp. 251ff. (Russell refers to Sorel's essay in his *Roads to Freedom* twenty years later; I do not know when he read it.)

18. *German Social Democracy*, p. 1.

19. ibid., pp. 1, 10.

20. Karl Marx and Friedrich Engels, *The German Ideology* (London, 1965), pp. 88–90.

21. *German Social Democracy*, pp. 39–40.

22. ibid., p. 35.

23. ibid., pp. 45–50.

24. *German Social Democracy*, p. 43.

25. Kirk Willis, 'The Critical Reception of Bertrand Russell's *German Social Democracy*', *Russell*, 1976, pp. 34–45.

26. 'The Uses of Luxury', in *Papers*, I, p. 322. (The headnote to this essay asserts, quite wrongly, that it is a *defence* of inherited wealth; it is a defence of inequality and of incomes earned other than by hard work, but explicitly attacks inheritance.)

27. *Papers*, 12, p. 11 among much else; *Autobiography*, pp. 150–52.

28. Russell to Couturat, 24 March 1900.

29. Thomas Packenham, *The Boer War* (London, 1983), pp. 10–35.

30. Russell to Couturat, 24 March 1900.

31. *Autobiography*, p. 149.

32. Russell to Couturat, 5 October 1903.

33. *The Entente Policy*, in *Justice in Wartime*, pp. 125ff.

34. *Autobiography*, p. 156.

35. *Papers*, 12, p. 229.

36. ibid., p. 188.

37. ibid., pp. 188–9.

38. *Life*, pp. 150–53.

39. *Autobiography*, p. 156.

40. *Papers*, 12, pp. 420–21.

41. ibid., pp. 298–9.

42. ibid., p. 301.

43. *Outline of Philosophy*, p. 233; *Philosophy of Bertrand Russell*, pp. 719–20.

44. *Portraits from Memory*, p. 207.

45. *Principles of Social Reconstruction*, pp. 137–41.

46. G. E. Moore, *Principia Ethica* (Cambridge, 1903).

47. 'The Elements of Ethics', in *Philosophical Essays*, pp. 20–21.

48. *Outline of Philosophy*, pp. 234–5.

49. *Human Society in Ethics and Politics*, pp. 15–20.

50. ibid., p. 25.

51. e.g., his 'call to non-violent action' of September 1960 in *Autobiography*, pp. 632–4.

52. *The Philosophy of Bertrand Russell*, pp. 719–20.

53. H. D. Lewis (ed.), *Clarity is not Enough* (London, 1965), argues this.

54. *Papers*, 1, p. 97.

55. Until their appearance in *Papers*, 1, pp. 78–116, 201–44.

56. *Papers*, 1, pp. 219ff.

57. *Philosophical Essays*, p. 20.

58. J. M. Keynes, 'My Early Beliefs', in *Essays and Sketches in Biography* (London, 1957), pp. 241–7.

59. *Portraits from Memory*, p. 59.

60. *Philosophical Essays*, p. 43.

61. ibid., pp. 54–5.

62. ibid., pp. 14–15, 19–21.

63. ibid., p. 26.

64. ibid., pp. 25–8.

65. ibid., p. 30.

66. It was read to the Apostles on 4 March 1922; it has been reprinted in *Russell*, 1987, pp. 144–9.

67. *Human Society*, p. 19.

68 The notion of 'persuasive definition' comes from C. L. Stevenson, *Language and Ethics* (New Haven, 1944); I do not know whether Russell read it or simply picked up an idea which was 'in the air'.

69. cf. J. J. C. Smart and Bernard Williams, *Utilitarianism, For and Against* (Cambridge, 1973).

70. *The Philosophy of Bertrand Russell*, p. 720; Nicholas Griffin, 'Bertrand Russell's Crisis of Faith', in *Intellect and Social Conscience* (McMaster University, 1986), p. 117.

71. e.g. 'Prisons', 'The Free Man's Worship' and much of the correspondence reprinted in his *Autobiography*.

72. 'Why I am not a Christian', in *Basic Writings*, pp. 586–91.

73. ibid., p. 596.

74. 'A Free Man's Worship', *Mysticism and Logic*, p. 51.

75. 'Why I am not a Christian', p. 591.

76. ibid., p. 594.

77. ibid., p. 594.

78. 'A Free Man's Worship', p. 59.

79. *Papers*, 1, pp. 109–10.

80. 'The Place of Science in a Liberal Education', *Papers*, 12, pp. 390–96.

81. ibid., p. 394.

82. ibid., pp. 295–6.

CHAPTER THREE

1. *The Entente Policy*, in *Justice in Wartime*, pp. 123–236.

2. In America, it was published as *Why Men Fight*, without Russell's permission or approval.

3. *Life*, pp. 412–15; *Autobiography*, p. 263; Jo Vellacott, *Bertrand Russell and the Pacifists in the First World War* (Brighton, 1980) is indispensable on Russell and the NCF.

4. See, e.g., Barbara Tuchman, *August 1914* (London, 1962) on how Europe 'tumbled into the war'; her account greatly influenced John Kennedy's response at the time of the Cuban missile crisis.

5. Notably, the *Labour Leader*, edited by Fenner Brockway.

6. 'Is a Permanent Peace Possible?', March 1915; ' The Future of Anglo-German Rivalry',

July 1915; 'War and Non-Resistance', August 1915; *Justice in Wartime*, pp. 83–104, 67–82, 40–59.

7. *Life*, pp. 328–32.
8. G. H. Hardy, *Bertrand Russell and Trinity* (London, 1941).
9. *Autobiography*, pp. 243–7, 277–8; *Life*, pp. 323–6.
10. *Bertrand Russell and the Pacifists*, pp. 31ff.
11. ibid., pp. 102–21.
12. ibid., pp. 223–30.
13. *Justice in Wartime*, p. v.
14. It was on this straightforward point that Russell and 'North Staffs' (T. E. Hulme) disagreed – as well as on more overtly philosophical issues, such as the existence of objective values and the merits of Bergson.
15. *Justice in Wartime*, pp. 136–7.
16. A. J. P. Taylor is such a figure; see *The Troublemakers* (London, 1957).
17. cf. K. B. Blackwell, *The Spinozistic Ethics of Bertrand Russell* (London, 1985).
18. 'On "Liberty" ', and 'Inevitability Inapplicable', *Cambridge Magazine*, 22 and 29 January 1916.
19. 'The Kind of Rubbish we Oppose', *Cambridge Magazine*, 5 February 1916.
20. *The Cambridge Review*, 1912, pp. 193–4; *Papers*, 12, pp. 385–6.
21. *The Monist*, vol. 22, 1912, pp. 321–47.
22. 'Why we are in Favour of this War', *Cambridge Magazine*, 12 February 1916.
23. 'The Kind of Rubbish we Oppose', *Cambridge Magazine*, 5 February 1916.
24. Alun Jones, *The Life and Opinions of T. E. Hulme* (London, 1960); W. E. Roberts, *T. E. Hulme* (London, 1982).
25. *Principles*, pp. 11–15.
26. That is, he has none of the difficulties which Mill encounters in *Liberty* by offering to show the importance of liberty on utilitarian principles.
27. 'Direct Action and Democracy', *English Review*, June 1919.
28. *Political Ideals*, first published in America in 1917, and published for the first time in Britain in 1963.

CHAPTER FOUR

1. *Roads to Freedom*, pp. 126–9. Royden Harrison, 'Bertrand Russell: from liberalism to socialism?', *Russell*, 1986, pp. 5–38, is interesting on much of what follows.
2. *Life*, pp. 395–6.
3. *Practice and Theory of Bolshevism*, p. 28.
4. *Autobiography*, pp. 333–5, 354.
5. ibid., p. 394; *Practice and Theory of Bolshevism*, pp. 17–18.
6. *The Tamarisk Tree*, vol. 1, pp. 83–146.
7. Stuart Schram, *The Political Thought of Mao Tse-tung*, (London, 1962), pp. 294–8.
8. Below, Chapter 6, pp. 136ff.
9. Below, Chapter 6, pp. 150ff.
10. *Power*, pp. 27–8.
11. *The Impact of Science on Society*, given as lectures in 1949 and 1950, published in 1952.
12. *Autobiography*, pp. 255, 321–2.
13. It was omitted from the second edition.

14. Many are reprinted in *Mortals and Others* (ed. Harry Ruja, London 1975).

15. Lord Allen of Hurtwood, *Plough a Lonely Furrow* (ed. Martin Gilbert, London, 1965), pp. 195–9.

16. 'Why I am a Guildsman', *The Guildsman*, September 1919; 'Socialism and Liberal Values', *English Review*, 1920, pp. 449–508.

17. 'Democracy and Direct Action', *English Review*, 1919, pp. 495ff.

18. *Roads to Freedom*, pp. 138ff.

19. *Practice and Theory of Bolshevism*, pp. 33–5.

20. *Roads to Freedom*, p. 87.

21. ibid., pp. 141ff.

22. ibid., pp. 8–9.

23. ibid., pp. 111–16.

24. ibid., pp. 118–19.

25. ibid., pp. 145–6.

26. *Autobiography*, pp. 506–22.

27. *Practice and Theory of Bolshevism*, pp. 90–96.

28. ibid., p. 90.

29. ibid., pp. 37–43.

30. ibid., pp. 47–9.

31. ibid., pp. 7–8.

32. ibid., p. 46.

33. Leon Trotsky, *Writings on Britain* (London, 1974), pp. 169–82.

34. *The Problem of China*, pp. 179–80.

35. ibid., p. 199.

36. ibid., pp. 49–51.

37. ibid., pp. 113–14, 172–5.

38. ibid., p. 172.

39. ibid., pp. 175–6.

40. *Tamarisk Tree*, I, p. 88.

41. *Prospects of Industrial Civilization*, p. 226.

42. ibid., pp. 20–21.

43. ibid., pp. 22ff.

44. ibid., pp. 226–8.

45. ibid., p. 61.

46. ibid., pp. 90, 225–6.

47. ibid., p. 86.

48. ibid., pp. 116–17; below, Chapter 6, pp. 140–41.

49. ibid., pp. 88–9.

50. T. Hobbes, *Leviathan* (London, 1914), pp. 64–5.

51. *Tribune*, 15 December 1961, p. 8.

CHAPTER FIVE

1. *Marriage and Morals*, p. 149.

2. *On Education*, pp. 73–4; Katharine Tait, *My Father Bertrand Russell*, pp. 58ff; *Autobiography*, pp. 386, 390.

3. *Autobiography*, pp. 389–90; *Tamarisk Tree*, II, pp. 6–51.
4. *Papers*, 12, pp. 390–97.
5. 'Freedom in Education: Against Mechanism', *The Dial*, February 1923.
6. *Autobiography*, pp. 461–2.
7. 'Should the Public Schools be Abolished?', *Listener*, 29 March 1933; 'Labour and the Universities', *The New Leader*, 14 September 1923; *Portraits from Memory*, p. 63.
8. *Tamarisk Tree*, II p. 12.
9. *On Education*, pp. 111–12.
10. ibid., p. 112.
11. ibid., pp. 41–2.
12. ibid., pp. 45–6.
13. ibid., pp. 58ff.
14. ibid., pp. 65–6.
15. 'Bertrand Russell on Education', *The Forward* (New York), 23 December 1928.
16. *On Education*, pp. 61ff.
17. ibid., p. 46.
18. Patricia Morgan, *Delinquent Fantasies* (London, 1978), pp. 5–35.
19. *On Education*, pp. 114–16.
20. ibid., pp. 138ff.
21. ibid., pp. 138–42.
22. ibid., p. 147.
23. ibid., pp. 156–9.
24. ibid., pp. 161–2.
25. ibid., pp. 200–201.
26. ibid., p. 28.
27. Plato, *The Republic*, Book X.
28. *Education and the Social Order*, p. 19.
29. ibid., p. 21.
30. ibid., pp. 23–4.
31. ibid., pp. 50ff.
32. ibid., p. 79.
33. ibid., p. 119.
34. ibid., pp. 119–21; below, pp. 144–8; 'Slavery or Self Extermination?', *The Nation* (New York), 14 September 1923.
35. *Marriage and Morals*, pp. 111–23.
36. *Autobiography*, pp. 461–2; *Life*, pp. 586–91.
37. *Marriage and Morals*, pp. 23–6.
38. ibid., pp. 114–20.
39. ibid., pp. 67ff.
40. ibid., pp. 83–6.
41. ibid., p. 151.
42. ibid., p. 83.
43. ibid., pp. 109–10.
44. ibid., pp. 94–6.
45. ibid., pp. 104–10.
46. ibid., pp. 106–7.
47. ibid., p. 108.

48. ibid., p. 151.
49. Patricia Ehrenreich, *The Hearts of Men* (London, 1983).

CHAPTER SIX

1. *Freedom and Organization*, p. 8 and erratum slip.
2. *Life*, pp. 556–7.
3. *Life*, pp. 595–606.
4. Below, pp. 157ff; *Life*, pp. 609–42.
5. *Which Way to Peace?*, pp. 144–6.
6. *Autobiography*, p. 430; Martin Ceadel, *Pacifism in Britain* (Oxford, 1980), pp. 215–20; *New Statesman*, 8 June 1940, p. 719.
7. *Scientific Outlook*, p. 75.
8. ibid., p. 153; *Papers*, 12, pp. 395–6.
9. cf. *Scientific Outlook*, 25, and Paul Feyerabend, *Against Method*, pp. 113–43.
10. *Scientific Outlook*, pp. 58ff; 'The Place of Science in a Liberal Education', *Papers*, 12, pp. 380–93.
11. *Scientific Outlook*, pp. 150ff.
12. ibid., pp. 186–9.
13. ibid., p. 250.
14. ibid., pp. 251–5, 176.
15. ibid., pp. 266–8.
16. 'Problems of Democracy', BRA.
17. Louis Greenspan, *The Incompatible Prophecies, passim*.
18. Russell reviewed *Brave New World*: 'We Don't Want To Be Happy', *New Leader*, 11 March 1932.
19. *Freedom and Organization*, p. 510.
20. ibid., p. 485; pp. 492–6.
21. ibid., pp. 57–62.
22. ibid., pp. 61–2.
23. ibid., p. 89.
24. ibid., p. 192.
25. ibid., pp. 25–52.
26. ibid., pp. 24–41.
27. ibid., p. 249.
28. ibid., p. 269.
29. ibid., pp. 356ff.
30. ibid., pp. 500–501.
31. ibid., p. 501.
32. ibid., p. 510.
33. *New Statesman*, 8 June 1940, p. 719.
34. *Which Way to Peace?*; *Autobiography*, p. 509 – but cf. p. 156.
35. *America*, II, pp. 311–14.
36. *Which Way to Peace?* , p. 37.
37. Max Hastings, *Bomber* (London, 1981) gives a chastening account of how severe losses were.

38. *Which Way to Peace?*, p. 14.
39. ibid., pp. 75, 95.
40. ibid., p. 139.
41. ibid., p. 145.
42. ibid., pp. 209–10.
43. Peter Calvacoressi and Guy Wint, *Total War* (Harmondsworth, 1972), pp. 692–702.
44. 'History's Lesson for the Nazis', *Sunday Referee*, 9 April 1933.
45. *New Statesman*, 8 June 1940, p. 719.
46. *Power*, p. 9.
47. ibid., p. 11.
48. ibid., p. 27.
49. ibid., p. 22.
50. ibid., p. 97.
51. ibid., p. 106.
52. ibid., p. 149.
53. ibid., pp. 135–6.
54. ibid., p. 137.
55. *Human Society in Ethics and Politics*, p. 19.
56. *Power*, pp. 193–8.
57. *Power*, p. 203; Karl Popper, *The Open Society and Its Enemies* (London, 1945).

CHAPTER SEVEN

1. *Autobiography*, p. 522.
2. *Portraits from Memory* reprints some of the best: 'Six Autobiographical Talks', pp. 13–47.
3. *Basic Writings,* pp. 729–32.
4. 'Voltaire's Influence on Me', *Voltaire Studies*, February 1958, pp. 157–62.
5. *Mortals and Others* (ed. H. Ruja, London, 1975), pp. 26–7.
6. *Autobiography*, p. 9; *Life*, p. 535.
7. *Life*, pp. 715ff.
8. *Sceptical Essays* (London, 1928), pp. 111ff.
9. *The Conquest of Happiness* (London, 1932), p. 12.
10. ibid., p. 18.
11. ibid., p. 133.
12. Janet Radcliffe Richards, *The Sceptical Feminist* (Harmondsworth, 1983) is a welcome exception.
13. Quoted in *Life*, p. 539.
14. *Authority and the Individual* (London, 1949), p. 20.
15. ibid., p. 80; above, Chapter 3, pp. 73–9.
16. *Authority and the Individual*, p. 60.
17. Carol Pateman, *Participation and Democratic Theory* (Cambridge, 1971); *Authority and the Individual*, p. 78.
18. *Authority and the Individual*, p. 72.

19. Given as lectures in 1949 and '50, published 1952.
20. *In Praise of Idleness* (London, 1936), p. 84.
21. ibid., p. 90.
22. ibid., p. 65.

CHAPTER EIGHT

1. *Autobiography*, pp. 509, 662.
2. *Tribunal*, 3 January 1918 (reprinted in *Autobiography*, pp. 308–10); above, pp. 62–3; *Autobiography*, p. 256.
3. *Autobiography*, p. 662; *Bertrand Russell's America*, II, pp. 274–5, 405; '16 Questions', in *Autobiography*, pp. 699–707.
4. *Tribune*, 15 December 1961, p. 8; *Life*, pp. 803–19 ('Schoenman Memorandum').
5. *War Crimes in Vietnam*, p. 99.
6. *Unpopular Essays*, pp. 80–87.
7. *War Crimes in Vietnam*, pp. 95–8.
8. *Russell Philosopher of the Century*, 'Introduction' – the gushing prose of which is suspiciously like much of *War Crimes in Vietnam* and utterly unlike Russell's.
9. 'Memorandum', *Life*, p. 819. The *Autobiography* is kinder, praising his 'almost super-human energy and courageous determination', p. 656.
10. *Has Man a Future?*, pp. 31–2.
11. *Has Man a Future?*, pp. 20–21; *Autobiography*, p. 554.
12. *Bertrand Russell's America*, II, p. 313.
13. *Autobiography*, pp. 508–9; *Bertrand Russell's America*, II, p. 314; *Common Sense and Nuclear Warfare*, pp. 88–90.
14. *Autobiography*, p. 509; *Bertrand Russell's America*, II, p. 312.
15. *Common Sense and Nuclear Warfare*, p. 90.
16. *Bertrand Russell's America*, II, p. 11.
17. ibid.
18. *New Statesman*, 21 April 1951; *Autobiography*, p. 509; *Common Sense and Nuclear Warfare*, pp. 89–90. Ronald Clark, *Life*, pp. 658–60, is extremely good on this 'lapse of memory'.
19. *Bertrand Russell's America*, II, p. 314.
20. *Has Man a Future?*, pp. 24–5; *Life*, pp. 652–7.
21. *Bertrand Russell's America*, II, pp. 16–34.
22. ibid., pp. 37, 43.
23. ibid., pp. 36ff.
24. *Autobiography*, pp. 574–5.
25. *Bertrand Russell's America*, pp. 13, 324–5.
26. *Autobiography*, p. 555.
27. *Life*, p. 735; *Has Man a Future?*, p. 39.
28. Jonathan Shell, *The Fate of the Earth* (New York, 1982); *Common Sense and Nuclear Warfare*, p. 19.
29. *Common Sense and Nuclear Warfare*, pp. 37–8; *Autobiography*, pp. 578–9.
30. *Autobiography*, pp. 555–6; *Life*, pp. 690–92.
31. *Life*, p. 692.
32. Anthony Kenny, *The Logic of Deterrence* (London, 1985); *Autobiography*, pp. 640–41.
33. *Has Man a Future?*, p. 63.

34. ibid., p. 31.
35. ibid., pp. 71–3.
36. *Common Sense and Nuclear Warfare*, pp. 85–8.
37. *Life*, pp. 705–6.
38. *Has Man a Future?*, pp. 125–6.
39. cf. *Has Man a Future?* and *Common Sense and Nuclear Warfare*.
40. *Life*, pp. 717–18.
41. *Autobiography*, pp. 604–5; *Life*, p. 742.
42. *Life*, pp. 742–3.
43. *Life*, pp. 757ff.
44. *Bertrand Russell's America*, II, pp. 388–9.
45. Ibid., p. 392.
46. *The Entente Policy, Justice in Wartime*, pp. 125ff.
47. *Bertrand Russell's America*, II, p. 392.
48. *Portraits from Memory*, p. 30.
49. cf. letters to Couturat, above, pp. 29–30.
50. *Autobiography*, pp. 381–3.
51. *Unpopular Essays*, pp. 156ff.
52. *Common Sense and Nuclear Warfare*, p. 30.
53. *Bulletin of the Atomic Scientists*, March 1962, p. 6.
54. Robert Kennedy, *13 Days*. especially pp. 110–25.
55. *Unarmed Victory*, pp. 53ff.
56. *Life*, pp. 744–53; *Unarmed Victory*, p. 59.
57. *Autobiography*, p. 647.
58. C. L. Sulzberger, 'Corpse on Horseback', *New York Times*, 4 April 1967; *War Crimes in Vietnam*, pp. 31–9.
59. I owe this recollection to Katharine Tait.
60. *War Crimes in Vietnam*, p. 35; p. 47.
61. *War Crimes in Vietnam*, pp. 66–7; pp. 99–100.
62. *Life*, p. 793.
63. *War Crimes in Vietnam*, pp. 32–3, 38.

A Note on Sources and References

I have not tried to provide a full list of Russell's writings, although I have listed every book referred to in the text. Because I have found them so illuminating, I have listed many of the ephemeral articles I have read in newspapers and journals, although very few are actually cited in the text. Similarly, I have not tried to supply complete references in my notes. There is little in Russell's political writings which does not appear in several different places and usually in almost identical words; I have confined myself to referring to what he says in the text under discussion at a given point. I have referred to so few books or essays by other writers that I have not listed them here, but have supplied brief details where they are first mentioned. I have thought long and hard about background reading, but have come to the conclusion that Russell's life straddles so many years and so many issues that a list would be almost endless. Mine, therefore, begins and ends with Russell's *Autobiography* but readers interested in Russell's politics will find *Russell*, published by McMaster University, uniquely useful.

BOOKS BY RUSSELL

German Social Democracy (1896)
Justice in Wartime (1916)
The Principles of Social Reconstruction (1916)
Political Ideals (1917)
Roads to Freedom (1918)
Mysticism and Logic (1918)
The Practice and Theory of Bolshevism (1920)
The Problem of China (1922)
The Prospects of Industrial Civilization (1923)
Icarus or the Future of Science (1924)

On Education (1926)
An Outline of Philosophy (1927)
Sceptical Essays (1928)
Marriage and Morals (1929)
The Conquest of Happiness (1930)
The Scientific Outlook (1931)
Education and the Social Order (1932)
Freedom and Organization (1934)
Which Way to Peace? (1936)
The Amberley Papers (1937)
Power (1938)
A History of Western Philosophy (1945)
Authority and the Individual (1949)
Unpopular Essays (1950)
The Impact of Science on Society (1952)
Human Society in Ethics and Politics (1954)
Why I am not a Christian (1957)
The Vital Letters of Russell, Khrushchev and Dulles (1958)
Common Sense and Nuclear Warfare (1959)
Has Man a Future? (1961)
The Basic Writings of Bertrand Russell (1961)
Unarmed Victory (1963)
War Crimes in Vietnam (1967)
Autobiography (1967, 1968, 1969)
Bertrand Russell's America (1983, 1985)

SELECTED NEWSPAPER AND PERIODICAL ARTICLES

(*The Collected Papers of Bertrand Russell* will eventually reprint all Russell's contributions to *The Tribunal*, the *Sunday Referee* and the like; this list may be useful to anyone with a good library close to hand.)
'The Meaning of Good', *Independent Review*, March 1904
'Spinoza's Moral Code', *The Nation*, April 1907
'Liberalism and Women's Suffrage', *Contemporary Review*, July 1908
'The Essence of Religion', *The Hibbert Journal*, October 1912
'The Rights of the War', *The Nation*, August 1914
'Russell and the War Office', *War and Peace*, October 1916
'Two Ideals of Pacifism', *War and Peace*, January 1917
'The Position of the Absolutists', *The Tribunal*, March 1917

'Russia Leads the Way', *The Tribunal*, March 1917

'The Russian Revolution and International Relations', *The UDC*, August 1917

'Bad Passions', *The Cambridge Magazine*, February 1919

'Democracy and Direct Action', *The English Review*, May 1919

'Why I am a Guildsman', *The Guildsman*, September 1919

'Socialism, and Liberal Ideals', *The English Review*, May 1920

'The Happiness of China', *The Nation*, January 1921

'What is Morality', *The Athenaeum and Nation*, November 1922

'The Sources of Power', *The Freeman*, May 1923

'Slavery or Self Extermination', *The Nation*, July 1923

'Labour and the Universities', *The New Leader*, September 1923

'On the Use of a General Strike', *The New Leader*, May 1926

'Rewards and Punishments in Education', *Teachers World*, January 1927

'Nationalism – A Blessing or a Curse', *Forward*, May 1928

'What I Believe', *The Forum*, September 1929

'Politics and Theology', *The Political Quarterly*, April 1930

'Who May Use Lipstick?', *New York American*, December 1931

'We Don't Want to be Happy', *The New Leader*, March 1932

'How to End War', *New World*, April 1932

'On the Fierceness of Vegetarians', *New York American*, April 1932

'Who Wants War?', *New York American*, August 1932

'Should Socialists Smoke Good Cigars?', *New York American*, November 1932

'Should the Public Schools be Abolished?', *The Listener*, March 1933

'History's Lesson for the Nazis', *Sunday Referee*, April 1933

'The Ideals of Fascism', *Sunday Referee*, October 1933

'Why I am not a Communist nor Fascist', *New Britain*, January 1934

'What Does Hitler Mean to Do?', *News Chronicle*, April 1934

'Your Duty in the Next War', *Sunday Referee*, July 1935

'How to Keep the Peace', *Sunday Referee*, August 1935

'Keep Out of War', *Sunday Referee*, September 1935

'Dictatorships that Pass in the Night', *Sunday Referee*, August 1936

'The Future of Democracy', *The New Republic*, May 1937

'The Bomb and Civilization', *Forward*, August 1945

'What is the Truth about Russia?', *Forward*, August 1945

'How to Avoid the Atomic War', *Common Sense*, October 1945

'Humanity's Last Chance', *Cavalcade*, October 1945

'The Atomic Bomb and the Prevention of War', *Polemic*, August 1946

'The Outlook for Mankind', *The Listener*, March 1947

'International Government', *New Commonwealth*, January 1948

'Communist Fanaticism the Chief Threat to Peace', *Daily Telegraph*, July 1950

'Lord Russell and the Atom Bomb', *New Statesmen*, April 1951

'Russell and "Preventive War" ', *The Nation*, October 1953

'The Hydrogen Bomb and World Government', *The Listener*, July 1954

'Man's Peril', *The Listener*, December 1954

'Scientists' Appeal for the Abolition of War', *New York Times*, July 1955

'Voltaire's Influence on Me', *Voltaire Studies*, February 1958

'The Case for Neutrality', *New York Times Magazine*, July 1960

'CND and Civil Disobedience', *Manchester Guardian*, October 1960

'The Negro Rising', *Minority of One*, October 1965

INDEX